HOW TO
UNDERSTAND
THE FINANCIAL
PAGES

KT-164-323

Jupiter 2005

Year-in, year-outperformance.

We believe it's what every serious investor wants. And it's what every manager at Jupiter aims to deliver. Over twenty years (and through varying market conditions) we've grown to become one of the UK's leading investment houses by focusing on beating the market — and nothing else. Now, with more Citywire rated fund managers than anyone else (as at 31.12.04)*, our talented team is dedicated to actively pursuing outperformance for over 400,000 investors. To find out more, visit **jupiteronline.co.uk**, call **0500 0500 98** or see your Independent Financial Adviser about Jupiter's ISA range for 2005.

Past performance is not a guide to future returns and the value of investments can fall as well as rise.

JUPITER

Call 0500 0500 98 or visit Jupiteronline.co.uk

On the planet to perform

*Source: Citywire fund manager ratings are based on assessing individual fund manager's outperformance against appropriate benchmarks over a period of 36 months. Jupiter Unit Trust Managers Limited is authorised and regulated by the Financial Services Authority. Registered address 1 Grosvenor Place, London SW1X 7JJ. It is a subsidiary of Commerzbank AG, one of Germany's leading banks. For the impact of charges and other expenses, reference should be made to the Key Features Document. Current tax levels and reliefs will depend on your individual circumstance and details are contained in the Key Features Document. For your security we may record or randomly monitor all telephone calls. If you are unsure of the suitability of this investment you should consult your Independent Financial Adviser.

Praise for *How to Understand the Financial Pages*

'This really is everything you wanted to know about financial jargon but were afraid to ask. Even long-serving investors will be astonished by the plethora of neologisms that reflect the dynamic nature of financial markets.'

Alastair Ross Goobey, CBE, Chairman, Hermes Focus Asset Management Ltd

'This book is an excellent introduction for anyone seeking to find their way round the financial pages. Whether for personal interest or because of a new career in financial services, this book takes us on a journey with the agreeable assumption that we do not know our way round the mysterious maze which unfolds before us. How I wish I had this when I first moved into the financial services sector to work and needed to understand the financial pages. I also thoroughly recommend it to anyone taking our examinations as a reference tool with a very clear and logical structure.'

Ruth Martin, Managing Director, Securities & Investment Institute

'The power of knowledge is knowing where to find it and how to use it. Here is the power!'

Justin Urquhart Stewart, Co-founder, Seven Investment Management

'Essential reading for anyone looking to improve their investment returns; not only is it clear, yet detailed, but also informative yet interesting.'

Alpesh B Patel, Managing Director, Agile Partners Asset Management, author, Financial Times *columnist, trader and financial broadcaster*

'Long-term investment success cannot be built on hunches and tips, but on confidence which has resulted from keeping in touch with business and financial information and having the ability to interpret that information. Alexander Davidson's guide can play an essential role in enabling that confidence, and should be within easy reach of all personal investors who wish to take control of their own share portfolio and investment prospects.'

Gavin Oldham, Chief Executive, The Share Centre

250 542 859

'The book represents both a comprehensive and accessible guide to *The Times*' financial pages covering all aspects from global economics to personal finance. Successfully demystifying the often complex jargon that surrounds financial markets, the author has broken the subject matter down into useful and manageable sections that give the reader a clear insight as to the detailed workings of the City and the varied markets that operate therein.'

Tim Bevan, Product Manager Market Services, London Stock Exchange

'At a time when we are all being urged to take greater responsibility for our long-term financial well-being, Alexander Davidson's book gives a sound background for how to get the best out of the information available through the financial pages in a newspaper. I would urge anyone wishing to improve their financial education to buy a copy.'

Brian Tora, Investment Communications Director, Gerrard Ltd

'This book is an excellent primer for people looking to invest in a share portfolio and a good reference guide for everybody. Of all investing skills, understanding the business numbers is most critical. How to Understand the Financial Pages covers the ground in a clear, jargon-free and reader-friendly style.'

Clem Chambers, CEO, ADVFN

'This book is just as important for people employing professional managers as for those who take a direct interest in markets. For success today is based on mutual confidence and a shared understanding of the task ahead -- and the tools with which to do it.'

George Lynne, New Business Director, Hichens Investment Management

'[Alexander Davidson has] achieved a good brief summary of the very complex subject of corporate governance. As a bank non-executive director, I thought the explanation of Basel 2 was particularly good, given it was so succinct.'

Rhidian Jones, independent director

THE TIMES

HOW TO UNDERSTAND THE FINANCIAL PAGES

a guide to money & the jargon

alexander davidson

KOGAN PAGE

Dedication

For my mother
And in memory of my father

Publisher's note

Every possible effort has been made to ensure that the information contained in this book is accurate at the time of going to press, and the publishers and author cannot accept responsibility for any errors or omissions, however caused. No responsibility for loss or damage occasioned to any person acting, or refraining from action, as a result of the material in this publication can be accepted by the editor, the publisher or the author.

First published in Great Britain in 2005

Apart from any fair dealing for the purposes of research or private study, or criticism or review, as permitted under the Copyright, Designs and Patents Act 1988, this publication may only be reproduced, stored or transmitted, in any form or by any means, with the prior permission in writing of the publishers, or in the case of reprographic reproduction in accordance with the terms and licences issued by the CLA. Enquiries concerning reproduction outside these terms should be sent to the publishers at the undermentioned addresses:

Kogan Page Limited
120 Pentonville Road
London N1 9JN
United Kingdom
www.kogan-page.co.uk

© Alexander Davidson, 2005

KIRKLEES CULTURAL AND LEISURE SERVICES		
250 542 859		
Askews		26-Feb-2007
332.6		£14.99
HF		CUL42960

The right of Alexander Davidson to be identified as the author of this work has been asserted by him in accordance with the Copyright, Designs and Patents Act 1988.

The views expressed in this book are those of the author, and are not necessarily the same as those of Times Newspapers Ltd.

British Library Cataloguing in Publication Data

A CIP record for this book is available from the British Library.

ISBN 0 7494 3957 2

Typeset by Saxon Graphics Ltd, Derby
Printed and bound in Great Britain by Cambridge University Press

Contents

Appendices

its THE ASSOCIATION OF
INVESTMENT TRUST COMPANIES

Welcome to the world of

investment trusts

Investment trusts are the oldest type of collective
investment. The AITC is the non-profit making trade
body of the investment trust industry and we ourselves
were formed in 1932.

We represent the majority of investment trust companies and
also work closely with the management groups that
administer them. The individual trusts provide our funding, and
our activities are focused on providing value to them and their
shareholders.

We regularly publish industry data and information on
our member companies which is available at our
website **www.aitc.co.uk**

Find out more at
www.aitc.co.uk

Issued by AITC Services Limited, wholly owned by the Association of Investment Trust Companies. AITC Services
Limited is authorised and regulated by the Financial Services Authority. Registered Office: 9th Floor, 24 Chiswell
Street, London EC1Y 4YY. Because these investments may go down as well as up, you may not get back
the full amount invested. If you have any doubt whether it is suitable for you, you should obtain expert advice.
Past performance is not a guide to future performance.

Investment trusts are public limited companies that are quoted on the London Stock Exchange, whose sole purpose is to make money for their shareholders. They do this by pooling investors' money and employing a professional fund manager to invest in a spread of companies. The range of companies an investment trust invests in is more than most people could practically invest in themselves. An investment trust therefore helps investors diversify their investments so they are not putting all their eggs into one basket.

Investment trusts are closed-ended which means that the number of shares in issue is fixed from the start – for every buyer of an investment trust share, there must also be a seller. This allows the fund manager to plan ahead and take a long-term view of the market.

Every investment trust has an independent board of directors. It is their legal duty to look after shareholders interests and to monitor the activities of the fund manager.

Investment trusts can 'gear up' or borrow money to invest. Gearing works by magnifying the investment trust's performance. If a fund has 'geared up' and the markets rise, investors' gains are enhanced, but if markets are poor investors' losses are correspondingly amplified. However, many investment trusts that do gear do so at very modest levels and some do not gear at all.

Investment trusts cover a wide range of sectors from the Global and UK sectors to Emerging Markets and Japan; therefore, they can accommodate a wide spectrum of risk profiles and meet different investment needs.

You can buy and get advice on investment trust shares through your stockbroker or financial adviser. If you already know where you want to invest, you can buy directly from many investment trust managers who offer ISA's and savings schemes with minimum entry levels from as low as £50 per month or a lump sum of £250.

advertisement feature

Foreword

The financial pages of today's newspapers are for everyone. Any idea that they might be a ghetto area, of interest only to a select few readers, is as antiquated as the belief that the City is the sole province of bowler-hatted chaps carrying tightly furled umbrellas.

The Times financial pages are put together with the intention that they should be interesting and accessible to all our readers. Share prices and profit figures play their part – the numbers are important – but all human life is also there. Money, power, politics and sometimes even sex are to be found featuring in the City pages. Business is, after all, part of life.

It is still only a minority of people who hold stocks and shares directly. Nevertheless, everyone has a reason to be interested in business. Those who work for companies can benefit from learning more about their activities or gleaning an independent view of their performance. It is also interesting to know about the progress of rival companies or those which might be attractive employers in the future. And we are all consumers, increasingly keen to know more about those businesses with which we deal, even if only at a distance.

The business pages come packed with insights into how companies operate and the people who lead them. There is news of drug discoveries and technology breakthroughs, takeover battles and boardroom rows. *The Times* business section includes profiles and interviews, international news and in-depth features. We have controversial columnists and insightful economists offering their views on what is going on in the world. Any reader should find plenty to hold his or her attention.

But while we insist that the paper should be accessible to those who have not done an MBA degree or spent years working in the Square Mile, it is undeniably the case that readers will benefit from having an understanding of the technical terminology the companies use and the way the City works.

That is why I am delighted to be introducing this book. Alex Davidson has produced a work which will give added confidence to those still harbouring a certain nervousness about matters financial. Not only is it an invaluable glossary of terms but it goes deeper, to throw light on how the City works. It also provides elucidation to those who may be coming to the share price tables for the first time and who want to be able to understand exactly what the various columns signify. A 'P/E ratio' is only worth reading if you understand that, while it does in some way act as a measure of profits in relation to expectations, it is in fact the ratio of a company's share price to its earnings per share. Simple once you know, but this is the sort of basic information which people are often reluctant to seek, for fear of looking silly.

Mr Davidson writes in a clear and straightforward manner, which should enable any reader to feel at home with the sometimes complicated subjects he addresses. Armed with this information, readers will find that share price tables have stories to tell and are not merely columns of numbers.

Those numbers are constantly changing. Now readers of *The Times* do not have to rely solely on their morning paper to find out what is happening to company share prices or the latest news on a takeover bid. Like many of those companies we write about, *The Times* is making the most of the opportunities offered by the internet. On our website there is extensive, constantly updated, business news coverage and share price information.

I hope that, with the aid of this book, many more people will be able to enjoy that and the daily business pages in our newspaper.

Patience Wheatcroft
Business and City Editor, The Times

Acknowledgements

To write this book at times seemed an endless task because the City was changing quickly and becoming increasingly complex. The work was not accomplished alone, and I am gratified that so many professionals took time from their busy schedules to comment on and, in some cases, amend my text, and to discuss related areas. Nobody was under any obligation to do so, and yet the help that I received was incredible. These acknowledgements are in no particular order.

Thanks to Jon Finch, my editor at Kogan Page, for his patience and guidance over this project which took so many unexpected – and interesting – turns. My gratitude is due to Patience Wheatcroft and others at *The Times* for allowing this opportunity and for early feedback. Thanks to ShareScope for the use of some charts.

Several investment professionals reviewed Part 1 of this book. I am grateful to Justin A Urquhart Stewart, co-founder and director of Seven Investment Management, a division of Killik & Co, for giving this part an inspired read, and making some enlightening comments. Thanks to Chris Evans, investment manager, Charles Stanley, for a lively and perceptive overview. I would like to thank Charles Newsome, investment manager, Christows, for a shrewd and enthusiastic reading. I thank Alison Cashmore, External Communications Manager, TD Waterhouse, for tireless and crucial help in checking the accuracy and improving the completeness of the book. I thank Vivian Coghill, Managing Director, City Asset Management, for useful broad perspectives.

On futures and commodities coverage in Part 1, my thanks are due for amendments and discussions to Jackie Bullimore, Head of Oil Markets, the International Petroleum Exchange, the London Metal Exchange, and Euronext.liffe, including Claire Terry, Statistician, Pavel Pinkava, Senior Manager, interest rate product, and Libby O'Rourke.

I thank Steven Poser, former Chief US Technical Analyst, Deutsche Bank, and author, *Applying Elliott Wave Theory Properly*, for reading Part 2, Sections C, K, V and W, as well as Section L, critically and making helpful suggestions. I thank Technical Analyst Zak Mir for a quick check on this material from a UK perspective.

I thank Heath Dacre, Equity Strategist, GNI, for explaining contracts for difference and related areas, and commenting on related material. My gratitude is due to Gareth Parker, head of Index Design, FTSE Group, for enormous help on indices, and for his amendment of relevant parts of the draft manuscript.

Thanks to the Association of Investment Trust Companies for commenting in detail on Section U. I am grateful for input from National Statistics, and The Chartered Institute of Purchasing & Supply. I am obliged to Chris Huhne, MEP for South East England, who found time to skim read material about the Financial Services Action Plan, and to HIFX for a quick check on Section G.

My gratitude is due to Marie-Louise Rossi, Chief Executive, the International Underwriting Association, Peter Staddon, Head of Technical Services, British Insurance Brokers Association, John Ellis, Group Public Affairs Director, The Chartered Insurance Institute, and to various senior officials at Lloyd's of London and the Association of British Insurers for commenting on sections related to insurance.

My thanks are due to KPMG where David Ward, Senior Manager, DPP – Accounting and Reporting, cast an expert eye over Section N, made some valuable amendments, and cleared up subsequent tricky points.

BDO Stoy Hayward lent its expertise, which enabled a significantly more precise focus on tax and accounting. I am most grateful to Stephen Herring, Tax Partner, who played a major part in shaping up Section F, and to James Nayler, Senior Manager, who gave a detailed reading to a draft of Section N, suggested important amendments and answered many subsequent questions.

I would like to thank Stuart Collins, Partner, PKF accountants & business advisers, who found time to provide detailed and valuable comments on an early draft of Section N. These caught the spirit of it and helped enormously.

In the IFA community, I thank Paul White of Belgravia Insurance Consultants for commenting in detail on early drafts of the sections covering life insurance, personal finance, bonds and tax. His expertise made a major difference.

Chase de Vere gave me access to its specialists who made valuable comments on early drafts, including Anna Bowes, Investment Manager, Elizabeth Gibling, Life and Pensions Manager, and Catherine Elphick, Moneyextra Mortgages.

I had help from Kevin Carr, Senior Technical Adviser, Lifesearch, and from Tom McPhail, Head of Pensions Research, Hargreaves Lansdown, and Justin

Modray, Bestinvest. Sanjay Shah of Smart Wealth Management gave feedback on the bonds section, and Home & Capital Trust Limited on equity release. Norwich Union helped on home income plans, and Halifax on mortgages.

I am grateful to the London Stock Exchange for reading and commenting on material mainly from Section S. At Ofex, I would like to thank Simon Brickles, Chief Executive, and Nemone Wynn-Evans, Head of Business Development (UK), for answering questions and checking a draft. I am obliged to National Savings and Investments for commenting on material.

My gratitude is due to the Serious Fraud Office for taking the trouble to dig up facts from its archives and to comment on a draft. My thanks are due to Joseph Tanega, Senior Lecturer, Finance and Business Law, Westminster Business School, for commenting in detail on Part 2, Section O. Thanks to Helen Parry, Reader in Law, London Metropolitan University, for an expert and enthusiastic review of Section S.

Thanks to Sandy Grey of the Timeshare Consumers Association for helping me to ensure that the timeshare material is up to date and accurate.

I could not have completed this book without the support at home from Aigulia and Acelia, my family. Thank you again. I thank Complinet for giving me so many perspectives on financial regulation. I am grateful to the Australian Securities Institute for a first class postgraduate training in technical analysis, which helped me to prepare relevant sections in this book.

There are others who have backed this project, in some cases anonymously. Even some who criticised this project have gone out of their way to assist. From all sides, the help has been great. Any errors are entirely my own.

Aequam memento rebus in arduis
Servare mentem

Remember when life's path is steep
to keep your mind even

Horace, Second Book of Odes, *3*

REDMAYNE-BENTLEY STOCKBROKERS

Award-winning Service

BEST ADVISORY BROKER

BEST ADVISORY/DISCRETIONARY BROKER

FREE Guide to Stocks and Shares

A newcomer's guide to stocks and shares

Contact Your *Local* Stockbroker

**Over 30 Branches Nationwide
visit www.redmayne.co.uk**

Members of the London Stock Exchange.
Authorised and Regulated by the Financial Services Authority.

Our Services Include:

- Share Dealing;
- Low-cost ISAs and PEPs;
- Advisory and Discretionary;
- Low Cost SIPPs;
- Monthly Investment (Plan Bee);
- Child Trust Funds.

REDMAYNE
BENTLEY
STOCKBROKERS

Your friend on the Stock Exchange

Free Information call us on 0113 200 6538

To receive more information on any of our services, just fill in this form and return to: Marketing, Redmayne-Bentley Stockbrokers, 84 Albion Street, Leeds LS1 6AG or fax to **0113 242 7735**.

- Newcomer's Guide to Shares
- Low-cost ISA / PEPs
- Advisory Portfolio Service
- Discretionary Management
- Self Invested Personal Pensions

- Monthly Investment (Plan Bee)
- Traded Options and Derivatives
- Overseas Share Dealing
- Child Trust Funds
- Fortnightly Newsletter

Title_____

Name_____

Telephone_____

Address_____

_____

_____

_____ Postcode_____

Apply for your *FREE* Guide to Stocks and Shares Today

Introduction

A lot of people who read a newspaper tend to skim over the financial pages under the mistaken impression that they are difficult. They lose out in more ways than they realise. The financial pages are a mirror on not just business and the economy but also how the world works.

Financial markets reflect, and help to forecast, almost anything that happens, from politics in Europe to presidential elections in the US. They serve as a barometer of sentiment. But finance still has a reputation for being a little dull. The explanations in this book will, I trust, destroy this myth.

You will be reading the financial pages most likely for personal interest, but also perhaps to help prepare for an examination, as part of your work, or simply to broaden your understanding of the news headlines, which are so often linked with financial events. If you are an investor, the financial press can make an important contribution to your success.

Whether you are a beginner to financial markets, or have some knowledge already, this book is designed to help you. It covers newspapers, with examples taken from *The Times,* as well as magazines, tip sheets, financial websites, stockbrokers' research, and company reports.

You may read Part 1 independently. It guides you through the financial pages of *The Times,* in print and online. Your priority will be to understand the share price tables and related data, and you may then progress from there. Part 2 provides the next stage. It is an A–Z of how money works and the jargon. Cross-references appear throughout the book, with the words or terms that are explained elsewhere highlighted in ***bold italic,*** followed by the relevant page or referral.

The book reflects the growth in financial regulation and shows you how to interpret financial ratios, economic indicators and news stories. It covers concepts in technical analysis. The text mainly covers the UK but also some of Europe and the US. Then follow up with the appendices, which list financial websites and further reading.

The financial pages are my world and I have worked with them for the past two and a half decades. If this guide kick-starts you into reading them with greater interest and understanding, it will have achieved its purpose.

Alexander Davidson, MSI

Wealth warning

This book is a general guide to reading the financial pages. It has a broad educational purpose and the author aims to communicate in easy-to-understand language that does not have the status of legal definitions. The author has made every effort to ensure that the text is up to date, accurate and objective, but the City changes daily. This book is no substitute for professional investment advice.

Online information

It is worth mentioning that the online services of *The Times* are constantly evolving and therefore some of the information quoted in this book may have changed by the time you read this.

Part 1

Your guide to the financial pages

FYSHE

Horton Finney Ltd

Stockbrokers & Investment Managers

Growing And Protecting Wealth

Since 1896

Chris Pook

cp@fyshe.co.uk

01480 811400

Member Firm of The London Stock Exchange, OFEX and APCIMS.
Authorised and Regulated by the Financial Services Authority
107, High Cross Street, Leicester LE1 4PH

How to understand the share price tables

Introduction

When you open the financial pages of your newspaper, you are faced with a vast sea of stock market figures and news. It can be difficult to know where to start.

In this chapter, I will show you how to focus on the share price tables in *The Times* and then work outwards. I will explain how to interpret the figures, and how they are linked with the rest of the stock market coverage.

The emphasis in this chapter is on the print, and not the online, edition of your newspaper. If you refer to a copy of *The Times* as you read this chapter and the rest of Part 1, it will speed up your grasp of the financial pages, but you can easily manage without.

The message for investors

Financial markets and the economy are interlinked. Movements in shares, bonds, interest rates, inflation indicators and much more tend to have a knock-on effect on each other, both within the UK and, to an extent, internationally.

For investors, one asset class may be doing well and another badly. The three main asset classes are shares, bonds and cash. A diversified investment portfolio will include a proportion of each. A young investor able to take risks will have more in equities, and less in bonds and cash, and a risk-averse investor approaching retirement will have the reverse. Two further asset classes are commodities and commercial property.

But even if your only investment is a pension, or your main financial dealings are with your bank account, you need to keep an eye on the financial pages. It is not a theoretical skill. Regular reading will help you to adapt your investment strategy to changing markets, and to talk meaningfully with your broker and financial adviser.

Numbers and sectors

In your newspaper

Everything starts and ends with the figures

The stock market has the lion's share of coverage in the business pages of *The Times*, and everything starts and ends with the numbers. If you invest in shares, you will need to know not just their price, but how this compares with the past. You will need to see how the stock is valued through, for example, the P/E (Price/Earnings) ratio and yield. The figures are given in your newspaper.

Millions of people look at the sports pages and can instantly unscramble the mass of names and figures in the football results that give players, substitutes (who and when), number of spectators, red cards, yellow cards and slices of orange consumed at half time. If only the millions realised that less info is attached to a share price but it can give them the opportunity to make real money!

Chris Evans, investment manager, Charles Stanley

The share price adjusts early to how specific events and the economy are thought by the market to be likely to affect the underlying company. It can be six months to a year ahead of events. Ratios are affected, and the company's valuation adjusts accordingly.

For medium- to long-term investors, the newspapers can give useful signals. But if you are a trader, you will need a faster news flow, and are more concerned with market sentiment than with buying stocks that are priced low or have growth potential. *Times Online* could be useful to you, and we will be looking at it from Chapter 2.

How to look up shares under sector headings

As a reader of *The Times*, turn to the two pages headed 'Equity Prices' at or near the end of the business pages. 'Equity' describes share ownership, and these pages cover what are often called the share price tables, although they contain more than just the prices. They are published Monday to Friday and are physically more manageable now that the newspaper is published in compact form.

Your key to the stock market

The share price tables are your key to the stock market. The share price in itself will react quickly to important rumours and events, and you should compare its latest level with the highs and lows. The P/E ratio and yield provide valuation perspectives.

In *The Times*, companies listed on the London Stock Exchange are divided into sectors that represent the broad category of business. In the share price tables, sector headings are highlighted in white against black, and are presented alphabetically. The first heading is 'Banking & finance', and the last one is 'Utilities'.

Under each sector heading, the stocks are listed alphabetically. For example under the sector heading 'Technology', the first share is AIT and the last is Zoo Digital. This order of presentation helps you to:

■ find a stock's details quickly;
■ compare a stock with others in the sector;
■ compare sectors.

When you look up a share under a sector heading for the first time, be prepared for a little trial and error. An investor looking up Reuters could be forgiven for searching under 'Technology' but it is included under 'Media'. It does not help that every newspaper uses its own sector headings and they may differ slightly from those of its rivals. The popular press uses fewer sector headings than *The Times*, and the *Financial Times* uses more. It will cause you no confusion if you stick to one newspaper. Once you are checking the same share price tables every day, you will soon get used to the layout.

Sectors covered in *The Times*

Here are the sector headings in the share price tables, with some examples from each:

Banking and finance	Alliance & Leicester, HSBC, Legal & General, Lloyds TSB, Royal & Sun Alliance
Construction and property	British Land, Hanson, Land Securities, Liberty International, Wolseley
Consumer goods	Allied Domecq, Cadbury Schweppes, Diageo, Imperial Tobacco, Scottish & Newcastle
Engineering	BAE Systems, Rolls Royce, Smiths Group
Health	AstraZeneca, GlaxoSmithKline, Reckitt Benckiser, Shire Pharmaceuticals, Smith & Nephew
Industrials	BOC, ICI, Johnson Mathey
Investment companies	3i
Leisure	Carnival, Enterprise Inns, Hilton, Intercontinental Hotels, Whitbread, William Hill
Media	BSkyB, EMAP, Pearson, Reed Elsevier, Reuters
Natural resources	Anglo-American, Antofagasta, Cairn Energy, Rio Tinto, Shell
Professional and support services	Bunzl, Capita Group, Compass, Hays, Rexam
Retailing	Boots, Dixons, GUS, Kingfisher, Marks & Spencer
Technology	Sage Group
Telecoms	BT, Cable & Wireless, mm02, Vodafone group
Transport	BAA, British Airways, Exel
Utilities	Centrica, National Grid, Transco, Scottish Southern Energy, Severn Trent

How to pick out the FTSE 100 companies

So there you have it, 16 sectors covering the London stock market. *The Times* has put FTSE-100 companies in bold type. The FTSE-100 is an index of the 100 largest companies listed on the London Stock Exchange and is the most widely followed indicator of UK stock market performance. Many do not realise that the *FTSE-100* (see page 265) is an international index because its component companies gain so much of their earnings from overseas.

In my own examples under sector headings above, I have included only companies in the FTSE-100. If you are starting out as an investor, you may prefer to invest in companies in this index because they are best supported by institutional investors. It means that the companies are usually heavily researched. The sheer size of FTSE-100 constituents, ranging from a minimum of £1.4 billion for United Utilities, a highly geared utility company, to £1.1 trillion for BP, the oil giant, offers some protection against hard times.

However, the inclusion of technology companies in the FTSE-100 in recent years has contributed to greater price fluctuations than before. It is a mistake to think that size alone can stop a company from near collapse. Marconi proved the point in 2001 when, in the first nine months, it lost more than 90 per cent of its value, although in 2003 it completed a lifesaving financial restructuring, and has since been recovering.

At about the same time, the press focused on businessman Asil Nadir because he was thinking of returning to England from Northern Cyprus to address fraud allegations related to his role as chairman of Polly Peck, a 1980s conglomerate which at its height was included in the FTSE-100 but by October 1990 had collapsed.

Facts and figures

In the share price tables, you should first find the column that carries the company's name and any relevant symbol (explained below). The other columns show the daily share price change, the 52-week high or low, the yield and the P/E ratio. In Monday's edition, the market capitalisation replaces the high and low, and the share price is weekly rather than monthly. Let us scrutinise each column.

Company name and symbol (Monday to Friday)

The company's name may be accompanied by a symbol, indicating something affecting the price or status of the shares. A key to the meaning of symbols is included at the bottom right of the second page of the share price tables. I will mention here just four main symbols:

- ■ AIM. A black diamond indicates that the company is quoted on the *Alternative Investment Market* (AIM). This is a market for small, risky companies where requirements are more relaxed than on the main market. See page 262.
- ■ Ex-dividend. A small crucifix denotes that the shares are ex-dividend. It means that the seller, and not the buyer, is entitled to the most recent dividend. This is a cash payment that a company can make to shareholders from available profit. UK companies will pay any annual dividend in two parts: an interim and a final dividend.

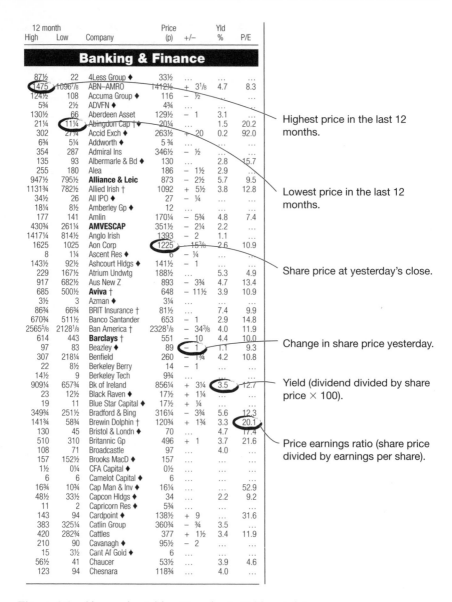

12 month High	Low	Company	Price (p)	+/–	Yld %	P/E
Banking & Finance						
87½	22	4Less Group ♦	33½	...	...	...
1475	1096⅞	ABN–AMRO	1412½	+ 3⅛	4.7	8.3
124½	108	Accuma Group ♦	116	– ½	...	...
5¾	2½	ADVFN ♦	4¾	...	...	...
130½	66	Aberdeen Asset	129½	– 1	3.1	...
21¼	11¼	Abingdon Cap †♦	20¼	...	1.5	20.2
302	27¼	Accid Exch ♦	263½	+ 20	0.2	92.0
6¾	5¼	Addworth ♦	5 ¾	...	...	...
354	287	Admiral Ins	346½	– ½	...	...
135	93	Albermarle & Bd ♦	130	...	2.8	15.7
255	180	Alea	186	– 1½	2.9	...
947½	795½	**Alliance & Leic**	873	– 2½	5.7	9.5
1131¾	782½	Allied Irish †	1092	+ 5½	3.8	12.8
34½	26	All IPO ♦	27	– ¼	...	...
18¼	8½	Amberley Gp ♦	12	...	...	...
177	141	Amlin	170¼	– 5¾	4.8	7.4
430¾	261¼	**AMVESCAP**	351½	– 2¼	2.2	...
1417¼	814½	Anglo Irish	1393	– 2	1.1	...
1625	1025	Aon Corp	1225	– 15⅜	2.6	10.9
8	1¼	Ascent Res ♦	6	– ¼	...	...
143½	92½	Ashcourt Hldgs ♦	141½	– 1	...	...
229	167½	Atrium Undwtg	188½	...	5.3	4.9
917	682½	Aus New Z	893	– 3¾	4.7	13.4
685	500½	**Aviva** †	648	– 11½	3.9	10.9
3½	3	Azman ♦	3¼	...	...	...
86¾	66¾	BRIT Insurance †	81½	...	7.4	9.9
670¾	511½	Banco Santander	653	– 1	2.9	14.8
2565⅝	2128⅛	Ban America †	2328⅛	– 34⅜	4.0	11.9
614	443	**Barclays** †	551	– 10	4.4	10.0
97	83	Beazley ♦	89	– 1	1.1	9.3
307	218¼	Benfield	260	– 1¾	4.2	10.8
22	8½	Berkeley Berry	14	– 1	...	...
14½	9	Berkeley Tech	9¾	...	...	...
909¼	657¾	Bk of Ireland	856¼	+ 3¼	3.5	12.7
23	12½	Black Raven ♦	17½	+ 1¼	...	...
19	11	Blue Star Capital ♦	17½	+ ¼	...	...
349¾	251½	Bradford & Bing	316¼	– 3¾	5.6	12.3
141¾	58¾	Brewin Dolphin †	120¾	+ 1¾	3.3	20.1
130	45	Bristol & Londn ♦	70	...	4.7	17.4
510	310	Britannic Gp	496	+ 1	3.7	21.6
108	71	Broadcastle	97	...	4.0	...
157	152½	Brooks MacD ♦	157	...	...	...
1½	0¼	CFA Capital ♦	0½	...	...	...
6	6	Camelot Capital ♦	6	...	...	...
16¾	10¾	Cap Man & Inv ♦	16¼	...	...	52.9
48½	33½	Capcon Hldgs ♦	34	...	2.2	9.2
11	2	Capricorn Res ♦	5¾	...	...	...
143	94	Cardpoint ♦	138½	+ 9	...	31.6
383	325¼	Catlin Group	360¾	– ¾	3.5	...
420	282¾	Cattles	377	+ 1½	3.4	11.9
210	90	Cavanagh ♦	95½	– 2	...	...
15	3½	Cant Af Gold ♦	6	...	...	...
56½	41	Chaucer	53½	...	3.9	4.6
123	94	Chesnara	118¾	...	4.0	...

Highest price in the last 12 months.

Lowest price in the last 12 months.

Share price at yesterday's close.

Change in share price yesterday.

Yield (dividend divided by share price × 100).

Price earnings ratio (share price divided by earnings per share).

Figure 1.1 Share price tables (Tuesday to Friday style)

By close on Ex-dividend day, which is when the company pays the dividend, the share price should have slipped back by about the amount of the dividend. If the share price is £1 before the dividend of 5p is paid, it should be 95p afterwards. But a stock can go ex-dividend *well,* in which case it might be 98p afterwards, or do so *badly*, when it might be 90p.

■ Ex-scrip. A horizontal line crossed by two verticals means that the shares are ex-scrip, or *after* a scrip issue. Through a scrip issue, existing shareholders will have been given free shares in proportion to their existing holdings. Following the scrip issue, there will be more shares in issue than before, at a proportionately reduced price.

■ Ex-rights issue. A small black triangle means ex-rights. A rights issue is when a company offers new shares to its existing shareholders, usually at a discount to the market price. Afterwards, the share price will be slightly cheaper than before because it is weighed down by the lower priced new shares. But shareholders who took up their rights will own proportionately more shares and the value of their overall shareholding will be unchanged. If they sold their rights in the market, they will have compensatory cash.

Rights and **scrip issues** are explained on pages 247 and 248 respectively.

The 52-week high and low (+/-) (Tuesday to Friday)

To the left of the company name there is a column for the mid-price high and low of the shares in the past 52 weeks. The bigger the difference between the high and the low, the more volatile the shares will have been, creating more opportunity for the share trader, who can profit from both up and down movement.

If a stock is trading at or near its high, and this trading level is far more than the low, the market will have priced in the investment potential. If the share price has risen more than the market average over the last month and the last year, it may indicate likely continued out-performance, according to the Relative Strength theory.

On the same theory, a stock's under-performance against the market is seen as likely to continue. In either case, the market will eventually turn, and the share trader tries to anticipate this. Medium- to long-term investors are more prepared to stay with the stock through its ups and downs.

If you searched for BSkyB in the share price tables of *The Times* of 15 October 2004 you would find it under Media. The previous night's close was 497¾p, not so far from the 52-week low of 465½p. But the high over the previous 52 weeks had been 786p. You might congratulate yourself that you had not bought at or near this price.

Investors will wonder whether a deflated share price will return to former heights. Technical analysts maintain that history repeats itself, but the theory often does not work in practice. Fundamental analysts look at each case on its own merits, researching the company's recent history and sifting financial fact from sentiment to assess whether the stock has become genuinely undervalued.

Market capitalisation (Monday only)

This column includes the market capitalisation, which is the value of the company in terms of issued share capital (share price multiplied by number of shares in issue). The size of market cap is the qualifying factor for inclusion in the FTSE-100 and some other *indices*. For details, see page 265.

The larger companies on the London stock market have a market cap of several billion pounds or more. At the smaller end, Coffee Republic, the coffee shop chain, has only £3.27 million, and there are companies with a smaller market cap.

As a general rule, the smaller the market cap, the less liquid the shares, and the wider the spread (the difference between the bid and offer price), but the more opportunity there is for large price movements. Institutional investors buy larger cap stocks more readily, although small cap funds are an obvious exception.

The share price (Monday to Friday)

To the right of the company name is the share price, expressed in pence at yesterday's market close, based on the most competitive quote from market makers. It is the mid-price, which is half way between the buying and selling price. It reflects the market's future earning expectations plus the rate at which the earnings are discounted.

Yesterday's share price can serve as a prompt for investigating likely investing opportunities today. But by 8.00 am on the day when you open your newspaper, the market will be open for trade and the prices (and other figures) may already have changed.

If you decide to trade, be warned that in the early morning the spread on stocks can be very wide because there are not enough buyers to meet selling demand. It is what brokers dub the 'margarine market', in which you may get the best price at the time, but not for the day.

The daily share price change (+/-) (Tuesday to Friday)

To the right of the share price is a column headed by a plus and minus, which includes any difference between yesterday's and the previous day's close. The change is expressed in pence and not as a percentage. If the share price was 30p and it goes up a further 10p in the day, it is a significant 33 per cent rise. But if the price was 1,000p, and it goes up 10p, it is a mere 1 per cent rise.

The weekly share price change (+/-) (Monday)

This gives you a longer perspective.

The yield (Monday to Friday)

Next to the right is the yield column. The yield is the dividend divided by the share price, multiplied by 100. The higher the yield, the higher is the income to investors as a proportion of the current share price. This may be useful to the investor who requires income more than capital gain.

Some sectors such as utilities are high yielding because of the nature of the business. But growth companies typically have a low yield. Companies are not obliged to pay a dividend, and growth companies often prefer to reinvest earnings in the company, which may prove the best way to maximise the return for shareholders.

Dividend cover tells you a lot

To assess dividends properly, you should also look at dividend cover, which is earnings per share divided by dividend per share. It tells us how easily a company can pay dividends from profits. If the cover is less than one, in a company that has earnings, there may be reason to become concerned.

This ratio is not available from the price tables in every newspaper, but you can obtain the component parts, the earnings per share and the dividend, over the last five years where available, from *Times Online* (www.timesonline.co.uk). You will need to go to the business page, and click on a box there headed 'Instant Market Data'. We will look at this resource in the next chapter.

A form of dividend not covered in the share price tables is the special dividend. This is non-recurring and arises when a company hands back excessive cash to shareholders, broadly speaking because it cannot do anything better with it. The initiative would usually be driven by demand from institutional investors.

The P/E ratio (Monday to Friday)

The last column in the share price tables is headed P/E. It represents the price/earnings ratio, which is the current share price, divided by the earnings per share in the most recent 12-month period. The P/E ratio moves in the opposite direction from the yield.

The ratio is useful mainly as a tool of comparison against either the sector or, to a lesser extent, the broad market. If a stock's P/E ratio is higher than for its peers, the market rates it highly. The share price will be high in relation to earnings – and could go higher, but could also fall. If the P/E ratio is comparatively low, the market is not rating the stock highly, probably for a good reason but perhaps because it has overlooked value.

In comparing companies on the basis of the P/E ratio, be sure to compare like with like. The share price used may vary, depending on when it was taken. In the annual report and accounts, all ways of calculating the earnings per share must be reconciled to the basic figure required under Financial Reporting Standard 14 for accounting periods ending on or after 23 December 1998. The basic earnings per share is net profit or loss after deduction of minority interests and returns to preference shareholders, divided by the weighted average number of ordinary shares. Under International Financial Reporting Standards (IFRS), in force from 1 January 2005 for all listed companies in the European Union, the earnings per share calculation is essentially unchanged.

However, analysts may calculate the earnings per share several ways to support their case – both in relation to the profits element and the calculation of the number of shares in issue. The financial press tends to use *headline* earnings, a definition provided by the Institute of Investment Management and Research (IIMR), now called the UK Society of Investment Professionals (UKSIP). The headline figure excludes non-trading and capital items from earnings, which is the main way it differs from the earnings figure required under Financial Reporting Standard 3 (provided for individual companies through 'Instant Market Data' on the business page of *Times Online*).

In light of IFRS, the UKSIP is talking about revisiting its definition of headline earnings. See entries for *P/E ratio* (page 218) and for *earnings per share* (page 211).

It is worth measuring a company's P/E ratio against its own past figures, although you will need to research beyond the price tables. If a company has no earnings per share because it has not yet broken into profit, it will have no P/E ratio. This makes it not necessarily a bad investment, but probably a riskier one.

Sectors have characteristics

Sectors of the stock market have their own attributes. Companies in the Health sector may spend heavily on research and development but the benefits may be slow to come. The Construction and Property sector is cyclical, which means that its stocks rise and fall quickly with economic conditions.

Sector idiosyncrasies can be reflected in share price patterns. In a bull market, stocks in the Telecoms or Technology sectors are likely to soar far above their fundamental value, which is what they are intrinsically worth, measured as the present value of future dividends or on earnings- or asset-related criteria. The companies may borrow heavily on the strength of the temporary price surge. In a bear market, the wonder stocks may reverse sharply in value, and stocks in defensive sectors such as Utilities or Retailing become more attractive.

Investment trusts, categorised in *The Times* as investment companies, are a special case. They are quoted companies that have the sole purpose of investing shareholders' money in the shares of other companies. To value investment trusts, you need to know the net asset value (NAV) per share, which is net assets (ie, total assets less total liabilities) divided by the number of shares in issue. On this basis, you may compare the figures of different trusts, and if one stands at a substantial discount or premium to its peers, you should look far more carefully.

The NAV is not included in the share price tables of *The Times* although it may be calculated from figures accessible from 'Instant Market Data', via the business page of *Times Online* (www.timesonline.co.uk).

The Association of Investment Trust Companies publishes daily statistics on investment trust discounts, performance figures and similar through its website (www.aitc.co.uk). Such information can also be found on www.trustnet.com. See also page 284 for more on *investment trusts.*

Sector diversification is prudent

Shares should form only part of your investment portfolio. The shares that you select should themselves be diversified across sectors because different parts of the economy perform differently at a given time. If your favourite sector goes through a bearish phase, a better performance elsewhere may compensate.

The theory breaks down once you have diversified your portfolio so much that you are closer to replicating the broad market than being positioned to beat it. But if you hold only a few stocks, a more likely problem is that you will have bunched them into one or two favourite sectors, leaving yourself vulnerable to an individual sector downturn.

To get the right balance is complicated because sophisticated portfolio diversification requires more than just spreading your shareholding across sectors. Size and geographical focus of companies should vary and, as we have seen, you should also include at least bonds and cash in your portfolio. Bonds are also covered in *The Times*, although not in so much detail as shares, and we will take an initial look in the next chapter.

News

If the share price moves significantly, be sure to check the news. In *The Times*, a page headed 'Need to know' has the same sector headings as the share price tables, but also Economics. Against each heading is the sector's percentage rise or fall yesterday, illustrated with an arrow. Below is a news summary. Look elsewhere in the paper for full news stories and comment.

A final word

In this chapter, we explored how to read the share price tables, and some ways to follow it through. In the next chapter, we look at further coverage of shares, including relevant tables and news, and online coverage.

More about shares

Introduction

In this chapter we will be looking at further shares coverage in *The Times*, including company announcements, large price moves, company results, trading volumes, recent new issues and indices. We will explore related sections of *Times Online* (www.timesonline.co.uk).

Stock market data

In your newspaper

Company announcements

A major source of news stories in the financial press is corporate statements. If companies are on the London Stock Exchange's full list or on its *AIM* (see page 262), they must first release information that might affect the share price through a regulatory information service to ensure equal access. RNS is the largest of these services. It is provided by the London Stock Exchange and accessible through its website.

The regulatory announcements, as they are known, may be interim and final results, or directors' dealings, operational updates, or mergers and acquisition information. Non-regulatory announcements may be made via services such as RNS Reach. *The Times* will pick up on important announcements but the following day; *Times Online* may be faster.

Sometimes, a company will make an announcement at 4.30 pm, after UK markets have closed, with the aim of minimising press coverage as well as impact on the share price in the market. But everybody will pick it up the following day. This tactic, initiated by some PR agencies, does not reflect well on the issuing company. The market hates surprises.

The day's biggest movers (Tuesday to Friday)

The biggest share price movements yesterday will almost certainly have resulted from *new* news. The City will already have known the *old* news and have discounted it in the share price.

THE DAY'S BIGGEST MOVERS

	Price	Change	
BHP Billiton	750½p	+19p	Australian Government begins talks on selling uranium to China
Kingfisher	295½p	+5p	Full-year figures reassure
Dimension Data	33½p	+2p	UBS upgrades to "neutral"
Alfred McAlpine	312p	+16½p	Full-year figures reassure
Paladian Resources	184p	+7¾p	Full-year figures reassure
Premier Farnell	185½p	+7½p	Full-year figures reassure

Figure 2.1   The day's biggest movers

The Times has a table headed 'The Day's Biggest Movers'. It shows the 16 companies whose shares moved most on the previous day. Against the company name is the share price, the change (plus or minus) from the previous day in pence, and a line of related news.

Let us look at a few of The Day's Biggest Movers in *The Times* of 15 October 2004. I have added my comments.

On the upside

Cadbury Schweppes rose 10¾p to 446p. Cazenove repeats outperform advice after UK site visit.
My comment: Share prices are driven by broker forecasts.

BP rose 8p to 549p. Oil price touches US $54 a barrel.
My comment: Share prices of oil-rich companies are influenced by the oil price.

Great Portland rose 13¾p to 295¼p. Liberty sells 25 per cent stake to Morgan Stanley at 297½p.
My comment: A stake sale has significant impact on the share price.

On the downside

Rexam declined 10½p to 423p. Ousts chief executive after six months.
My comment: Staff changes can have a positive or a negative effect on a company's shares.

Smith & Nephew fell 11½p to 481½p. Jitters ahead of Stryker trading update.
My comment: Negative sentiment about one company will typically hit others in the sector. Companies will remain 'guilty until proven innocent'.

Corin Group was down 5½p to 311p. Says offer talks terminated.
My comment: A share price will usually rise on bid talks, but decline if the talks have ceased.

All is not what it seems

The line of news given above may not have caused the share price change. City folk may give reasons which, whether they know it or not, are false. The share price could soar, and everybody talk of takeover rumours, but it could be a smokescreen and a few big buyers might be acquiring the stock as an investment.

The market makers have the job of making a wholesale market in shares and they sometimes manipulate the share price in a way noticed most easily by those working in the market. They may drop back the share price to shake out nervous sellers and to get stock back onto their own books. They are under pressure because they are required to quote firm two-way prices in the stocks in which they make a market.

In 1997, SETS (The Stock Exchange Electronic Trading Service) was introduced as an electronic order book for large stocks, and trading in these is much less exposed to share price manipulation than in small stocks which still use the conventional market maker system, but it happens.

In the short term, rumours or speculation can have as powerful an impact as events on the share price. If the price has already risen sharply, you will probably be too late to snap up shares for a quick profit. But after the share price has eased because of profit-taking, it may be worth buying.

In assessing the odds, check news and comment in *The Times*. Be willing to dig beyond your newspaper, perhaps putting questions to the company's investor relations department or, in the case of small companies, the finance director. If there is one message that you take from this book, it should be that the financial press is only your starting point.

RESULTS IN BRIEF

Name	Period	Pre-Tax Figures (profit+, loss -)	Dividend
P&MM Group (support services)	Yr to Dec 31	+£1.4m (+£822,000)	0p (0p)
Paladin Resources (natural resources)	**Yr to Dec 31**	**+£109.7m (+£84.8m)**	**1.7p (1.575p)** final 1.14p (1.05p) payable May 27
Palandri (consumer goods)	HY to Dec 31	-AS$1.05m (-AS$1.1m)	0c (0c)
Portmeirion Group (consumer goods)	**Yr to Dec 31**	**-£1.6m (+£2m)**	**13.25p (13.25p)** Final 9.95p (9.95p) payable May 20

Figure 2.2 Results in brief

Results in brief (Tuesday to Friday)

In *The Times*, company results are reported in the table headed 'Results in Brief'. It has four columns:

1. Company and (in brackets) sector.
2. Year or half year covered, for example Yr to 30 June, or HY to 1 August.
3. Pre-tax profit or loss.
4. Dividend per share (if none, 0p) and payment date.

In the UK, results are reported on a year or half-year basis. For pre-tax profits and dividends, the figures for the same period the previous year are given in brackets. The comparison puts the latest performance in perspective. If a company should report £110 million pre-tax profit for the financial year, it may impress if it were up from £80 million, but not if down from £130 million.

However, the movement in profit is never the full story. If a drug manufacturer reports a sharp earnings rise because it has cut its research and development expenditure, it may impress now, but not in future years when earnings will suffer the consequences. Conversely, a decline in a company's profits now could be a price worth paying if it is due to heavy marketing expenditure from which benefits will show through in future years.

Not every company pays a regular dividend. But when it happens, the City prefers to see the annual figure rising, or at least not falling. If a company is in good financial health, it should be able to pay its dividend comfortably from current earnings. If it cannot do this, it may use its reserves to keep up the payment in an effort to avoid giving the City a negative message about its prospects.

FTSE VOLUMES (000s)

3i	1,989	Johnson Matth	2,061
AB Foods	677	Kingfisher	23,423
Allnce & Leic	9,228	Land Secs	8,050
Alnce UniChem	1,476	Legal & Gen	76,899
Allied Dom	6,178	Liberty Intl	2,092
Amvescap	5,040	Lloyds TSB	29,532
Anglo Amer	5,492	Man	3,196
Antofagasta	1,446	Marks Spr	24,558
AstraZeneca	4,521	Morrison (W)	95,884
Aviva	11,510	Nat Grid Transco	9,224
BAA	8,714	Next	2,856

Figure 2.3 FTSE Volumes

FTSE Volumes (Tuesday to Friday)

Increasing interest in a share is usually accompanied by rising trading volume. Exceptions are when the share price moves entirely on unconfirmed trading interest or other psychological factors. Technical analysts see volume as useful to confirm price movement but do not make the mistake of putting the cart before the horse.

Trading volume is usually measured as the number of shares traded, with buyers set against sellers. In *The Times*, trading volume for individual companies in the FTSE-100 index is recorded under 'FTSE Volumes'. If you access a share price quote on *Times Online* (www.timesonline.co.uk) through Business Market Data, you will find the average and, sometimes, the historic absolute trading volume for the company.

When you measure trading volume, look for relative, and not absolute, size. Note breaks in consistency. If the average number of Vodafone shares traded in a day suddenly doubles, you should ask what is going on. If you keep back copies of *The Times*, you will have previous volume figures for comparison and could create your own chart.

It is worth finding out the number of bargains traded, which is different from the number of shares. If a sudden rise in a small company's shares is due to increased volume from just one or two buyers, this is more fickle than if it is from a large number, and is perhaps grounds for being wary.

If you visit the London Stock Exchange's website (www.londonstock exchange.co.uk), you will find in the statistics section the number of bargains for individual securities on a monthly basis. If you divide the figure by the number of trading days in the month, you will have an average daily figure. You can obtain an actual daily figure from a Proquote (www.proquote.net) or Bloomberg (www.bloomberg.co.uk) screen.

In *The Times*, a daily figure for the number of bargains traded across the market, but not for individual stocks, is provided under 'Major Indices' (discussed below).

RECENT ISSUES

Harbinger Capital	6	...	
Calyx	63½	...	
Gladstone Pacific N	145½	...	
Wraith	107½		
Gasol	9	−	¼
Ant	187½	+	1½
Ventus VCT	100	...	
Brooks Macdonald (140)	157	...	
Afren	57	+	2½

Figure 2.4   Recent issues

Recent issues (Tuesday to Friday)

In the table headed 'Recent issues', you will find stocks that were recently launched on the stock market, including the AIM. The table shows yesterday's closing price, and any rise or fall on the day.

The book runners to a new issue will try to price a deal to reach a small premium, perhaps 10–15 per cent, over the issue price in early secondary market trading. In a bull market, this is often possible. In a bear market, there are almost no new issues and, if they do happen, the price may start trading at a discount to issue price.

The book runner tries to discourage flipping, which is to buy a new issue and sell the shares quickly in secondary market trading. But it may welcome a little of it – ideally from favoured institutional investors – because it needs liquidity to establish value in the shares. If buyers are looking for stock, the book runner will need stock to sell to them. For more about how *new issues* work, see page 245.

New issues do occasionally run amok. In early February 2005, White Nile, an oil exploration company chaired by former England spin bowler Phil Edmonds, was floated on the AIM at 10p, and the share were suspended four days later at the company's request after they had risen to 138½p, and the London Stock Exchange asked White Nile for full details of its plans to buy a 60 per cent stake in an African oil company. Market sources considered that the shares rose so sharply because they were tightly held.

US and Europe (Tuesday to Friday)

Stock markets have expanded their international links in recent years. Markets in the US and, to a lesser extent, in the Far East, influence those in Europe. The time difference oils the wheels. New York closes in the evening and opens mid-morning, UK time, and the Far East trades overnight.

Within Europe, markets have a fast knock-on effect on each other. If merger rumours have arisen in Italy's banking sector, it will boost bank stocks across Europe. Check out the tables in *The Times* (see Figure 2.5).

WALL STREET

	Mar 17 close	Mar 16 close		Mar 17 close	Mar 16 close		Mar 17 close	Mar 16 close
3M Company	85.97	86.00	Crown Holdi	16.98	16.58	McGraw Hill	88.98	88.16
ADC Telecom	2.09	2.18	Daimler Chrys	45.15	45.20	MeadWestvaco	32.89	32.40
AEP	33.91	33.82	Dana Corp	13.78	14.00	Medtronic	53.37	53.07
AMR Corp	8.66	8.65	Deere	67.75	67.20	Merck Inc	31.72	31.70
AT&T	18.88	18.80	Dell	38.20	38.70	Merrill Lynch	59.02	59.40
Abbott Labs	44.53	45.42	Delta Air Lines	4.12	4.29	MetLife	39.63	39.61

Figure 2.5 Wall Street

Wall Street (Tuesday to Friday)

The Times lists 32 large US stocks with yesterday's close, as well as the previous day's for comparison.

EUROTOP 100

	Close	+/-	12mHi	12mLo	Yld%	P/E
ABN Amro NI €	20.25	+0.11	21.40	16.47	4.94	8.27
AEGON NI €	10.49	-0.12	11.74	8.24	4.00	9.99
Air Liquide Fr €	140.50	+1.00	141.90	123.35	2.49	19.51
Alcatel Fr €	9.70	+0.05	13.99	8.95		46.19
Allianz G €	97.25	-1.45	100.95	73.87	1.54	20.39

Figure 2.6 Eurotop 100

Eurotop 100

This includes stocks in the Eurotop 100, an index consisting of Europe's 100 biggest companies by market capitalisation. You will find here the share price close, the rise or fall on the day, the 12 month high and low, the yield and the P/E ratio.

The stocks are priced in euros. It enables like-for-like cross-border price comparisons. But if you compare with stocks priced in sterling (or another currency), you must do a currency conversion.

Major indices (Tuesday to Friday)

Under the heading 'Major indices', you will find the last closing value, and the day's rise or fall, of important indices. They cover the stock market across Europe, as well as UK government bonds and inflation, and currencies.

Stock indices

Have you sometimes wondered why the FTSE-100 could be up, and the FT Ordinary Share Index down, or the reverse? Both represent the stock market but from a different overview. But the FTSE-100, as we have seen, covers the top 100 stocks, and the FT Ordinary Share Index has its own choice of 30. The

MAJOR INDICES

New York:
Dow Jones .... 10626.30 (-6.80)
Nasdaq Composite .... 2016.42 (+0.67)
S&P Composite .... 1190.20 (+2.15)

Tokyo:
Nikkei Average .... 11775.50 (-97.68)

Hong Kong:
Hang Seng .... 13817.99 (-14.53)

Amsterdam:
AEX Index .... 368.36 (-0.01)

Sydney:
AO .... 4217.3 (-12.6)

Frankfurt:
DAX .... 4315.92 (+6.81)

Singapore:
Straits .... 2159.89 (-9.75)

Brussels:
BEL20 .... 3075.89 (-0.18)

Paris:
CAC-40 .... 4032.07 (+12.67)

Zurich:
SMI Index .... 5929.05 (-15.70)

DJ Euro Stoxx 50 .... 3039.80 (+7.67)

London:
FT 30 .... 2049.3 (-7.3)
FTSE 100 .... 4922.1 (-15.5)
FTSE 250 .... 7194.7 (-9.7)
FTSE 350 .... 2514.1 (-7.3)
FTSE Eurotop 100 .... 2336.11 (+1.55)
FTSE All-Share .... 2474.37 (-7.03)
FTSE Non Financials .... 2419.40 (-3.77)
FTSE Fixed Interest .... 137.19 (-0.38)
FTSE Govt Secs .... 100.22 (-0.40)
techMARK 100 .... 1171.92 (-2.55)
Bargains 286870
SEAQ Volume 3227.2m
US$ .... 1.9237 (-0.0047)
Euro .... 1.4376 (+0.0017)
£ SDR 1.2523
Exchange Index .... 103.0 (n/c)
Bank of England official close (4pm)
CPI ...... 111.9 Jan (1.6%) Jan 1996 = 100
RPI ...... 188.9 Jan (3.2%) Jan 1987 = 100
RPIX ..... 185.2 Jan (2.1%) Jan 1987 = 100

1. The most widely used UK stock market index.

2. An index of index-linked government bonds.

3. An index of government bonds, excluding index linked.

4. Inflation indicators.

Figure 2.7   Major indices

former is weighted by market capitalisation, but the latter has an equal contribution from each of its constituent stocks, regardless of size. For details of how the stock market *indices* are made up, see page 264.

You can compare one stock market UK index with others to assess where major market changes may have been most prominent. If the FTSE-100 is up, but the broader-based FTSE All-Share – also weighted by market capitalisation – is down, it indicates that the top 100 market stocks have swum upwards against the tide.

The techMARK 100 index comprises the UK's small and medium sized technology companies. If it has fallen more than the FTSE All-Share, you can pin disproportionate blame on technology stocks for the broad market fall.

Bond indices

You will find here the FTSE fixed interest, which contains 25 UK index-linked government bonds, and the FTSE Government Securities, consisting of 111 UK government bonds, excluding index-linked. The two indices together give an indication on how gilts as a whole are progressing.

This is useful not only if you are a gilts investor. Share prices and bond prices have had long periods of moving in broadly opposite directions although, at the time of writing, have been running together. To compare the FTSE All-Share with the FTSE Fixed Interest is a way to monitor the uneasy relationship.

Volume

You will find here the number of bargains traded in London. Separately, there is yesterday's volume from SEAQ (Stock Exchange Automated Quotations), a quote-driven market for mid-cap stocks listed on the London Stock Exchange and for the most liquid stocks on the AIM.

Look for any big change in these figures from one day to the next and, if it happens, consider the reasons, which may be unconnected with market sentiment. SEAQ volume tends to rise when derivatives contracts are about to close.

Currency

The value of both the dollar and the euro against sterling is shown. The sterling/dollar rate matters most to the British economy, and the relationship between the two currencies in the foreign exchange market is stable. The US is the UK's largest *single* export market, and accounts for almost two-thirds of all foreign direct investment in the UK, compared with less than a fifth in the EU. The UK is the largest overseas investor in the US.

Inflation indices – CPI, RPI, RPI-X

You will find here the best known indicators of inflation. They are the Retail Prices Index (RPI), the RPI-X, which is the RPI excluding mortgage payments, and the Consumer Prices Index (CPI), which excludes house prices. In the seven years to November 2004, RPI-X inflation averaged 2.4 per cent, and CPI inflation averaged 2.3 per cent.

In December 2003, the CPI replaced the RPI-X as the official measure for inflation. Cynics say that it has made it easier for the Government to be seen as successful in its aim of keeping inflation low. But to compensate, the Chancellor reset the inflation target to 2 per cent a year, compared with the 2.5 per cent for RPI-X inflation since May 1997.

The switchover made no difference to economic conditions, but only to how they were measured. The RPI-X is an arithmetic average of inflation rates and CPI inflation is a geometric average, but they both track the changing costs of a fixed base of goods and services over time.

The key point here is not to get bogged down too much in the minutiae of how the RPI-X differs from the CPI, but to keep an eye on both with the aim of understanding the deeper thinking of the Bank of England's Monetary Policy Committee (MPC) when at its monthly meeting it decides on whether or not to change interest rates.

The Times publishes a monthly figure for the RPI-X and CPI in absolute and in percentage growth terms, subject to revisions. It enables you to compare one with another. If you look at back issues of your newspaper or visit the website of National Statistics (www.statistics.gov.uk), you will be able to check how the figures have moved over a period of months. Read related news stories in *The Times*, and the minutes of the latest MPC meeting on the website of the Bank of England (www.bankofengland.co.uk).

From the government's perspective, it is as important not to be below the inflation target as not to be above it. If inflation strays more than 1 per cent either side of target, the Governor of the Bank of England must write an open letter of explanation to the Chancellor of the Exchequer. The pundits have it that a 'Goldilocks economy', neither too hot nor too cold, is the ideal, although they are not slow to add that it tends to be followed by bears.

The RPI and its derivatives remain in use for measuring the inflation-linked calculations of pensions, benefits and index-linked gilts. The CPI is preferred for making inflation comparisons between countries. For more about the *CPI* and *RPI,* see pages 141 and 154, respectively. The CPI is also included in the 'Data' table in *The Times*, to be discussed in the next chapter.

Online

General

We will now take a break from the print edition of *The Times* and turn our attention to stock market coverage in the online version. *Times Online* complements, and partly repeats, the print version of *The Times* and *Sunday Times.* There is some duplication but the website offers faster news updates, and organised access, including to archives. Most of the online facilities are free. It is worth remembering that the online services of *The Times* are constantly evolving, and so some of the details mentioned may have changed by the time you read this.

Visit the site at www.timesonline.co.uk. On the left, under the *Times Online* heading, you will find a contents list in light grey blocks, including 'Business' and 'Your Money', which are the only two sections that concern us. Click on 'Business'.

Business Market Data

A blue box on the top right of the business page is headed 'Instant Market Data', which is a joint venture between *Times Online* and stockbroker comdirect. It gives access to Business Market Data, which provides company profiles, share prices, news, statistics and data, and a charting facility.

Company information and statistics

To access a company's data via Business Market Data, you must enter its name or symbol in the Quote Search box provided. Against the company's appropriate name or symbol on screen are boxes representing the following (put the mouse over it to read):

Research – only for comdirect customers

JCF Analysts info – only for comdirect customers. It includes the analysts' consensus forecast, a useful steer on City thinking. This will initially influence the share price even if it is wrong.

Company Profile – contact details and date of the ***annual general meeting*** (see page 177) are included, as well as the results date and details of the financial year. A *latest* share price is provided, with when it was last updated, and the change since the last close, the number of shares in issue, and the sector. The share symbol is given, which is useful to obtain share prices from brokers' and other financial websites.

Key people in the company, including non-executive directors, are named. The company's history and aims are outlined. Probably the most valuable resource is five years of figures from the profit & loss account and balance sheet, and related key ratios. Earnings that have consistently risen present a stronger case than if they are down one year and up the next.

You may use all this data to dig further. Let me flag an omission. 'Company Profile' provides no detail of the cash flow statement, and you must obtain this from another source (such as the company's latest report and accounts). If cash flow is at odds with operating profit, it suggests possible creative accounting.

Chart – you may pull up a chart for any company. It will show how the share price has performed, whether intraday or over one week, three months, one year, or five or 10 years. Your choice is between a line chart, a bar chart, candle-sticks or open/high low/close. Each has its strengths and weaknesses, and your choice depends on your priorities. For example, line charts cut out the *noise* of intraday price action, but lack detail. Some consider candlesticks particularly good for short-term trading. Bar charts are a popular all round choice. For more on *charts,* see page 82.

You can fit a benchmark, such as a major index, into your chart. You can see the chart on a *linear* scale, which is absolute, or on a *logarithmic* scale, which is percentage-based and more suitable if price movements are signif-icant. If you are a technical trader, you can pull up a chart of any key technical indicator alongside the share price to help time your long and short sells. For details of *technical indicators,* see page 179.

For point and figure charts, or chart patterns, look elsewhere on the internet or use separate charting software. The best software on the market for starting investors is probably ShareScope. It is not necessarily the most sophisticated of its kind but is user-friendly, reasonably priced, and with a good backup service.

Quote – here are the latest bid and offer prices for the stock. They are not up to date, so use as an indication. The change since last close, the price and the volume are included.

With the quote comes historic trading activity, including today's opening price, the high and low, and details of trading turnover and volume. For a 20-day and 52-week period, average price and volume, volatility, and the highest and lowest price are shown.

Data provided includes market capitalisation and dividend/share. There is the earnings per share in accordance with Financial Reporting Standard 3, issued in October 1993, under which, as we saw in Chapter 1, the earnings figure used includes non-trading and capital items.

Relative performance against the FTSE All-Share index is shown over different time periods. There is the beta factor, which measures the share's sensitivity to the market, and correlation. Recent news, including from RNS and the AFX agency, is available.

Related news – news sourced from AFX.

Trade now – for comdirect customers only.

After the boxes, the following items are recorded:

Latest – a recent share price.

Trend – a blue upward arrow represents a price gain of more than 1 per cent since the market opening and a red downward arrow an equivalent decline. A green horizontal arrow shows movement between minus and plus 1 per cent.

Last update – time and date.

Change since last close – in absolute and (in brackets) percentage terms.

Other

Besides corporate statistics, as discussed above, Business Market Data offers the following equities-related data, accessible via its front page:

World indices – you will find here latest closing values of major world stock market indices. Click on any one, and you can access details of each of the various indices, including constituents, chart, quote, related news, latest level, trend (coloured arrow, as described above for individual companies), time and date, and change (absolute and percentage) since last close. You can see the indices together, which enables easy comparison.

UK, European and US shares – there is a section for each, with main indices, including the same entries as for 'World indices', above. It is far more than you will find in the print version of *The Times*, and enables you to make detailed comparisons within a chosen jurisdiction.

Popular shares – nine large and well-known shares are included here, including ARM Holdings, BP, British Airways, Shell and Vodafone. You may access a charting facility, price quote, related news, the latest share price, trend, time and date of last update and the change since the last close.

Closing share prices – four sector groups are listed: Banks–consumer, Engineering–investment companies, Leisure–Professional services, and Retailing. If you click on one of these groups, you will find stocks included listed in alphabetical order, with last night's closing price. To the right of the company's name are the closing price, the daily share price change, the weekly change, the yield, and the P/E ratio. To the left are the market capitalisation and the high and low.

These items are in the price tables in the print version of *The Times*, but inclusion of the weekly share price change and the market cap there is restricted to Mondays.

Closing unit trust prices – see Chapter 4, page 58.

Let us now take a break from *Times Online* and return to the print version of the newspaper to check out news and comment on shares.

News and comment on shares

In your newspaper

General

In the business briefing in *The Times*, the biggest news items are summarised on the first page, enabling you to follow up and read the full story elsewhere. News gives you facts and comment provides interpretation, but the two can complement each other. Let us look at an example.

On 15 October 2004, a news story headed 'Argos and Experian make Gus "a winner"' opened with: 'A rise of 60 per cent in purchases over the internet helped Argos, the catalogue shop owned by GUS, to deliver a 7 per cent increase in underlying first-half sales.'

The business editor's commentary in the same edition of the newspaper gave an analytical perspective in comparing Argos's success with the loss of ground at W H Smith.

Stock markets (Tuesday to Friday)

A daily Stock Markets column in *The Times* summarises the previous day's market news. One half covers larger capitalisation shares, and the other the small-caps, where investment risk is higher but so is the potential reward. The column includes analysts' views, which may alone have moved markets.

Tipping

The Tempus column (Tuesday to Friday) analyses three companies most weekdays and may make a buy or sell recommendation. Like any tipping service, it can get it wrong. But the column is well reasoned and you should treat it as a source of ideas. There is also a daily column, Smaller Stock to Watch.

There is Bet of the Day. This is for those who place spread bets. Many who become involved are gamblers. But these do not last long, and some better informed traders are now attracted to spread-betting partly because profits are free of capital gains tax. The charges are, however, often higher than for trading contracts for difference (CFDs), which the spread-betting firms typically use to lay off their own bets.

US futures trader Jake Bernstein has dubbed ***spread-betting*** (page 114) firms 'user friendly', as they are, as the modern equivalent of the bucket shops in the early 1900s, making money in the same style of casinos.

City Diary (Tuesday to Friday)

The Times has a City diary. It gives colour to the hard news. Read this in conjunction with the rest of the business briefing. You may contribute via the contact e-mail address provided.

Other

Columns include a Stop Press column with latest news, and Deal of the Day, Rumour of the Day (not always coming to anything), and Look Ahead.

There is a Quote of the Day from a key financial markets player. In *The Times* of 15 October 2004, there was a juicy example from David Prosser, chief executive of Legal & General, which brought the pensions crisis home: 'We've studied the iceberg. We know it's an iceberg. And we know it's coming towards us.'

You may read interviews with business leaders, Brian McArthur's paper round, which focuses on newspaper developments. There is sometimes an Economic agenda.

Do not ignore the photos and cartoons. Complete with the telling captions, they bring news to life.

Online

General

On the front page of the Business section of *Times Online* are headings and summaries of the latest news stories in *The Times*, and you may click for full access. There is a features section, and latest news is provided on a streaming basis. A 'daily graphic' provides a colour photograph of a topical news event. You may register for a daily e-mail news bulletin.

Industry sectors gives access to each stock market sector through a blue box. They are the same sectors as in the print edition of *The Times*, except that they exclude investment companies. If you click on a sector, you will pull up news under such headings as 'Top stories', 'In focus', and 'Recent headings'.

Times Online gives website access to columns in the print edition including Tempus, Small Stock to Watch, Results in Brief and City Diary. There are Analysis and Economics sections.

Today's stock market report

In the contents on the Business page of *Times Online*, you will find a Markets section, which includes a stock market report, also accessible via news. This report is updated, sometimes hastily, through the day. It presents latest news first, which is convenient if you are reading quickly. Through links, you may follow up a company's financials, a sector, a market, or related news. You may get in touch by e-mail, and some feedback is published.

A final word

Our scrutiny of share coverage in *The Times* is now over. In the next chapter, we turn our attention to other financial markets.

3

Beyond the stock market

Introduction

In this chapter, we will look beyond shares at bonds, derivatives, commodities and foreign exchange. We will see how they are covered both in your newspaper and online.

Bonds, derivatives and commodities

In your newspaper

Bonds

The bond is a loan certificate issued by a government or company to raise cash. Bonds are also known as fixed interest securities because the borrower pays interest at a fixed rate. In most cases, repayment of the amount borrowed is on a specified date.

As an asset class, bonds are relatively low risk and offer more stable returns than equities, but over the long term, much lower ones.

> *The Times* will educate you about investments. It is all about clarity. If you don't like what's going on with your investments, you should then ask. You can't always make investment fun, but you can make it interesting.
>
> Justin Urquhart Stewart, co-founder and director of Seven Investment Management, a division of Killik & Co.

British funds (Monday to Friday)

British funds are UK government bonds, also known as gilt-edged stocks or gilts. They are backed by the government which has never defaulted on its obligations and so are considered extremely low risk. The returns are slightly lower than on corporate bonds, which have some risk of default.

Gilt prices tend to go down when interest rates go up because investors in gilts can get better returns elsewhere. It is more complicated for corporate bonds because prices take into account the credit rating of the issuing entity and the risk of going bust. Because gilts are repaid at their nominal value, the price moves towards this level as the redemption date approaches. This is the *pull to redemption.*

A table in *The Times* headed 'British Funds' includes gilts under Shorts (under five years until maturity), Mediums (5–15 years), Longs (over 15 years), as well as Undated (no fixed redemption date), and Index-linked, which pay a coupon and capital redemption adjusted for inflation according to the Retail Prices Index, and are for risk-averse investors. The longer dated the gilt is, the more its price will tend to fluctuate in line with interest rate changes.

Let us look at the table in more detail. The name of the gilt is important to distinguish it from others. There follows the coupon, which shows the percentage of the nominal price, always £100, that the owner will receive annually, and is decided by the level of interest rates in the market at the time of the gilt issue. Next is the year of redemption, when the government repays the gilt, always at nominal price.

If there are two years given, redemption will take place at some point between them. Some gilts such as Consols and War Loan are undated and have no fixed redemption date, which means that investors can retrieve their capital only by selling to other investors.

The table shows the current price of the gilt. This is clean, and so excludes the interest that has accrued between interest payments. The 12-month high and low of the gilt's price and yesterday's rise or fall is shown. Next is the current yield, which is the annual interest of the bond, divided by the current price. The lower it is, the higher the gilt price will be, and vice versa.

The table ends with the gross redemption yield, which is widely used to compare returns on bonds. It is the current yield plus any notional capital gain or loss from the current date to final exemption. In selecting gilts, investors will consider both types of yield, and also duration, which measures price sensitivity to interest rate changes. For more on **gross redemption yield**, see page 77, and on **duration**, see page 75.

Let us look at an example from Figure 3.1. Find the Mediums section, and you will see that the first gilt included is Tr 8% 09. In this case, 'Treasury 8%' is the full name of the gilt, indicating that the coupon is 8 per cent and is

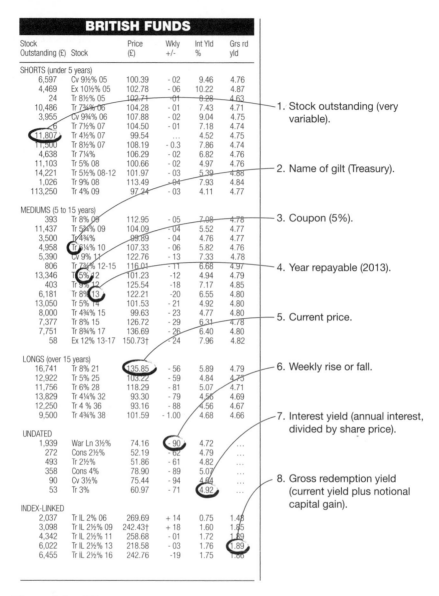

Figure 3.1 Gilts

repayable in 2009. The price is 112.95. So although the government will pay you £8 for every £100 nominal of stock, your real return, known as the current or running yield, is the smaller amount of 8/112.95 per cent, which is 7.08 per cent a year.

In Monday's edition of *The Times*, the weekly rather than the daily rise or fall is recorded. The 12-month high and low prices are omitted, but 'Stock Outstanding' is included. This figure varies significantly between gilts because the Government's Debt Management Office issues different stocks at various times, and sometimes will redeem a stock by converting it to another.

If a gilt is purchased cum dividend, the buyer will receive the interest payment for the period, and so must compensate the seller. But if the gilt is purchased ex-dividend, the buyer will not receive the dividend. Gilt prices may be quoted either clean, as in the tables in *The Times*, where accrued interest will need to be added to the bargain because it has been excluded, or dirty, where an interest adjustment is made to the clean price.

Gilts column (Tuesday to Friday)

A news column headed 'Gilts' appears in *The Times*. It covers market performance, stock issues, and relevant macro-economic statistics. If a gilt moves by £1 per £100 nominal, it is by one point, but smaller movements are also seen as significant. Over the long term, stocks have outperformed bonds by far, but it does not necessarily happen in the short term. For more on **bonds,** including gilts, see page 71.

Futures and commodities

Futures are a form of derivative. The futures contract, when based on a commodity, is an agreement for the seller to deliver to the buyer a specified quantity and quality of an identical commodity at an agreed price and time. The contract may also be based on a financial instrument such as a share, index or interest rate.

Futures contracts are highly standardised and can only be traded on a recognised exchange. They are considered an attractive alternative asset class for portfolio diversification because of high liquidity, low correlation between commodities and other asset classes such as equities, and the potential for dramatic price movements, which is linked to gearing. But traders in futures can lose more than their entire investment.

When you are reading *The Times*, there are three reasons for watching futures prices.

1. Commodity futures (see below) can give you indications of movement in the underlying commodity, and this can sometimes help you with timing your stock investments. For example, movements in the copper price may influence the share price of Antofagasta, a FTSE-100 copper mining company that operates mainly in Chile. The price of oil, as reflected in the futures, may have an impact on fuel costs, and so influence the prospects of quoted companies such as British Airways.

2. You can trade futures yourself through a broker. You can lose more than the money that you put up, and so will need to understand what you are doing and to have had investment experience before getting involved.

The amount of a commodity futures trade need not always be substantial. In March 2005, one broker had set a minimum trade of £9,200 for a cocoa futures contract, based on a price of £911 per tonne for the March contract, which is made up of 10 tonnes. If you trade futures, you may put up initial margin rather than the entire value of the contract. In this case, it is simply a deposit, usually about 10 per cent of the contract size, to show your good faith and on which your broker can draw should you incur losses. Some commodities have mini contracts, which are half the size, and so require half the margin.

Every day, any profits will be added to the balance on your margin account, and if your funds are reduced below a certain level, you will need to top up your margin account. This dual process is known as 'variation margin'. If you buy a futures contract you can place a stop loss to sell an off-setting contract if the price should fall to a specified level – or if the market is falling too rapidly to do this, at the best price available.

3. Futures are part of the broader market, which you need to be watching. Fund managers may use futures to hedge against risk and to diversify an investment portfolio, and speculators trade them in the expectation of profit. Market makers with a risk position in options may hedge it with futures.

Commodity futures

The prices for some commodity futures are included in tables under 'Commodities', a section in *The Times* published Tuesday to Friday. The tables provide an overview, although more detail is available from the exchanges. Let us take a look.

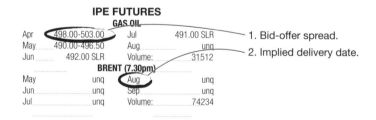

Figure 3.2 IPE futures

IPE futures

Energy is the largest market in commodities futures. In March 2005 crude oil had a 35 per cent weighting in the Rogers International Commodities Index (www.rogersrawmaterials.com). Crude oil is the raw material that comes out of the ground, and gas oil, among other products, is derived from it.

Under the subheading 'IPE futures', you will find prices for futures on gas oil and Brent crude, which are the only oil contracts traded on the International Petroleum Exchange, Europe's energy futures and options exchange.

You will find in the futures tables the month representing the implied delivery date in which the underlying commodity is to be delivered if the contract has not been closed. There is a snapshot (from a quote vendor) of yesterday's bid-offer spread for gas oil futures and Brent futures. A figure is given for volume, which helps to indicate liquidity. The IPE claims a dramatic growth in volume and in open interest, which is the number of contracts still open at close, since inception.

Today's prices are more useful if you compare them with those in previous periods. One way to do this is, as we saw for inflation statistics in Chapter 2, to keep back copies of *The Times*.

The 'basis differential', which is the difference between the futures price and the underlying commodity, is volatile, and has no stability, according to the IPE. In recent years it has been backwardated, which is where the physical commodity is more expensive than the future, but recently there has been a contango, which is the opposite. The degrees of either can vary.

At the same time, prices of futures generally are closely aligned to those in the underlying industry because of the physical option built into each contract. Higher oil prices are seen as likely to persist into the medium term if there is an associated increase in futures prices. A rising oil price can reflect political tensions, strong demand growth, and weather-related and other supply disruptions, and is supported by concerns about terrorism.

More expensive oil may encourage substitution of gas, so increasing its price as well, although many manufacturers will have entered into long-term contracts with gas suppliers when prices were weak, and so the impact will be staggered as they renew their contracts.

Euronext.liffe

Euronext.liffe is the international derivatives business of Euronext. In 2004, it traded over 790 million futures and options contracts, up 14 per cent on 2003, making it the second largest derivatives exchange in Europe. The Exchange also offers financial futures.

Cocoa, Robusta coffee and white sugar futures are traded on Euronext.liffe. Under the subheading 'Liffe', a table for each shows the expiry month, and the bid-offer spread, as well as the daily trading volume, which is a good measure of liquidity. The contracts are the global price benchmarks for the underlying physical markets and are actively traded by managed funds, institutional and short-term investors. These markets are much smaller than crude oil, and are driven more by supply than demand.

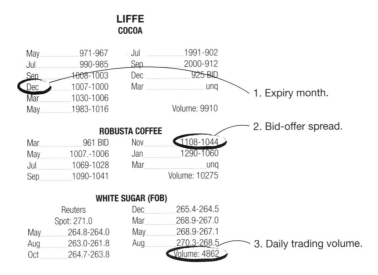

LIFFE
COCOA

May	971-967	Jul	1991-902
Jul	990-985	Sep	2000-912
Sep	1008-1003	Dec	925-BID
Dec	1007-1000	Mar	unq
Mar	1030-1006		
May	1983-1016		Volume: 9910

ROBUSTA COFFEE

Mar	961 BID	Nov	1108-1044
May	1007.-1006	Jan	1290-1060
Jul	1069-1028	Mar	unq
Sep	1090-1041		Volume: 10275

WHITE SUGAR (FOB)

	Reuters	Dec	265.4-264.5
	Spot: 271.0	Mar	268.9-267.0
May	264.8-264.0	May	268.9-267.1
Aug	263.0-261.8	Aug	270.3-268.5
Oct	264.7-263.8		Volume: 4862

1. Expiry month.

2. Bid-offer spread.

3. Daily trading volume.

Figure 3.3 Liffe commodity futures

Cocoa is traded also on the Coffee, Sugar and Cocoa Exchange (CSCE) in New York in contracts strongly correlated to those on Euronext.liffe, and there are arbitrage opportunities. The New York Board of Trade lists futures in Arabica coffee, more widely produced than Robusta, and the main international raw sugars contract as well as a domestic raw sugar contract.

The Times also shows prices for Liffe wheat and barley futures, provided by GNI London Grain Futures.

London Metal Exchange

This section includes a table of futures on the London Metal Exchange (LME). It is the leading non-ferrous metals market, with a turnover of US $2,000 billion a year. The largest metals traded are aluminium and copper. Metal prices tend to be synchronised with global industrial production.

The futures prices are closely aligned to those in the underlying metal industry because of the physical option built into each contract, according to the Exchange. But they may be expected to fluctuate in the short term.

In July 2003, the LME initiated a formal investigation into irregularities in the trading of primary aluminium, triggered by a severe backwardation that appeared at odds with supply in the underlying physical market. Following a five-month investigation, the LME referred the matter to the Financial Services Authority (FSA).

The FSA spent a year investigating allegations of collusion and misconduct by non-LME members in relation to the trading activity. In January 2005 it announced that it had decided, on the basis of current evidence, not to pursue the matter further. The investigation mirrored a separate 1999 probe into the aluminium market that also failed to find evidence of collusion on the LME.

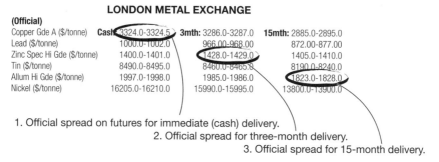

LONDON METAL EXCHANGE

(Official)

	Cash	3mth:	15mth:
Copper Gde A ($/tonne)	3324.0-3324.5	3286.0-3287.0	2885.0-2895.0
Lead ($/tonne)	1000.0-1002.0	966.00-968.00	872.00-877.00
Zinc Spec Hi Gde ($/tonne)	1400.0-1401.0	1428.0-1429.0	1405.0-1410.0
Tin ($/tonne)	8490.0-8495.0	8460.0-8465.0	8190.0-8240.0
Allum Hi Gde ($/tonne)	1997.0-1998.0	1985.0-1986.0	1823.0-1828.0
Nickel ($/tonne)	16205.0-16210.0	15990.0-15995.0	13800.0-13900.0

1. Official spread on futures for immediate (cash) delivery.
2. Official spread for three-month delivery.
3. Official spread for 15-month delivery.

Figure 3.4   London Metal Exchange

In the table above, you will see prices for futures on six metals for immediate (cash) delivery (two-day settlement), and with the higher priced three- and 15-month delivery. There are the official bid and offer spread prices, derived from the LME's second 'ring' of the day, starting at 12.30 pm and ending at 1.05 pm.

Other

There is a price table for Rubber futures, and a table for pig, lamb and cattle average fatstock prices from the Meat & Livestock Commission, which is mainly of interest to farmers and traders.

London Financial Futures

The Times publishes a table of details related to financial futures contracts traded on Euronext.liffe, the derivatives business of Euronext. The prices include expectations of future interest rate moves. In early November 2004, they pointed to rises in rates in the euro zone and Japan over the next few years.

Among others in the table are three-month Euribor futures prices. At expiry, these futures contracts are set to a price of 100 minus the three-month European Banking Federation's EURIBOR rate. EURIBOR stands for the Euro

Inter-Bank Offered Rate, and has been the benchmark of the euro deposit market since 1999.

The benchmark rates are fixed from a daily poll of the most significant banks in the euro zone. There are daily EURIBOR rates across the deposit lending curve, but each futures contract uses only the three-month benchmark rate and only on the day that the future finally ceases trading.

LONDON FINANCIAL FUTURES

	Period	Open	High	Low	Sett	Vol	Open Int
Long Gilt	Mar 05	109.59	109.59	109.21	109.35	9313	17907
	Jun 05	109.38	109.40	108.93	109.14	56524	227225
Japanese Govt Bond	Jun 05...	138.42	138.45	138.38	138.42	485	0
	Sep 05...				137.78	0	0
3-Mth Sterling	Apr 05...				94.970	0	500
	Sep 05...	94.860	94.900	94.850	94.890	51771	293152
	Dec 05...	94.870	94.900	94.860	94.890	62136	256316
	Mar 06...	94.900	94.920	94.880	94.910	26319	130498
3-Mth Euribor	Apr 05...	97.850	97.850	97.845	97.845	3128	49140
	Jul 05...				97.750	0	0
	Dec 05...	97.485	97.505	97.465	97.475	181166	530767
	Mar 06 ...	97.345	97.370	97.315	97.330	125396	395216
3-Mth Euroswiss	Jun 05...	99.170	99.210	99.150	99.200	15803	138459
	Sep 05...	98.980	99.030	98.960	99.020	9244	66552
2 Year Swapnote	Jun 05...	106.235	106.235	106.195	106.210	346	12287
	Sep 05..				105.905	0	0

1. Front month (current month of trading).

2. Second month.

3. This indicates market expectations that the March 2006 three-month euro deposit rate will be 2.670 per cent.

Figure 3.5   Liffe financial futures

Before expiry, the futures price is set by market forces on the Exchange. It indicates market expectations of what the three-month EURIBOR benchmark rate will be at expiry. For example, in Figure 3.5 above, the 97.330 settlement rate for Mar 06 indicates that the market expected that March three-month euro-deposit rate would be 2.670 per cent. This 97.330 price was the market expectation as at the end of the day on 18 March 2005. As expectations change, *The Times* includes this useful updated market information in its daily pages.

The table also includes the three-month Euroswiss, which is based on LIBOR, the London Interbank Offered Rate, offering exposure to three-month Euroswiss Franc deposits at 11.00 am on the last trading day.

Other contracts listed under Liffe financial futures (not all in Figure 3.5) include the Japanese bond, which is a way for professional investors to hedge Japanese exposure; the UK's long gilt and the three-month short sterling interest rate future, offering exposure to UK interest rates; futures on the

FTSE-100 (page 265) and *Eurotop 100* (page 267) indices; and the swap note, which consists of bond futures referenced to the swap market of 2, 5 and 10 year duration.

The discount at which the three-month short sterling interest rate future contract trades is an indication of the three-month sterling interest rate expected by the market at the time of the future's expiry.

The price table in more detail

Let us look at the price table for the above financial futures contracts in more detail. It includes the period until expiry, the opening price, the high and low, the settlement price, and trading volume, as well as open interest.

The period includes the front month, which is the current month of trading, as well as the second month. For example, in *The Times* of 9 December 2004, 'Long Gilt' includes under 'Period' the following two months: December 04 and March 05. In the case of three-month sterling, a third and fourth month are also included. A trade will be based in a given month, although it may be executed at any time.

The open, high and low columns for the futures price are self-explanatory. Once the market has closed, if you have an open position in the market and you would like to calculate its value, you would use the settlement price for this. This is the process of marking to market. The settlement price also serves as a benchmark for OTC contracts.

Volume and open interest give a good indication of liquidity, which is required by sellers looking to find buyers, and vice versa.

Gold and precious metals

The Times publishes price data for gold and other precious metals. Gold is traditionally a safe haven, in demand in times of war and upheaval. When the dollar weakens, people put money into gold.

In the table in *The Times*, the bullion price is shown at open, and at close, with the high on the day. Prices are also shown for Krugerrand, platinum, silver and palladium, and yesterday's prices are shown for comparison. Under 'Data Day', a two-month graph of the gold price, as of North Sea oil, is shown, which tells you a longer story.

A few banks make a market in gold, but the easiest and cheapest way to invest is not to buy bullion directly, which requires storage and does not pay an income. Instead, buy shares in gold companies. In the US, the StreetTracks Gold trust attracted publicity when it started trading in 2004. It is an *exchange-traded fund* (page 284), which trades like an ordinary share but issues units like a *unit trust* (page 288).

Foreign exchange

In your newspaper

General

Today's foreign exchange market is driven by trading from a few major banks. It reflects economic issues and developments within countries. In early 2005, the US dollar was weak because of weakness in the US economy.

Speculators exploit anomalies, and are seen as vultures. The most famous case was in September 1992, when George Soros took a US $10 billion short position in sterling in the belief that it was overvalued. The Bank of England withdrew the pound from the European Exchange Rate Mechanism and it fell in value, and Soros made an estimated US $1 billion from his bet.

At such times, foreign exchange hits the headlines. More generally, news reports focus on the most important currencies, including the US dollar, sterling, the Euro and the Yen.

Currencies are usually valued against the dollar, although sterling is the exception and it is usual to talk of dollars to the pound. Not to take account of this gives rise to the biggest misconception about foreign exchange. When a newspaper talks of the strength of the euro, it is measuring it against the dollar. The statement is about the weakness of the dollar and not the strength of the euro zone.

Currencies may be expressed against each other as cross-rates. These are exchange rates directly between two currencies, expressing a ratio of two foreign exchange rates that are both individually defined against a third currency. As a variation, a currency may be expressed against a currency basket. The sterling effective exchange rate index, known as ERI, is a measure of the UK exchange rate against a basket of other currencies, weighted by importance in UK trade.

The different ways of expressing a currency can lead to statements that appear to conflict but are based on different premises. A currency could be down against the dollar but up against the index, and the distinction is not always made clear.

Sterling can rise or fall in value for various reasons. If it depreciates, it may have been perceived as more risky, or the move may have been simply to equalise returns across currency. If the pound is weaker, British exporters benefit, but this can increase inflation by making imported goods more expensive.

In February 2005, sterling had weakened because it was perceived as over-valued. Interest rates were close to the top of the cycle, and the market expected them to rise a little more and then go flat or fall.

The importance of sterling comes home to us if we buy shares on another country's stock market, where capital gains will ultimately be affected by the local currency's exchange value against the pound. For more on *foreign exchange,* see page 147.

EXCHANGE RATES		
	Bank Buys	Bank Sells
Euro €	1.53	1.36
Australia $	2.58	2.30
Canada $	2.482	2.213
Cyprus Cyp £	0.8874	0.7930
Denmark Kr	11.45	10.21
Egypt	11.73	10.19
Hong Kong $	16.13	14.28
Iceland	126	104
Indonesia	20819	16654
Israel Shk	8.86	7.79
Japan Yen	212.05	192.68
Malta	0.669	0.590
New Zealand $	2.77	2.43
Norway Kr	12.51	11.18
S Africa Rd	12.49	10.95
Sweden Kr	14.02	12.47
Switzerland Fr	2.396	2.121
Turkey Lira	2.7298	2.4153
USA $	2.068	1.835

Rates for banknotes and traveller's cheques as traded by Barclays Bank yesterday.

Figure 3.6 Retail exchange rates

Retail exchange rates

The Times publishes daily a table of exchange rates for banknotes and traveller's cheques traded by Barclays Bank yesterday. There are two columns: 'Bank Buys' and 'Bank Sells'. These show retail rates, which are higher than rates available to traders. Consumers must pay for the convenience of buying foreign exchange in the High Street.

General

In the Monday edition, under the heading 'Change on the Week', you can find changes in the US dollar, the euro and the exchange index, giving the present figure and the rise or fall within a week.

Sterling spot and forward rates

The Times has a table headed 'Sterling Spot and Forward Rates'. It shows the amount of a foreign currency on the day exchangeable for a UK pound. The spot market is where participants buy or sell a currency for immediate delivery

STERLING SPOT AND FORWARD RATES

Market Rates for March 17	Range	Close	1 month	3 month	
Copenhagen	10.684-10.721	10.710-10.719	305-178pr	841-622pr	1. Spot rate selling price.
Euro	1.4347-1.4396	1.4385-1.4388	14-17ds	46-50ds	
Montreal	2.3066-2.3238	2.3130-2.3136	49-38pr	139-120pr	2. Spot rate buying price.
New York	1.9184-1.9285	1.9236-1.9241	32.8-30.8pr	92-87pr	
Oslo	11.668-11.732	11.709-11.715	361-213pr	959-755pr	
Stockholm	13.037-13.109	13.082-13.092	37-25pr	102-85pr	
Tokyo	200.08-201.39	201.15-201.25	89-74pr	256-235pr	
Zurich	2.2154-2,2276	2.2249-2.2259	83-71pr	244-218pr	
Source: AFX			Premium = pr	Discount = ds	

Figure 3.7 Sterling spot and forward rates

and cash settlement (within two working days), and is the most common type of foreign exchange transaction. The forward market is where participants agree to trade foreign exchange at a fixed price today for future delivery on a specified date.

For the spot rate, the buying and selling price are recorded, as well as the day's range (high and low). For the forward rate, the spread is given is for one month and three months ahead, with either 'pr', which means that it is at a premium to the spot rate, or 'ds', which means that it is at a discount to spot.

DOLLAR RATES

Australia	1.2623-1.2627
Canada	1.2035-1.2039
Denmark	5.5733-5.5773
Euro	0.7483-0.7485
Hong Kong	7.7994-7.8004
Japan	104.68-104.70
Malaysia	3.7995-3.8005
Norway	6.0990-6.1015
Singapore	1.6238-1.6248
Sweden	6.8152-6.8184
Switzerland	1.1580-1.1584

Figure 3.8 Dollar rates

Dollar rates

The table headed 'Dollar Rates' shows the exchange rate of foreign currencies against the US dollar. The foreign currency is quoted as a variable amount for one US dollar. For example, the table shows you how much you would receive in Australian dollars if you were to sell one US dollar. It is irrelevant where you were based and in which currency you asked for a quote.

The table shows the indicative market *spread* between buying and selling. The lower price shown in the spread is that at which you can sell, and the higher price is that at which you can buy. The spread can vary significantly from the indicative level, particularly in a large transaction. The table excludes sterling because, as we have seen, it is not normally expressed as a variable amount against the dollar.

OTHER STERLING

Argentina peso*	5.6017-5.6543
Australia dollar	2.4263-2.4277
Bahrain dinar	0.7244-0.7246
Brazil real*	5.2968-5.3577
Cyprus pound	0.8334-0.8427
Euro	1.4376-1.4386
Hong Kong dollar	14.9887-14.9906
India rupee	83.69-84.02
Indonesia rupiah*	17965-18027
Kuwait dinar KD	0.5614-0.5617
Malaysia ringgit	7.3015-7.3042
New Zealand dollar	2.5865-2.5904
Pakistan rupee	113.69-113.70
Saudi Arabia riyal	7.2071-7.2101
Singapore dollar	3.1212-3.1241
S Africa rand	11.7190-11.8188
U A E dirham	7.0589-7.0608

Lloyds Bank

Figure 3.9   Other sterling

Other sterling

This table shows other currency rates against sterling. The information is similar to that in the column on sterling spot and forward rates, explained above, but it is for less major currencies, and there is less detail. It shows what you will receive if you trade sterling for another currency. The amount is expressed in the other currency, and a spread is shown.

Online

General

At Business Market Data, accessible via the business page at *Times Online* (www.timesonline.co.uk) you will find a 'Currencies' section, which gives access to exchange rates. You can find a latest quote, the time and date of the last update (very recent), and the change since the previous quote.

To put each quote in historical perspective, you will also find the change over one week, one month and one year included. For a still broader perspective, click on the box headed 'Detailed quote'. You will find in this pop-up section the average price for 20 days or 52 weeks, together with average volume and volatility and the highest and lowest period over the year, and over 52 weeks. The section has data relating to the current exchange rate, including the open, high and low.

You have access to a charting facility on currencies, as on company data. It will present the currency's fluctuations not just intraday or for a year but also for various periods, including 5 or 10 years.

There is a table for euro fixing rates, which are conversion rates at which some currencies are fixed against the euro. Another table provides cross rates.

A final word

This concludes our look at financial markets in *The Times*. In the next chapter, we focus on the economy and personal finance.

4

The economy and personal finance

In this chapter, we will look at how the economy and personal finance are covered in our newspaper and online.

The economy

The British economy has performed remarkably well for more than a decade and the transformation of Britain's economic performance since the mid-1980s had reduced to irrelevance many of the previous worries about inflation, unemployment and strikes.

These are the observations of Anatole Kaletski, economics columnist of *The Times*, in an article on 1 March 2005. He concluded that the general election campaign in April 2005 would not be about economics.

Two factors have underpinned this state of affairs, according to Kaletski. First, the collapse of communism shattered hopes of creating an economic system superior to capitalism. Second, the dispute between those who wanted a laissez faire economy driven by private market forces and those who believed in government intervention has come to a truce.

Other commentators suggest that the growth in recent years combined with low inflation has not led to a widespread feeling of prosperity, partly because of rises in taxes and in expenditure on non-luxury items such as insurance premiums and education. *The Times* analyses such economic issues. For a snapshot of the UK economy, you should look at statistics in your newspaper, but consider these five points:

1. Statistics are approximate. The numbers may be presented in fractionalised detail but this does not mean precision. Statistics such as GDP (Gross Domestic Product) are frequently revised, and are a guide.
2. They may be calculated in more than one way. Statistics, like financial ratios, may sometimes be calculated in more than one way. Unemployment is an example. Your newspaper will not always explain how it has been done. Treat the figures as a broad indication.
3. Interpret the figures in the context of others. Economic statistics are pieces in a jigsaw and you need to consider the whole picture. Never consider one figure in isolation.

    If, inflation is low, based on CPI, you need to check how it compares on RPI-X and what accounts for the difference. The level of inflation is only half the story. Delve into the underlying causes. A broad inflation threat may be countered by a slowdown in house prices or retail sales.
4. Compare numbers over several periods. View the numbers over a period. A one-off figure could be a temporary blip. If inflation has been rising over several quarters, the message is more powerful than if just over one.
5. Probe deeper. To obtain a broad picture, probe deeper and try to find the themes underlying statistical changes. If you look at interest rates in isolation, you may become nervous but, in context, you can perhaps be more complacent.

    To find out more about what the statistics imply, I recommend two websites. These are National Statistics (www.statistics.gov.uk) and Bank of England (www.bankofengland.co.uk). See Appendix 1, ***Economics, statistics and money markets,*** (page 320) for further suggested web resources.

    Check that your sources are reliable. Statistics are usually based on a sample, but this should be genuinely random, and you should take into account any unusual factors. Statistics from some countries may not be of the same kind (or quality) as from the UK.

Let us now look at the tables.

Money rates (Tuesday to Friday)

The tables headed 'MoneyRates %' in *The Times* include the one shown in Figure 4.1.

Base rate

The base rate is the UK's core interest rate. It is technically known as the 'repo rate', at which the Bank of England deals with the market. As we saw in

MONEY RATES %

Base Rates: Clearing Banks 4.75 Finance House 5 ECB Refi 2 US Fed Fund 2.5
Halifax Mortgage Rate: 5.5
Discount Market Loans: O/night high 4.70   Low 4.58   Week fixed: 4.78
Treasury Bills (Dis): Buy: 2 mth 4.78, 3 mth 4.84. Sell: 2 mth 4.68, 3 mth 4.74

	1 mth	2 mth	3 mth	6 mth	12 mth
Interbank Rates:	4.82-4.77	4.89-4.84	4.95-4.90	5.04-4.99	5.14-5.09
Clearer CDs:	4.80-4.76	4.87-4.83	4.93-4.89	5.02-4.98	5.15-5.11
Dep CDs:	4.81-4.77	4.88-4.84	4.94-4.90	5.02-4.98	5.13-5.09
Overnight: open 4.68, close 4.58					
Local Authority Deps:	4.78	n/a	4.90	5.00	5.10
Eurodollar Deps:	$2^{19}/_{32}$-$2^{1}/_{2}$	n/a	$22^{27}/_{32}$-$2^{3}/_{4}$	$3^{3}/_{32}$-3	$3^{9}/_{32}$-$3^{1}/_{16}$
Eurodollar CDs:	2.75	n/a	2.97	3.23	3.61

Figure 4.1   Money rates

Chapter 2, the Monetary Policy Committee (MPC) sets the base rate at monthly meetings. The MPC consists of five members from the Bank of England and four appointed externally by the Government.

The MPC bases its interest rate decisions on the requirement to keep annual inflation on target, and it considers all economic factors, including the Consumer Prices Index, earnings growth, the Purchasing Managers' Index, Producer Prices Index, Gross Domestic Product, retail sales, house prices and the performance of sterling. For details of these and other measures, see Part 2, Section G (page 140).

The base rate is the major influence on lending rates in the retail sector. The MPC has kept it unchanged more often than not over the last eight years. In the 91 meetings from 1997, when the Bank of England was given the power to set the base rate, to early January 2005, there were 14 rate rises and 15 cuts, but in 63 meetings, there was no change.

If the MPC changes the base rate, retail banks react by changing key lending rates, to keep them at a margin above it. The margin varies according to product and financial institution. A bank may occasionally lend at the base rate itself, which means that it is lending money for no more than the rate at which it borrowed it, and the transaction will be intrinsically unprofitable. The bank that does this will doubtless see a long-term compensatory advantage, such as in gaining market share, or in making profitable sales in products related to the loans.

In the broader context, higher interest rates will slow consumer spending and make it more expensive for companies to borrow, so slowing their performance. Investors will move from shares into cash, which will help to depress share prices.

Halifax mortgage rate

This is the standard mortgage rate, and is set a little higher than the base rate to ensure the lender a profit. In early March 2005, it was 6.75 per cent, compared with the Bank of England's base rate of 4.75 per cent. The figure is the annual percentage rate, or APR, which I define later in this chapter. Halifax is a brand name of HBOS Group, which is the largest mortgage lender in the UK, and has a 22 per cent market share nationwide.

Discount market loans

This covers lending in the money markets. The discount is the difference between the price at which money is lent and that at which it is repaid. It represents interest payable. Figures shown are for the overnight high and low, and the week fixed.

Treasury bills

These are bills of exchange with a short-term maturity (three or six months), issued by the Debt Management Office. The bills do not pay interest, but lenders derive an effective income from the difference between the price at which they bought and at which they sell. The buying and selling prices are given for specified time periods between 1 and 12 months.

Interbank rates

These are the interest rates at which banks lend each other money. Interbank rates are the best indication of short-term rates and are shown here for periods of 1, 2, 3, 6 and 12 months. A range is given, showing the highest and lowest rate within each period. Interbank rates can vary according to the borrower's credit risk, and this table is only a guide.

Certificates of deposit

Certificates of deposit or CDs, also known as 'time deposits', are bearer instruments certifying that the holder has deposited money with a bank or building society at a fixed or floating rate of interest. The holder cannot withdraw the deposit before a specified date without a penalty. The CDs shown here are for respective periods from 1 to 12 months, on a clearer or repo basis. The interest rate is fixed every six months.

Local authority deposits

These are non-tradable instruments issued in the money markets. They are surplus funds belonging to local authorities and are shown here for respective periods from 1 to 12 months.

Eurodollar deposits

Eurodollar deposits are US dollars held outside the US. Banks holding these deposits may lend in dollars to avoid credit controls and exploit differences in interest rates. The range of interest payable is shown here for respective periods from 1 to 12 months. As an example, in *The Times* of 9 December 2004, the range for six-month deposits was recorded as 2 5/8–2 16/32.

Eurodollar CDs

These are **certificates of deposit** (see page 50), issued in dollars and held outside the US, commonly in London. The range is again shown for respective periods of between 1 and 12 months.

EUROPEAN MONEY DEPOSITS %					
Currency	1 mth	3 mth	6 mth	12 mth	Call
Dollar:	2.85-2.72	3.05-2.92	3.29-3.16	3.69-3.56	2½ -2½
Sterling:	4¹³/₁₆-4²⁵/₃₂	4¹⁵/₁₆-4²⁷/₃₂	5¹/₁₆-4³¹/₃₂	5¹/₈-5¹/₃₂	5¹/₄-3³/₄
Euro:	2³/₃₂-2	2¹/₈-2¹/₃₂	2³/₁₆-2³/₃₂	2⁵/₁₆-2⁹/₃₂	2-2
Yen:	¹/₁₆-¹/₃₂	³/₃₂-0	¹/₁₆-0	³/₃₂-¹/₃₂	1-0
Canada:	2⁵/₈-2¹/₂	2²¹/₃₂-2¹⁷/₃₂	2²⁵/₃₂-2²¹/₃₂	3¹/₁₆-3	3-2

Figure 4.2   European money market deposits

European money deposits (%) – Monday to Friday

This table in *The Times* contains money market rates for five major currencies. They apply in all the countries in the euro zone, which excludes London.

The table shows what a dollar deposit with a bank, perhaps in Paris or Frankfurt (the key financial centres in the euro zone), would pay if the cash were deposited for a specified period. This is for 1, 3, 6 or 12 months, or it is 'on call', which is where money is borrowed overnight in cash and the lender has the right to retrieve it at short notice. The same is shown for a deposit in sterling, the euro, the Yen or the Canadian dollar.

Data (Mondays)

This is a weekly column on Mondays in *The Times*. It provides a snapshot of basic macro-economic statistics, which the market will already have discounted. What influences markets now is the forecast figure, and the direction over a period. The following four statistical measures are included under country headings.

DATA	
UK	
Base rate	4.75%
Inflation (CPI, Jan)	1.6%
Unemployment (Oct-Dec)	4.7%
GDP growth (Q4)	0.7%
US	
Fed funds rate	2.5%
Inflation (Dec)	3.3%
Unemployment (Jan)	5.2%
GDP growth (Q4)	0.8%
Eurozone	
Refi rate	2.0%
Inflation (Jan)	2.1%
Unemployment (Dec)	8.9%
GDP growth (Q4)	0.2%
Japan	
Official discount rate	0.1%
Inflation (Dec)	-0.2%
Unemployment (Dec)	4.4%
GDP growth (Q3)	0.1%

Figure 4.3 Data

UK

1. Base rate
As discussed under 'Money rates', page 48.

2. Inflation (CPI)
This is the inflation figure based on the Consumer Purchase Index.

3. Unemployment
Unemployment shows how tight the labour market is, which reflects economic conditions. With rising unemployment, fewer companies may be expanding their businesses. When unemployment is low, this could indicate economic growth and potential overheating.

There is more than one way to calculate unemployment. The method used in *The Times* is based on the ILO (International Labour Organization) definition, which counts jobless people who want to work, who are available to work and who are actively seeking employment. A separate series, the claimant count, measures how many unemployed people are claiming unemployment-related benefits, which is always a lower measure. There is a major difference between the two series.

A quarterly ILO unemployment figure is shown here, using data from the household-based Labour Force Survey. In the three months to December 2004, it was 4.7 per cent, and had not been so low in a previous phase since 1975. The figures back to 1984 are available free online from National Statistics (www.statistics.gov.uk).

In February 2005, some economists felt that the next move in interest rates would be decided by the labour market. When the economy is strong, investors still tend to react adversely to a decline in unemployment because they fear that it might be inflationary. When the economy is weak, investors see a decline in unemployment as an improvement.

In the 1970s, UK monetary policy was based on the perception of a trade-off between unemployment and inflation and, by 1975, the rate of inflation had risen to 25 per cent. Economists now acknowledge that there is no strong link, partly because the unemployment rate does not fully reflect the slack in the labour market, which includes those who are not looking for a job.

4. GDP quarterly growth

The Gross Domestic Product (GDP) of a country is a measure of a country's economic output. It is the most important indicator of the economy's health, representing the combined market value of final goods and services produced in the economy, excluding exports and imports, over a given period. It omits unpaid and domestic work, bartering and the black economy, as well as some intangibles.

The GDP is only an approximate figure, and the government periodically revises it. Economists will break down the GDP into its component parts, and analyse its link with investment in new machines and perhaps changes in employment trends.

This table in *The Times* compares GDP growth in the latest quarter with the figure in the previous one. The figures used are real, which means that they are adjusted to remove the effects of price changes. They are seasonally adjusted.

Generally, a rising GDP in a strong economy gives rise to inflation fears and can cause share prices to fall, although in a weak economy, it is seen as a sign of expansion. If GDP rises by more than 3 per cent in each of four quarters in succession, the Bank of England will probably raise interest rates to restrain it.

For the investor, GDP data come too late to help forecast market trends. Industrial production (not included in *The Times*) is more useful for forecasting because industrial production (up to 25 per cent of GDP in industrialised countries) rises and falls faster than sales.

Other

The above four statistics, or equivalents, are shown for the US, the euro zone and Japan. You may compare the UK base rate with the Fed funds rate in the US, and the euro zone's Refi (ie refinancing) rate, issued by the European Central Bank.

The statistics can vary widely, depending on the economic circumstances of the individual country or region. In November 2004, GDP in the US was high, driven by consumer spending that economists considered unsustainable. At the same time, in the euro zone, GDP was recovering from low levels.

Online

Interest rates

Go to *Times Online,* Business, enter 'Business Market Data', and you will find on the bottom left, under the heading 'Market Focus', click-on access to interest rates. It covers UK rates including ***LIBOR*** (see page 198) and European rates including ***EURIBOR*** (see page 197).

Against every UK or European rate in the table is the current rate, time of the last update, and most recent change. A quote provides, among other things, the average rate, volatility, and highest rate over both the last calendar year and 52-week period. The change over a week, a month and three months is recorded, and there is access to charting.

Economics

In this section, accessible via the front page of Business at *Times Online,* you will find news stories and access to the following.

The Times Monetary Policy Committee

A *shadow* MPC appointed by *The Times* meets every month to recommend the Bank of England's next move on interest rates, and its reports are published here. This is ahead of the monthly meeting of the Bank's MPC to review rates.

The euro

You will find here news stories and web links. The euro is the single currency introduced on 1 January 2002, as part of Economic and Monetary Union, when 12 European currencies replaced their national currencies with it. Participating countries, which do not include the UK, share interest rates set by the European Central Bank in Germany, whose main task is to maintain the purchasing power of the ***euro*** (see page 145).

Target 2.0 – Target Two Point Zero

Here are details of the Bank of England's national competition for schools, sponsored by *The Times*. A-level students are invited to set interest rates to achieve the government's inflation target. The site provides relevant economic briefings.

Personal finance

In your newspaper

General

'Money' is a Saturday subsection of *The Times* that focuses on personal finance. It explains new products, and offers an education in running your personal finances. It covers mortgages, insurance tax and credit, as well as fund selection and the stock market.

There is a news roundup under 'In Brief', and there are the 'Stockwatch', 'Adwatch' and 'Whine of the Week' columns. A letters section focuses mainly on reader complaints about poor service from financial institutions. You can learn a lot from the example of others.

'A Question of Money' provides responses from a financial agony aunt to selected reader queries and complaints. *The Times* may take up the cudgel with the financial institutions involved.

Financial makeover

'Makeover' every week invites a panel of financial services professionals to comment on a member of the public's financial affairs. Their opinions are published, and a journalist may provide an overview. Readers may apply to be profiled.

Collecting

'Money Collecting' focuses on rare items, often on sale at new exhibitions, and provides contact details.

Unit trusts and OEICs

The Times Money Unit Trust and Open-ended Investment Company Prices Service lists unit trusts and open-ended investment companies (OEICs). Funds are grouped under the name of the fund provider, with its contact telephone number(s). There is the sell and buy price, the weekly rise and fall, and the yield. A 'Funds in Focus' column provides comment. See also Part 2 for more on *unit trusts* (page 288) and *OEICs* (page 287).

Money Shop

Under 'Money Shop' you will find best buys under the following subheadings.

1. Savers' Best Buys

Here are bank and building society accounts. The notice accounts pay higher interest than the no-notice, and internet accounts pay the highest because running costs are lowest, but there are some exceptions. Included are details of accounts with an introductory bonus, as well as cash *ISAs* (see page 135 for details of this tax-efficient wrapper).

New accounts that pay high interest may reduce the rate after the first rush of customers. To keep your cash deposits working hardest, you may need to switch accounts.

2. National Savings & Investments

Here are accounts and tax-efficient products available from National Savings & Investments. Included are a mini-cash ISA and guaranteed equity bonds.

3. Permanent interest-bearing shares

These are 'Fixed Rate' and 'Permanent Subordinated Bonds'. The gross coupon, buying price, gross yield, issue price and minimum purchase amount are shown.

4. Mortgages

Here are the most cost-effective mortgages, with a contact number. The headings are: Fixed Rates, Capped Rates, First Time Buyers, Discounted Variable Rates, Variable Rates and 100% Mortgages. (For more, see page 234).

In 2004, the standard variable rate on mortgages rose at the lenders' margin above the Bank of England's official interest rate, and fixed rates were offered and withdrawn in line with fluctuations in one- to five-year swap rates. Mortgage arrears were low but the size of deposits required on property purchases rose, according to industry sources.

The APR

The APR is the annual percentage rate, which must be given in every credit advertisement and promotional piece. Use it as a yardstick when you compare loans or mortgages. The APR represents not just the interest charge, which some lenders make the mistake of looking at alone, but all the costs charged over the lifetime of the loan.

The lower the APR, the better, but check further. If the loan has a discounted rate, as in a discount mortgage, the APR may only apply to that and will not take account of a rate change after the initial discounted period. How regularly interest is paid will impact on the APR.

5. Unsecured personal loans

The best rates for unsecured personal loans are included. Check the APR (see box above).

6. Credit cards

Credit cards with the better lending terms are listed. At the time of writing, the most enticing is from Sainsbury's Bank with 0 per cent APR for 12 months, but note that it is for a restricted period, as is typical for such deals.

7. Cheapest level term assurance

Term assurance is the simplest and cheapest life cover. It has no savings element, and the insurance company will pay out if the insured dies within the specified term. If terminal illness cover was included, a payment may be made if the insured is likely to live for only a short period. For more on life insurance, see page 164.

8. Best with-profits personal pension

Personal pensions are available to the self-employed or anybody not in a company pension scheme.

The with-profits personal pension enables investment of your contributions into a with-profits fund. Annual bonuses are added to the fund by increasing the value of units, or adding more units, and cannot be removed. This should partly protect the investor from stock market fluctuations.

The unitised with-profits personal pension combines a with-profits fund with a share in investment growth, which makes it slightly higher risk. It buys units in an insurance company's with-profits fund, and they will rise in value with the insurer's investment performance and profits. A terminal bonus may be awarded on maturity.

The best performers in each of these two categories are listed. Bear in mind that past performance may not be repeated. For more on pensions, see page 167.

9. Unit Trust Funds over five years

The top few performers are shown, with the results of £1,000 invested over five years. Small company and specialist funds have more scope for a volatile performance than large company funds. For selection criteria, see under 'unit trusts', page 58.

10. Investment Trusts over five years

The top few performers are shown with the results of £1,000 invested over five years. They have recently proved a better investment than the top unit trusts although, as in any investment, past performance is no guarantee of the future. For an overview of investment trusts, see page 284.

11. Pension annuities

A pension annuity is a contract that converts pension capital into income. An insurance company pays income regularly to the annuitant based on the lump sum that he or she has accumulated in the pension.

The table shows the gross annual annuity based on a £100,000 lump sum for the highest paying providers. It is guaranteed for five years, and paid monthly in arrears.

The older the applicant, the shorter is his or her life expectancy, and so the higher the annuity rate. For details, see 'annuities' on page 169.

Unit trusts

	Sell	Buy	+/−	Yld %
AXA FUND MGRS LTD				
Admin & Enq 0117 989 0808				
UK/Global Investment Companies				
Extra Inc Inc B #	94.33	... †	− 0.08	5.37
UK Eqty Inc Acc #	130.50	... †	− 0.40	3.84
UK Eqty Inc Inc #	104.90	... †	− 0.30	3.84
UK Gwth Acc A ‡	89.47	...	− 0.46	1.93
UK Gwth Acc B ‡	86.81	...	− 0.45	1.43

Figure 4.4   Unit trust information service

Unit trust information service (Tuesday to Friday)

I have left discussion of unit trusts until the end of Part 1 because what I have covered in the text up to now will help you to understand and select them. To have unit trusts is ideal if you are disinclined to select individual shares and other investments, because a fund manager will do the work for you. Your investment will be well diversified, which reduces the risk. The unit trust is open-ended, meaning that the fund may create as many more units as are required to meet investor demand.

The Times carries a paid-for unit trust information service, which lists some fund managers and their funds. Included are the fund's buy and sell price, the daily up or down movement, and the yield (dividend, expressed as a percentage of the current fund price). In unit trusts, as in shares, the yield is usually only a small part of the overall return.

There is access to slightly more detailed information about these unit trusts via Instant Market Data on *Times Online* (www.timesonline.co.uk), through four alphabetical groupings. The online listing gives the yield in absolute as well as in percentage terms, and the weekly, as well as daily, rise.

If you are a serious unit trust investor, this information service is a springboard for further research. There are more than 1,800 funds in this country, but most of the money invested goes to a few, which have the biggest marketing budgets but not necessarily the best track record.

The invasion of the OEICs

Many unit trusts have already converted to open-ended investment companies (OEICs), which are a more modern alternative. Unlike unit trusts, the OEIC has a single price for buying or selling, and it discloses any initial charges separately.

By the time this book is in your hands, the conversion process will have developed. But the term 'unit trust' will probably, as now, cover both products generically, just as some users of Dyson vacuum cleaners still call them Hoovers.

Selection criteria

For both unit trusts and OEICs, the risk profile, management style and five-year track record vary. In choosing which to buy, you will need to do your own research. Consider these four points:

1. how it fits into your investment portfolio;
2. performance;
3. charges;
4. price.

Let us look at each.

1. How it fits into your investment portfolio

Unit trusts can include any combination of equities, bonds, commodities or commercial property. They are diversified themselves but can also be part of a diversified portfolio.

2. Performance

Performance is tricky to assess. The mantra of collective investments – sourced to regulatory requirements – is that the past is no guide to the future. But it is all that we have to go on. Experience shows that a fund that has been in the top quartile of its sector for performance over at least the last five years is more likely to stay there than not, provided that its present management has not changed for the worse. But an absolute top (or bottom) performer in one year is unlikely to repeat the trick the next.

It is not usually a good idea to come in and out of unit trusts too frequently, because of the high charges. But it can be a good idea to take profits on, for instance, a holding in a technology unit trust where you have doubled your money in the last year. Not only may it not repeat such a good year but it may have developed over the period into a bigger percentage weighting of your funds invested than you had planned.

3. Charges

Charges on unit trusts have a significant impact on performance and, unlike on OEICs, are partly opaque.

On either form of collective investment, there is an initial charge, also known as a 'front-end charge', which includes the commission that you pay to the adviser or broker who sold you the fund. It can vary from nothing, as in the case of some trackers and money market funds, to a highest level for equity funds of up to 6 per cent of the capital sum invested.

In addition, there is an annual management charge. This is typically between 0.75 and 2 per cent a year, but can be more. Across the industry, the charge is increasing, but is broadly offset by a reduction in servicing fees, according to analyst Fitzrovia. Other fees cover administration, custody, audit and legal expenses. They total between 0.2 and 0.6 per cent and are not part of the annual management charge. They are detailed in the annual report and accounts.

To obtain a useful figure for the charges on a unit trust or an OEIC, find the total expense ratio (TER), which enables like-for-like comparisons across the industry. The TER is a single percentage figure showing fees as a proportion of a fund's average assets. It reflects charges more accurately than the widely quoted management charge, although it excludes commission paid to brokers by fund managers.

The implementation of the TER has been under consultation by the Financial Services Authority (FSA), which regulates the unit trust industry. It is likely to become required reporting for all unit trusts and OEICs in the UK, in accordance with European proposals.

The level of charges should not have as much priority as performance. Some funds more than compensate for high charges with a high performance, although there is no guarantee that it will continue. Some *multi-manager funds* (see page 286) are in this category.

4. Price

The Unit Trust Information Service in *The Times* shows the sell price and the buy price of unit trusts reset daily. If you buy or sell, you will not know the exact price of your deal until the next revaluation, often at midday.

From the tables in *The Times* you can check how wide in percentage terms is the spread, which is the difference between buying and selling prices, and compare it with peers. The manager may widen the spread if there are either more buyers or more sellers. At most, it will amount to the gap between maximum price perimeters set by the FSA.

How to find out more about unit trusts and OEICs

The simplest way to find out information about unit trusts and OEICs is directly from the fund managers. Contact those listed in *The Times* Information Service through the telephone numbers provided. Compare track record and charges, but set like against like. An emerging market fund is not comparable with one investing in pan-European blue chip companies.

You can also discover a fund's track record in the magazines *Money Management* or *Bloomberg Money,* or through a good website focusing on funds such as Morningstar.co.uk (www.morningstar.co.uk).

You will find an overview of unit trusts, OEICs, investment trusts and similar investment schemes – including low-cost tracker funds – in Section U (page 284).

A final word

We have now finished exploring the financial pages in *The Times*. If you want to read another newspaper as well, a good choice would be the *Financial Times,* which has been described as the City's bible. The Sunday newspapers are good for more leisurely articles, as well as for rumours and gossip. Of the magazines, *Investor's Chronicle* has stock tips, how-to articles and market perspectives, and is reliably researched. *The Economist* is an excellent read, and has a surprising amount of financial markets coverage.

Be cautious about stock market newsletters, which are typically written to impress but not necessarily well informed. They may sometimes have good tips, but also have plenty of poor ones. Internet message boards can be still more dubious. Many who post messages have a vested interest in either promoting or denigrating a stock. If a message seems important, check its veracity with a reliable source. For recommended investment books, see Appendix 2.

In the rest of this book we will define and explain terms and concepts that arise in the financial pages. You may use Part 2 for reference, or to browse, or even to read straight through.

Your A–Z guide to money and the jargon

Analysts in the stock market

Introduction

City analysts are frequently quoted in the financial pages. They can be very influential in the stock market but are required, among other things, not to compromise research that is held out to be objective. In this section, we will look at how analysts work, and some related regulatory issues. See also Section R, page 250.

Analysts

Analysts are the intelligentsia of the stock market. Most are fundamental analysts, but others are technical. In this subsection we will look at each.

Fundamental

Fundamental analysts focus on the company's fundamentals. They assess value from trading statements and the report and accounts, liaise with the management, and interpret news affecting the sector.

Sell-side analysts at investment banks and brokers publish research, which they disseminate to salespeople at their firm, and to clients. Buy-side analysts work for the fund managers and are in a less high-profile position.

The analyst produces valuation models on spreadsheets based largely on forecasts of the company's future plans and prospects, and comes up with figures that are often in line with those of other analysts. The sell-side analyst may cover only six or seven companies in a sector and will be issuing new notes on each to keep up with corporate or market developments affecting valuation.

Over the last two decades, investment banking, including securities issues and mergers and acquisitions, has become far more lucrative than trading. A bank may take 6 per cent of the proceeds of any IPO (new issue of shares) that it launches as book running, or 2 per cent of any secondary share offering.

In the past, analysts linked with this success were taking some of the cash in the form of bonuses. In the US it led to some biased recommendations, particularly on high tech stocks in the bull market until the end of March 2000. UK regulators found no conclusive evidence of systematic bias but noted that retail investors were at a disadvantage.

Regulators on either side of the Atlantic have since focused on *conflicts of interest* (see page 69) between research and investment banking. At the time of writing, we are in a new regulatory environment in which disclosure of these conflicts is required, and perceived *market abuse* (see page 258) leads to regulatory action.

Analysts in today's markets still give specific recommendations to buy, sell or hold, or similar, although, in at least one investment bank, they have started moving away from it. Unlike in the US, financial institutions in the UK are not required to disclose what proportion of their research consists of *sell* recommendations and, even in today's highly regulated climate, it is not many.

This is understandable because *sell* recommendations can offend the companies, which, after all, provide analysts with most of their information. The companies may be potential or actual corporate clients of the firm's investment banking division. In the past, analysts, particularly for smaller firms, have been terrified that if they are not kind about companies, they will be cut off from essential information. But companies are now constrained from favouring one analyst over another, and are required to disseminate information equally and simultaneously to all.

The analyst must play a similar game and not distribute *price-sensitive information* (see page 70) that has not been properly disseminated to the market. *Chinese walls* (see page 68) must be in place. The regulatory pressure is on the analyst not to obtain, or provide, the exclusive information that alone investors really seek. In their written research and e-mails, analysts play it by the book. In oral communications with favoured clients, there is the opportunity to speak off the record.

There is no doubt that the old days when former heads of equity capital markets in investment banks would instruct analysts in what to write about prospective actual or corporate clients are over, as are many of the huge bonuses. But analysts have gone too far down the route of backing up salespeople to become again the backroom number crunchers that they had been until the 1970s.

Analysts use informed guesswork to compensate for the lack of key company data available. Some of this is necessary even for those who come from an industry background. Anecdotal evidence suggests that only about a quarter of analysts are qualified accountants. This is not necessarily a drawback in a job that requires a lot more than understanding the intricacies of the annual report and accounts.

Analysts in major firms can work up to 12 hours a day, up to 6 or 7 days a week, with work split perhaps 50:50 between dealing with clients and actual research, and the job security is nil. The average age of City analysts is, according to one survey, only 27.

Technical

Technical analysts focus on price movements and, to a lesser extent, trading volume, and make forecasts based on perceived past trends. They tend to work independently or for large financial institutions and are far fewer in number than their fundamental counterparts.

As a secondary source, the analyst uses oscillators that focus on, among other things, whether the market is overbought or oversold, its relative performance and its rate of change. The oscillator's movement, viewed against that of the share price, often on the same chart, can indicate, among other things, when to open or close a long or short position.

The analyst's aim is to identify *trends and cycles* (see more, see Section W, page 293), although they are notoriously fickle. In its strongest form, the technical approach rejects the fundamental, although the two can be used concurrently.

Many successful investors give no credence to technical analysis. US hedge fund entrepreneur Victor Niederhoffer believes that trends do not exist, which undermines the concept at root. Fund manager Ralph Wanger considers that technical analysis has a following because of the illogical appeal of patterns.

Wall Street trader Jim Rogers once said that he had never seen a rich technician except those who sold their services. Academics have largely dismissed technical analysis as inconsistent with financial theory.

There are others who value technical analysis more. They are, on balance, more likely to be traders than investors. They will be in currencies, where fundamental analysis is not available, and in commodities more than in shares. Wall Street trader Marty Schwartz had only lost money in 10 years' trading on fundamental analysis. When he switched to technical analysis, he became rich.

National newspapers give technical analysis an occasional – and guarded – hearing. In late 2004, *The Times* presented a case for the **golden cross** (see page 182). Some of the magazines are more generous, reflecting the growing interest in technical analysis from private investors, which is partly driven by the investment software companies. *Shares* offers stock tips based on chart readings and covers the subject educationally. *Investor's Chronicle* publishes a version of the Coppock indicator. The tip sheet *Chart Prophet* educates readers in technical analysis at the same time as it makes stock recommendations. For specifics of **technical analysis,** see Sections C (page 82), K (page 179), V (page 291) and W (page 293).

Chinese walls

Chinese walls are procedures within a firm to ensure that information gained when acting for one client does not leak to someone else in the firm acting for another client for whom that information may be significant. They are required in City firms, including investment banks, stockbrokers and law firms.

In an investment bank, Chinese walls are the main divide between **analysts** (see page 65) and corporate financiers. They are designed to stop the analyst from being influenced by his or her own firm's corporate activity, and so giving a biased recommendation. The aim is to protect client confidentiality and ensure fair treatment of clients.

Chinese walls will involve some or all of the following:

- compilation of a list of individuals in the firm working for each client;
- the physical separation of advisers working on different sides of a project;
- separation of files;
- use of separate file servers to store information on a central computer base, so information on clients is segregated, and use of passwords and codes to restrict access;
- storage of information in a physically separate location such as a strong room;
- ensuring that advisers are aware of client confidentiality rules and possibly issuing these in writing.

Pundits have described Chinese walls as an extreme test of self-regulation. In mid-2004, an appeal court upheld a landmark ruling that law firm Freshfields could not work for Philip Green in his bid for Marks & Spencer because it had previously been the target company's main legal adviser. On 5 June 2004, the Business Editor's commentary in *The Times* said that the judge's reasoning in the case seemed to have cast doubt on whether any Chinese walls could be trusted.

Conflicts of interest

Conflicts of interest arise when sell-side *analysts* (see page 65) produce research that could be either independent or slanted to suit their employer's interest in attracting and looking after investment banking business, a main profit driver.

The Spitzer settlement of April 2003 in the US arose from perceived conflicts of interest of this kind. It was made between Elliot Spitzer, the New York Attorney General, and 10 leading global investment banks: Bear Stearns, Credit Suisse First Boston, Goldman Sachs, Lehman Brothers, J P Morgan Securities, Merrill Lynch, Morgan Stanley, Citigroup Global Markets, UBS Warburg and US Bancorp Piper Jaffray. They settled with the *Securities & Exchange Commission* (see page 260), the *New York Stock Exchange* (see page 271) and, the National Association of Securities Dealers, as well as with Spitzer.

They agreed on a US $1.4 billion Wall Street settlement. As part of the redress, they agreed to amend their practices, whereby they would physically separate research and investment banking departments to prevent the passing of information. Senior management would decide the research department's budget without input from investment banking. Research analysts could no longer be compensated in a way that reflected investment banking revenues.

Investment banking was to have no part in decisions on company coverage, and analysts were prohibited from participating in pitches and *road shows* (see page 248). The firms had to have firewalls that restricted interaction between research and investment banking. They would provide independent research to ensure that individual investors had access to objective investment advice.

Each firm was to make its analysts' historical ratings and target forecasts publicly available. The firms entered into a voluntary agreement to restrict *spinning* – the allocation of securities in hot *IPOs* (see page 244) to certain company executives and directors.

Other countries took their cue from the Spitzer settlement. On both sides of the Atlantic, investment banks and brokers are being forced to reorganise their working arrangements to ensure greater segregation of analysts and corporate financiers.

The UK reaction

In early 2004, the *Financial Services Authority* (see page 255), the UK regulator, issued conduct of business guidelines for firms that hold investment research as objective. These require firms to establish a policy to manage conflicts of interest.

As part of the process, a firm may use *Chinese walls* (see page 68), may issue guidelines dealing with conflicts, and may establish procedures to ensure compliance. The analyst should not take part in marketing shares if this gives an impression of failing to be impartial, and no inducements should be permitted for providing favourable research.

Full details of these guidelines are available from the FSA's helpful website at www.fsa.gov.uk.

Price-sensitive information

Price-sensitive information is data or information which, if made public, would be likely to have a significant effect on the price of a company's securities. The Listing Rules, issued by the UK Listing Authority, part of the *Financial Services Authority* (see page 255), require that such information is announced to the market as a whole without delay.

Suspected breaches arise after the share price has moved sharply ahead of takeover rumours that turned out to be true, or ahead of a trading statement of unexpected losses. It could lead to a regulatory investigation, and charges of *market abuse* (see page 258) including insider dealing.

If listed companies give *analysts* (see page 65) a selective briefing or leaking, they could be in breach of this part of the Listing Rules. Suspected incidents have led to regulatory investigations. In this climate, companies are careful to give the same bland information to all the analysts together. There is consequently less reporting of company news, and so more share price volatility – ironically, so cynics have it, hitting the very private investors that the rules are designed to protect.

Bonds and fixed income

Introduction

Bonds and fixed income products are most often a buy-and-hold investment for conservative investors. They can provide a useful diversification to an equities-based portfolio. Bonds are widely traded in capital markets, with the US bonds market being the largest securities market in the world. You will find here explanations of the main terms and concepts. See also page 303, on *cost of capital*, which is inclusive of bonds.

Basis point

Basis points are used to specify a change in the interest rate. One basis point is a hundredth of 1 per cent.

Bond

The bond is a debt instrument. The issuer of a bond pays interest to the lender throughout its term and repays the principal sum borrowed on redemption. An exception is the case of undated bonds, which are not redeemed. The bond is traditionally for cautious investors, offering a safe haven against equity price volatility. But it is also for traders who want to exploit price differentials. The short-term bond is also called a 'note'.

Through bonds, investors receive a higher proportion of their return from income than they do through equities. Bond prices are less volatile than stock prices, particularly as the redemption date approaches. Historically, bonds have underperformed equities, but have out-performed deposits in building societies.

The issuer of a bond may be a government or a company. The issue may be timed so that capital repayment will coincide with anticipated income from specified projects.

In the UK, government bonds are known as 'gilt-edged securities', or 'gilts', and they are issued by the UK Debt Management Office, an executive agency of HM Treasury, to raise cash so that the government can fund its annual spending requirements. In the US, they are called Treasury Bonds. Bonds issued by governments of developed countries are considered risk-free, acknowledging that taxes could be paid to honour commitments.

If a company issues a bond, it is a way to raise cash for a long period without using up conventional credit sources. For investors, corporate bonds carry a risk of default and so pay a fixed interest rate at a higher level than government bonds to compensate for the greater risk incurred by the investor. The default risk varies according to the financial status of the company, and the **credit ratings agencies** (see page 74) attempt to measure it.

Corporate fixed interest bonds can be secured on specified assets, which is reassuring to investors as an insurance against insolvency. They can also be unsecured, which is most usual for international bonds, in which case they have higher yields to compensate for the greater risk. Restrictive covenants may be in place to set a borrowing limit.

Bonds are classified by the time until maturity. If they are 1 to 7 years, they are classed as short term. If they are 7 to 12 years, they are medium term. If they are more than 12 years, they are long term.

A bond will be issued and redeemed at nominal value, known as 'par', which for UK bonds is £100. At any time in the bond's lifetime, the market price may deviate from nominal value. When two redemption dates are shown, the bond must be redeemed after the first but before the second.

Bonds in the UK, as in Italy and the US, pay interest twice a year. In some countries, including France and Germany, the payment is only once a year. In the period between interest payments, interest accrues. The pricing on bonds is normally *clean*, which excludes accrued interest.

A buyer of bonds pays not just for the financial instrument but also for any income accrued since the last interest payment. This is *cum* (with) *dividend*. If he or she buys it ex-dividend, it is the seller who has retained the right to the pending interest payment.

The coupon is the annual rate of interest on the bond, and is stated as a percentage of the nominal value. If, for example, a stock offers a 3 per cent coupon, it will pay £3 a year in interest for every £100 of nominal value. For UK bonds, it will be in two instalments. The coupon is decided by the level of interest rates in the market at the time of the bond issue.

The dividend yield that you receive from buying a bond on the secondary market can vary from the coupon because it consists of the return expressed as a percentage of the selling price of the bond, and the bond can sell at a different price from its nominal value. The yield can also be expressed in different ways. See *current yield* (page 75) and **gross redemption yield** (page 77) for definitions.

Both the yields and *duration* (see page 75) are criteria for selecting bonds. Investors also consider the spread between the yields for a given bond and the benchmark government bond, and any indication that it might narrow or expand.

The bond is priced precisely. In the case of a US corporate bond, the price is calculated to 1/8 of a dollar, and, for a US Treasury Bond, to 1/32. In continental Europe, decimals are used. The smallest price movement is known as the 'tick'. If a UK bond price moves by £1 per £100 nominal, it is one point. The press takes note of smaller movements, expressed as fractions of a point.

Pension funds are the largest traditional holders of bonds because these instruments help to match their liabilities more precisely than equities or other types. The factors affecting demand for bonds, whether government or corporate, are economic growth, inflation and interest rate expectations.

For example, if interest rates fall, bond prices will rise. The underlying logic is that investors rush to buy bonds when their yields look attractive compared with the declining rates on bank deposit accounts. The bonds will then rise to a level that reflects the increased demand, and the yields will reduce accordingly until they no longer look attractive. A converse process also arises. If interest rates rise, bond prices will decline.

Bonds may be registered, as in the UK. Others, such as **Eurobonds** (see page 76), have bearer status, which means that the physically held certificate is the proof of ownership. In the secondary market, bonds are sometimes traded on a stock exchange.

In the past, private investors who were higher rate tax payers used to buy gilts and practise **dividend stripping** (see page 133) for tax efficiency. The practice is no longer allowed.

Bond insurance

If a bond issuer cannot achieve a good rating from a **credit rating agency** (see page 74), it may buy bond insurance. It would pay a premium to a highly rated private firm that guarantees timely servicing of the bond.

Alternatively, the issuer may set aside cash in a fund for redemption of the bond, or undertake to buy bonds in the market on specified dates.

Brady bond

Brady bonds are issued in Latin America and some other developing countries and are considered riskier than most other types of bond. They are denominated in dollars and backed by US Treasury Bonds.

Bulldog bond

A bond issued in sterling in the UK by a non-UK issuer.

Commercial paper

Commercial paper is debt, issued by corporate borrowers, which has less than 270 days until maturity. It is traded in the international money markets.

Convertible bond

The convertible bond is a debt instrument that the investor can convert into a fixed number of shares. It pays a fairly low fixed coupon in return for the conversion opportunity.

This gives an issuing listed company a cheap way to raise capital, and is an alternative to the *rights issue* (see page 247). It is often used by companies going through an expansion period.

Coupon

The coupon is the interest rate on a bond. It is the annual percentage of its nominal value. For a working example, see *bond* (page 71).

Covenant

This is an issuer's legal commitment to limit its debt. It is made at the time of issuance to protect bondholders against downgrades default.

Credit rating agencies

The credit rating agencies rate the ability of issuers, corporate or government, to service bonds that they issue. The higher the rating, the better the credit terms a borrower will receive.

The three largest agencies are Standard & Poor's, Moody's Investment Services and Fitch IBCA. The rating is a paid-for service. If a company does not buy a rating, some agencies have been known to publish it unsolicited, even if based on incomplete information.

In rating a company, the agencies will only estimate its default risk. The criteria used vary slightly between agencies, but will include social and political risk, the regulatory environment, and level of Westernisation of the borrower's country. Critics say that the agencies react to events rather than anticipate them.

The agencies will grade borrowers on their own scale. For example, Standard & Poor's awards AAA as its best risk, and D as its worst. The agencies do not always agree on their ratings, even after allowing for differences in grading structure, but bonds highly rated by the major agencies are unlikely to default.

If an agency reduces its rating on a bond, the price is likely to decline. Bonds with ratings below investment grade, which is set at a specified level, are considered likely to default. Pension and insurance groups may hold only a limited number of these bonds in their funds.

So far, credit rating agencies have resisted regulation, saying that they don't need it because their business depends on the trust of the companies that pay for a rating. It is noted that such regulation worked out badly in Japan. The agencies have cooperated in the preparation of a code of conduct published in December 2004 by the International Organization of Securities Commissions.

Current yield

The current yield is the annual interest of a bond, divided by the current bond price. It is also known as the running yield, flat yield, simple yield, or annual yield. The higher the bond price rises, the lower the current yield will be. The reverse is also true, with a falling bond price triggering a higher yield.

Debentures

Debentures are straightforward bonds. They are the most usual way of issuing securities to obtain a long-term loan.

Debentures trade on a stock exchange and are often secured on specific company assets. In return for this security, the interest rate paid is lower than for many other debt instruments.

Dual currency bond

Dual currency bonds are bonds for which an investor pays in one currency but returns are in another, at a prearranged rate.

The borrower protects its own position against adverse exchange rate movements through the *forward market* (see page 148).

Duration

Duration shows how risky a bond is by measuring its price sensitivity to interest rate changes. It is the weighted average period until maturity of a security's cash flows. The longer the duration of a bond, the more volatile it is likely to be.

To calculate duration, find the present value of annual cash flows (coupon payments) on the bond, and its principal repaid on maturity. Multiply cash flow in year one by one, and in year two by two, and so on. Add the figures to the bond's principal, and divide the result by the bond's price. This is duration.

'Modified duration' measures changes in the bond price as a result of small changes in the yield. It is calculated as duration/(1 + yield).

Equity convertible

The equity convertible is a bond that the holder may convert into a given number of shares in the underlying company. Because of this advantage, the issuer may offer a lower level of interest than on a conventional bond.

Eurobond

The Eurobond is a **bond** (see page 71) denominated in the currency of neither the issuer nor the country where it was issued. It is a tradable instrument with a maturity of at least two years.

The Eurobond market started in 1964 when the US imposed compulsory interest equalisation tax on interest that Americans took from stocks and bonds that Europeans had issued. As a result, borrowers left the US. A market for dollar-denominated bonds started to flourish in London, where non-US buyers did not have to pay interest equalisation tax. In 1974, the US requirement for interest equalisation tax was abolished, but by then Eurobond business was well established in London. It had extended to lending business, which from 1965 had also been affected by the tax.

Banks and companies use Eurobonds to borrow cheaply in a highly liquid market. The issue process is as follows. A lead bank will run a syndicate of banks to underwrite the issue. A group of selling banks that need not be underwriters will retail the bonds to investors.

The bond pays interest only once a year, compared with a six-monthly payout on domestic bonds. It puts investors in Eurobonds at an obvious disadvantage.

The Eurobond is in bearer form, which means that it is held physically, in the form of a certificate. The holder can claim interest by tearing off and sending in coupons. On maturity, the loan will be repaid. There is no register of owners. It gives investors anonymity for tax purposes, an attraction of this type of investment.

The larger Eurobond issues are global, to high net worth individuals as well as institutions.

Eurocurrency

A currency held outside its country of origin is called a eurocurrency. For example, dollars deposited in a French bank account are euro-dollars. Euros kept outside the member countries of the European Economic Union are called euro-euros.

Eurocurrencies are traded in the interbank market. The average offer rate at which the bank will lend these is the *LIBOR – London Interbank Offered Rate* (see page 198).

Floating rate note

Floating rate notes (FRNs) are a form of debt with interest rates linked to a standard rate such as LIBOR. The rates change every six months.

Banks in particular, but also companies and governments, become issuers of the FRNs, which are most prevalent in the euro markets.

For borrowers, the FRN is less certain than fixed rate debt. It appeals when interest rates are high because the alternative of issuing fixed rate debt at the time would commit them to making high interest rate payments.

Banks have sometimes issued perpetual FRNs, and these never need to be repaid. As another variation, there are hybrid notes, which pay initially a fixed coupon and, after a specified date, a floating rate.

Gilt

A term for UK government bond. See *bond* (page 71).

Gilt-edged market maker

This is a market maker in gilts, which are UK government bonds. Gilts can be easily purchased via the National Savings Register.

Gross redemption yield

The gross redemption yield, also known as 'yield to maturity', is widely used to compare the returns on bonds. It is the *current yield* (see page 75) plus any notional capital gain or loss at redemption. If an investor pays £85 for a stock that is repaid at £100 in 15 years, there will be a gain of £15 over the 15 year period, amounting to £1 a year.

It is slightly more complicated than this as, in calculating the redemption yield, future interest and redemption revenue are discounted to today's value. It is assumed that the interest rates used for discounting will be identical to the redemption yield, although this applies only if the stock is held until redemption.

Index-linked bonds

Index-linked bonds are issued in the UK by the government, and in a number of other countries including Australia, Canada, the US and France. They are guaranteed to keep pace with inflation.

The bonds pay interest and a redemption value adjusted for inflation. In the UK, the adjustment is based on the change in the *Retail Prices Index* (see page 154). Because of the RPI's eight-month time lag, the adjustment is for eight days before the bond was issued. In return for the security of an inflation adjustment, the coupon is lower than for conventional bonds.

In May 2004, *Times Online* reported that this type of bond was popular amidst forecasts of pending inflation, and that experts were recommending it.

In the US, index linked bonds are called Treasury Inflation Protected Securities. They are linked to the *Consumer Prices Index* (see page 141).

Inter-dealer brokers

The inter-dealer brokers give on-screen prices to gilt-edged market makers, and conduct deals with them. This enables the market makers to avoid revealing their positions to competing firms. The gilt-edged *market makers* (see page 270) obtain screen-based prices from the inter-dealer brokers, and deal through them to avoid revealing their positions to competing firms.

International Securities Market Association

The International Securities Market Association is the regulatory body for *Eurobonds* (see page 76). It has affirmed its belief in competition, which puts it at conflict with European bureaucrats looking to impose tax and regulatory restrictions.

Investment bond

See under Section I, Insurance and Pensions (page 161).

Junk bond

'Junk bond' is a derogatory term, widely used in the press, for a bond that is below investment grade, as defined by one of the major *credit rating agencies* (see page 74). It may have fallen in price due to problems in the underlying company. There is a risk that interest or capital may not be paid.

Junk bonds that previously had investment grade status are known as 'fallen angels', and investment grade bonds that once had junk status are 'rising stars'.

In the 1980s, junk bonds were commonly used to finance takeovers. Drexel Burnham Lambert, a US broker, dominated the junk bond market, and its key representative, Michael Milken, was known as the junk bond king. In 1990, Milken was jailed for 22 months on charges of felony and racketeering related to his junk bond activities. He had to pay more than US $1 billion in fines and repayments, and was banned from working in the financial services industry for life.

'Sub-investment grade bonds', as junk bonds are more kindly often termed, are widely used in today's high income funds, which are used in portfolio planning. The increased return to investors on this type of fund, which is due to the greater risk of default, can be harnessed in a pooled investment, where one company defaulting would not significantly affect the fund's overall purpose.

Mortgage-backed securities

These are special purpose vehicles that pool a large number of residential mortgages.

Multi-option facility

This is a loan arrangement. How the borrower receives his or her money, and the time span, are variable.

Partly paid bond

Investors who buy a partly paid bond pay only part of the face value on issue. They will pay the rest later. In this way the bond is geared, with heightened gains or losses in proportion to cash put up.

Precipice bond

'Precipice bonds' is a derogatory umbrella term for bonds that guarantee high income but do not protect against the loss of original capital invested to finance this, and has been much used in the press. These bonds were marketed in the late 1990s and early this century, and are generically known as 'structured investments'.

How much of the original capital invested in precipice bonds is eroded, if any, depends on the performance of a stated index, or indices, or a basket of shares.

Recent mis-selling scandals related to the selling of these bonds to retired people have received widespread press coverage. There were no proper explanations of the risks to capital in order to finance income payments. Since December 1999, the Financial Services Authority has issued warnings about the products.

Samurai bond

This is a Yen bond that a foreigner issues in Japan's domestic market.

Sovereign debt

This consists of bonds issued by a government. Semi-sovereign debt is issued by the lower branches of government.

Swap

This is a derivative that allows a user to swap one liability for another. Each user's aim is to borrow money in the required form less expensively than if it had done so directly. If for example, one company can raise fixed but not floating rate money, and another company can do only the reverse, it may suit them both to do an interest rate swap.

The most frequent swap is on interest rate payments in the same currency.

Syndicated loan

This is a loan offered by a syndicate of banks. Every bank involved provides part of it. The interest rate may be above or below *LIBOR* (see page 198), depending on the borrower's credit history.

The borrower pays interest only on the amount still owed, which compares favourably with the requirement for a bond issuer to pay interest on the full amount until it is repaid.

In the 1980s, syndicated loans fell out of popularity because of repayment problems.

Tombstone

This is an advertisement by an investment bank in a business publication announcing a securities offering. It includes details.

Yankee bond

A security issued in dollars in the US by a non-US issuer.

Yield curve

The yield curve shows the different interest rates on government bonds that mature at different times. The vertical axis shows the yield, and the horizontal axis shows the number of years.

Normally the slope of the yield curve rises, which is positive. It reflects the greater compensation required by bond investors for holding their asset over a longer period, in which they will be exposed to inflation.

Sometimes the yield curve is inverted, which means that interest rates are higher over the short than the long term. This negative sign may arise if the government has announced interest rate changes.

Zero coupon bond

The zero coupon bond is issued at a discount to the face value at which it will be redeemed on maturity after a fixed period. It pays out no interest during its life.

It appeals to investors who prefer capital gain to income due to the more favourable tax treatment. To compensate, the return may be slightly lower than on interest-paying bonds.

This type of bond is sometimes recommended to those planning for future school fees.

Charts, patterns and reversal signals

Introduction

The charts are the main working tool of technical analysts. The general premise is that they are a representation of the market's psyche: hope, fear and greed. Charts also depend on markets not being efficient. Not everybody gives them credence, but in this section we will look at how they work.

In the layout of this section there are three parts. They are: charts, patterns and reversal signals. Much of this section will make better sense once you understand such basics as how a trend works, and support and resistance (see Section W, page 293).

Charts

Overview

Charts differ a little in what they convey, as well as in how they do it. For instance, a bar chart is more informative than a line chart, but cuts out less *noise*. Candlesticks are arguably more useful for short-term traders than investors. In this subsection I will explain the main types of chart.

Bar chart

The bar chart is a popular form of chart. It plots the share price against time. For each time period, a bar is drawn. The top of the bar represents the high, and the bottom the low. On the left of the bar, a tick shows the opening price. On the right, another tick shows the closing price.

Candlesticks

Candlesticks, also known as candles, are a form of technical analysis that originated in Japan. They are increasingly popular, but are a little controversial. Some years ago, when I was a student on courses run by the Society of Technical Analysts, I was warned against them. Some top traders do not find them particularly useful, and I know of one acclaimed expert on candles who has never used them for his own trading.

The candlestick, as it appears on the chart, is based round a vertical line that extends from the high to the low of the share price (or of any other instrument) over the given period, which is usually a day. One horizontal line crosses this vertical line at the stock's opening price, and another crosses it at the closing price, making a rectangle that is known as a 'real body'. If the real body is white, the price at close was higher than at opening. If the real body is black, the price at close was lower.

There may also be shadows, which are any vertical lines that extend above or below the real body. The straight line above it is the upper shadow, and that below it the lower shadow. The shadows represent price action not encompassed by the open and close.

The names of candlestick patterns are often visual, such as Hammer or Morning Star, and may have Japanese linguistic origins, such as the Harami. These patterns are grouped together under the subsection **Patterns** in this chapter (see page 90).

Candlesticks are aimed at traders more than investors. They give more priority to *reversal* than *continuation* signals, signalling a reversal faster than Western trend analysis (see page 300, 'Trend') or ***moving averages*** (see page 183).

Candlesticks have limitations. They can only be created when the opening share price is available. They do not claim to indicate the likely extent of a turn and so are not used by technicians to set price targets.

Equivolume chart

Equivolume charting, invented by Richard Arms, Jr, focuses on the relationship between price and volume. It is not widely used. On the chart, the horizontal axis represents a combination of volume and time, and the vertical axis shows

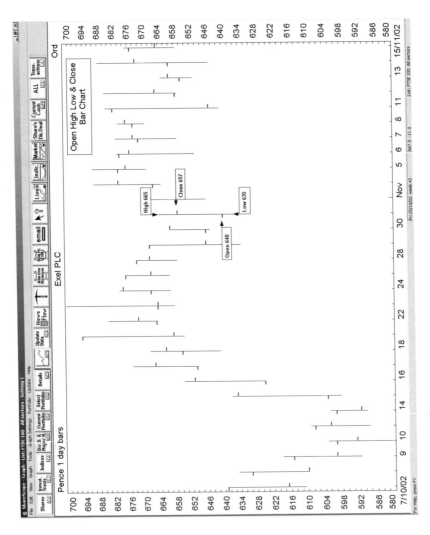

Figure C1 Bar chart

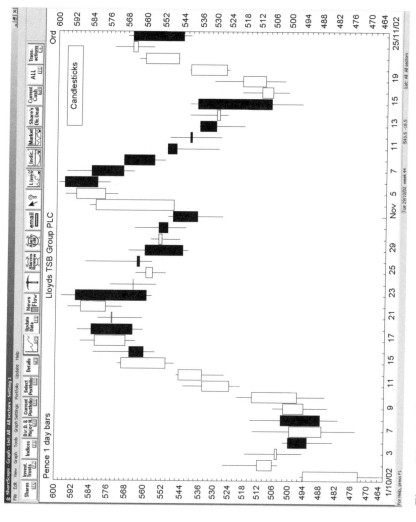

Figure C2 Candlesticks

the high and the low of the share price. Every trading period gives rise to a bar shaped like a rectangular box. The broader the box, the heavier is the volume, and the higher the box, the bigger the range.

Some examples will demonstrate the equivolume chart. A tall but narrow box shows share price movement on the day and is known as a *narrow day*. A box where the height and breadth are equal indicates substantial volume but a lack of movement, representing a *square day*.

An oversquare box has more breadth than height and so indicates a share price that moves little on still greater volume. Within a trend, the square and oversquare boxes can indicate a trend reversal, according to technicians.

Line chart

The line chart is the simplest kind. It plots the price on the Y-axis, which is vertical, against time on the X-axis, which is horizontal.

The line plots only the closing mid-price of a share, and so cuts out the *noise* of intra-day price changes. The chart is short on detail, but the flip side is that it never appears cluttered.

Point and figure chart

The point and figure chart can look obscure to the uninitiated, and a bit like a noughts and crosses game. It has a reputation for being hard for beginners to understand.

The chart is based on the premise that supply and demand dictate the share price, and it shows the struggle between the two.

Point and figure has its limitations. It records only significant movements, so it is not good for short-term trades. Point and figure charts have no time element. The same space on a chart could represent several minutes, or several weeks, if prices remain in a tight trading range.

In preparing the charts, the analyst will often use the day's high and low prices as a shortcut. However, this will not always result in an exactly correct chart. An alternative approach is to use intraday price movements.

When the share price rises by a given measure, an X is marked. When the share price falls by the given measure, an O is marked in the next column, which always starts one square across. The measure is known as the box. The higher the share price of the company on which the chart focuses, the bigger the box will be. For UK shares, the box is typically between 1p and 4p.

To provide a time perspective, the month's first entry may be recorded as the initial letter of the month, such as 'F' for February. On computer-generated charts, upward-pointing chevrons indicate price rises, and downward-pointing chevrons the reverse.

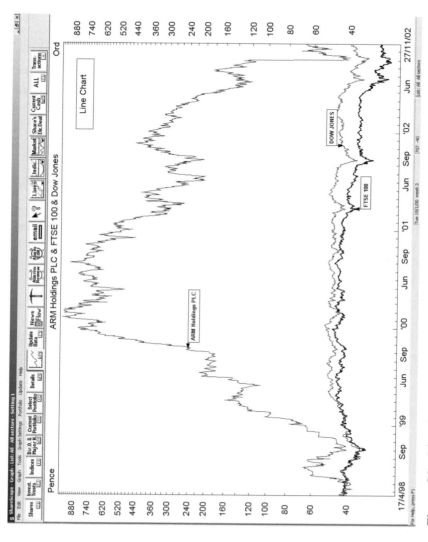

Figure C3 Line chart

If the share price breaks the trend and changes direction, it must register a reversal before the movement is recorded on the chart. The reversal is often larger than the box size. The most usual type is the three-box reversal, which is three times the box size.

If there is a reversal upwards, an X will be marked in the next column, one square horizontally across, changing from an O. If the reversal is down, an O will be marked in the next column, changing from an X.

The Count

The Count is a method of forecasting share price movements on a point and figure chart. It gives the technician a price objective. Of the two versions available, the *Vertical Count* is used more frequently. It sets a target price move based on significant rises and falls that have already happened. The *Horizontal Count* is preferred when the technician is projecting a breakout from a wide horizontal base on the chart.

Range

The range is the difference between the high and low transaction prices of a security during a trading period.

Scale

There are two alternative scales for charts: arithmetic and semi-logarithmic. In the charting facility of Business Market Data at *Times Online*, they are described as linear and logarithmic. Technical software packages allow you to switch between the two.

The arithmetic scale shows absolute share price movements, and the semi-logarithmic scale shows percentage price movements. In an arithmetic chart, a price move from 10p to 20p would take up the same vertical distance as from 20p to 30p. In a semi-log chart, 10p to 20p would take up the same distance as a move from 20p to 40p, since they are both 100 per cent price increases.

In short, the arithmetic scale is more sensitive and so is suitable for short-term charts or when the share price is moving only slightly. When charts are long-term or if the share price is moving substantially, the semi-log chart presents a less distorted picture.

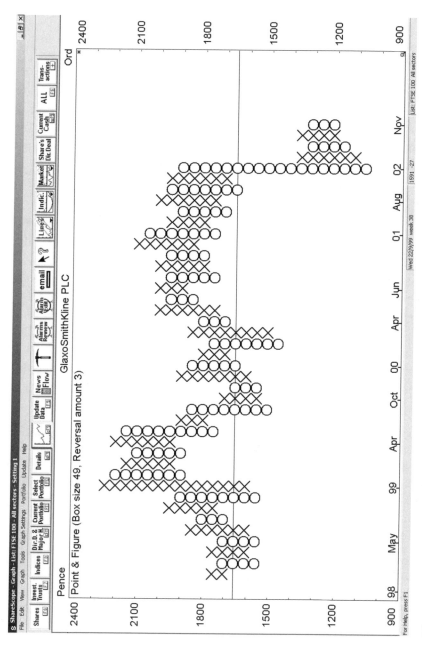

Figure C4 Point and figure chart

Patterns

Overview

Repeating price patterns arise in the charts, according to some technicians. Some patterns indicate continuation, others reversal, and a few both. In this subsection, I will show you how to recognise them, and what they mean. I have divided the patterns into 'General' and 'Candlesticks'.

General

Breakout

A breakout is a move away from a congestion zone on a chart where the price has been confined to a range.

If the breakout is in the direction of the previous trend, the pattern is seen as a continuation, and if in the opposite direction, a reversal. A breakout may be false. As a reality hurdle, traders sometimes use a filter, for example that the breakout must be at least 5 per cent of the share price.

On breakout, technical traders set price targets. In a continuation pattern, they measure from the start of the previous trend to the furthest boundary of the pattern, and project this length from and in the direction of the breakout as a minimum target. In a reversal pattern, they take the breadth of the pattern and project this length from breakout.

In general, *volume* (see page 292) should expand on the move into the pattern, and contract as the pattern is formed, but expand again on breakout, according to technicians.

Broadening formation

The broadening formation, also known as the 'megaphone', is a rare reversal pattern, with a tendency to fail. It arises when successive peaks are higher, accompanied by rising *volume* (see page 292), and successive troughs are lower, accompanied by contracting volume.

To form the pattern, join the pattern's tops, of which there should be at least three, in a line. You should join the bottoms, of which there should be at least two, in a diverging line. The pattern is the reverse to the *triangle* (see page 97).

Cup and handle

The cup and handle is a U shape on a bar chart, resembling a cup, followed by a line slanting slightly downwards, which is the handle. As the share price rises to the top of the cup for the second time and tests an old high, there is selling pressure. The price will move slightly down along the handle for up to a few weeks. It should then rise again, reaching above the top of the original cup. An increase in volume should accompany the breakout from the formation. The pattern lasts from 2 to 17 months.

Diamond top

The diamond top is a rare reversal pattern in active markets. It is a ***broadening formation*** (see page 90) that converts into a symmetrical ***triangle*** (see page 97). The pattern has the appearance of a ***head and shoulders*** (see page 95) with a V-shaped neckline.

Double top and bottom

A double top signals the reversal of an up trend. The pattern is formed by two similar price highs, separated by at least several days. The price highs do not need to be exactly the same, but should be close.

It is formed after the share price rises to a new high, and then declines from this first top to a trough. The share price will then rise to the second top, and volume should expand, but less than it did towards the first top, which is itself a bearish indicator. The price is likely to reach the previous peak but it will not succeed in going higher.

Once the price has made a ***breakout*** (see page 90) below the trough set between the two peaks, typically on expanded volume, the pattern is complete. It is rarely perfectly formed.

The double bottom is a double top in reverse, and is a bullish sign. Technicians consider the pattern reliable only if trading volume rises as the second bottom is formed.

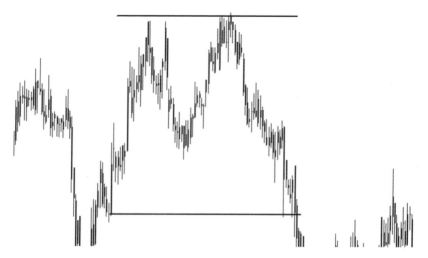

Figure C5　Double top

Flag

The flag is a continuation pattern with a reputation for reliability among technicians. It is a brief consolidation in the share price with a small price *range* (see page 88), formed on declining volume, and is followed by a sharp move like a flagpole. A flag looks much like a very tight channel (parallel support and resistance lines).

You will find the flag mainly on short-term charts, as it is typically completed in less than three weeks. In a down trend, completion is often faster. The flag forms in, and sustains, a strong trend, which may be up or down. In an uptrend, the flag will slope downwards and the *breakout* (see page 90) from the pattern in price action will be above the highs. In a downtrend, the flag will slope upwards and the breakout will be below the lows.

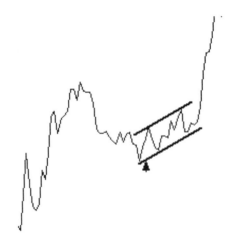

Figure C6   Flag

Gap

The gap is a physical break in price movement on the chart. It arises when a price has jumped from one level to another. Technicians consider the gap stronger if it is backed by trading volume.

The gap can signal a reversal but it is more often a continuation pattern, according to technical analysts. It is infrequent gaps in the share price of heavily traded stocks that are considered significant. Technicians ignore intraday gaps, which arise when the share price jumps more than one point during the day's trading, and gaps in stocks going ex-dividend.

Gaps may be divided into the following four categories.

1. *Common.* The common gap arises when buying and selling are congested within a range. Trading volume is expected to be low, and the gap should be filled quickly. It will have arisen because buyers and sellers had little interest in the market. This type of gap is familiar in less liquid stocks. In most cases, technicians ignore it.

2. *Breakaway.* The breakaway gap arises when the price breaks out of a ***range*** (see page 88), shortly after a price reversal. It indicates the start of a new trend. The gap is bullish after a downturn or bearish following a rally or consolidation, according to technicians. In their view, it may serve as a ***support or resistance*** (see page 299) level, and is unlikely to be filled, particularly when trading volume is high, as anticipated.

3. *Runaway.* The runaway gap, also known as the continuation or measuring gap, appears less frequently than the breakaway, and after a trend has started.

   This kind of gap arises in a continuing trend. The share price will have gapped on significant momentum but insubstantial volume. If the market is fast moving, two or three runaway gaps may appear in succession.

4. *Exhaustion.* The exhaustion gap arises when a fast move in the share price, up or down, has almost reached an end. It indicates that the trend is weakening, according to technicians. It can lead to a reversal, closing the gap, and perhaps an ***island reversal*** (see page 104) or, no less often, to a continuation.

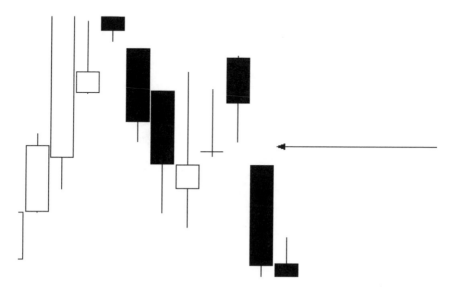

Figure C7   Common gap

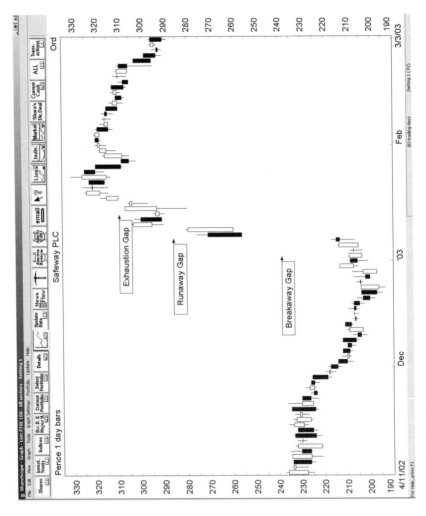

Figure C8 Breakaway, runaway and exhaustion gap

Head and shoulders

Head and shoulders is the best-known reversal pattern and is said to precede a downturn. If it appears on a chart, believers become bearish. Others have found it unreliable.

To form the pattern, the share price moves up and reverts to form the first shoulder, which is a peak in the trend. A sharp reaction will follow, and the share price dips to form a trough. It will then rise to a higher peak, which becomes the head, and will drop back again to form a second trough. The share price will rise to form another shoulder, a lower peak. It will then drop back passing the neckline, which may be drawn between the two troughs. Prices will often move back to retest the neckline before falling. You can compute a price target by measuring the distance between the high at the head and the neckline on that date, and projecting that distance lower from the neckline break. This is the downward *breakout* (see page 90).

In a textbook scenario, volume should rise on the first shoulder, fall as the shoulder declines, and then expand as the head arises. It should fall on the correction from the head, and should rise again as the right shoulder is formed, although less than with the head. It should rise on the breakout.

If the 'head and shoulders' is turned upwards, it indicates resistance to reversal. But should the pattern complete, the reversal is expected to be especially strong.

Some technicians suggest that a head and shoulders pattern can also be used reliably as a continuation pattern within a downtrend.

Inverse head and shoulders

This is an upside down head and shoulders. It arises at the end of a bear market and is considered a bullish reversal pattern.

The pattern, sometimes known as a head and shoulders bottom or a pendant bottom, is considered less volatile than its upright counterpart.

Pennant

The pennant is a continuation pattern. It consists of straight lines drawn through highs and lows that converge to create a small symmetrical triangle. It is formed on declining volume, after the share price has moved up or down quickly. In this respect, it is like a *flag* (see page 92), which looks similar except that its boundary lines run parallel.

The pennant is similarly completed within three weeks or, in a strong trend, perhaps faster. In an uptrend, the *breakout* (see page 90) is above the line drawn through the highs. In a downtrend, it is below the line drawn through the lows.

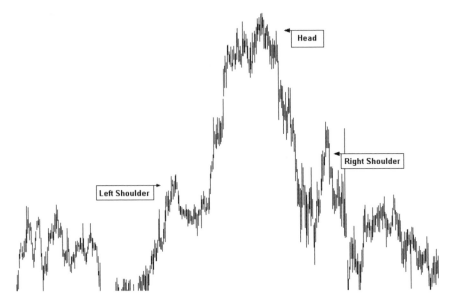

Figure C9   Head and shoulders

Rectangle

The rectangle is a chart shaped like it sounds. It represents the struggle between buyers and sellers in a stock – essentially, it is a trading range. It is proportionate, first swinging up to a resistance line, then down to a support line, until **breakout** (see page 90). The trader may profit from price swings within the *congestion* area.

There is no rule on how many times price movements must touch the upper boundary in order to define a rectangle. But the bigger the rectangle, the more powerful it is. If it is a continuation pattern, the rectangle forms quickly and has a small price **range** (see page 88). It is a frequent and rather weak pattern that has greater significance if it nestles within a larger rectangle. If the rectangle is a reversal pattern, which is less often, it tends to form more slowly and the price range is larger.

Saucer

The saucer is a triple round pattern without defined peaks or troughs. It is also known as a rounding top or rounding bottom.

This is a rare pattern, although less so on longer-term charts. While the saucer starts to form, volume tends to fall. The longer the pattern lasts, the more likely it is to lead to reversal, according to technicians. In the event of a reversal, volume tends to rise.

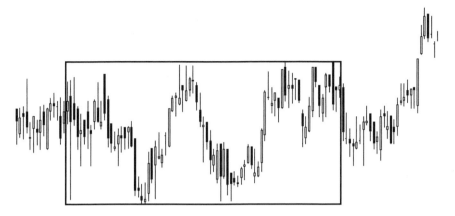

Figure C10   Rectangle (continuation)

Sometimes, one saucer follows another quickly, which indicates continuation. In all cases, the lack of obvious breakout makes the pattern very difficult to trade. Saucers are more common at tops than at bottoms for markets, but for individual stocks a saucer is more likely to develop at a bottom.

Spike day

A spike day (also known as a V-bottom or inverted V-top) on a chart is when the price or index reaches a level significantly higher (at a top) or lower (at a bottom) than on other days surrounding it. The pattern resembles a spike. The low in the stock market in October 1998 is an excellent example of a spike bottom.

Triangle

The triangle is a pattern on the chart shaped as it is named. It is a pair of two lines, one representing support and the other resistance, which eventually converge at the apex. The more often the share price touches the sides of the triangle, the more reliable the pattern is considered.

Following a *breakout* (see page 90), the share price should continue in the direction in which it started before the triangle was formed, according to technicians. Trading volume is said to provide early clues of the breakout direction. If volume expands on the up thrusts within the triangle, an upward breakout is seen as likely. If volume expands on the down thrusts, a downwards breakout is expected.

A breakout very early in the pattern, before halfway to the apex, is often a false breakout, meaning that the pattern is likely to continue again. The most reliable breakouts are believed to arise between 50 and 75 per cent towards the apex, as is also true of the *pennant* (see page 95).

There are three main types of triangle: symmetrical, ascending and descending. Let us look at each.

1. *Symmetrical*. A symmetrical triangle may arise in either an uptrend or a downtrend. It has lower highs and higher lows in a trading *range* (see page 88). In its smallest form, it is a pennant.

   If the price breaks out of the symmetrical triangle in the same direction as the previous trend, it is likely to be a continuation. If it breaks in the opposite direction, which is a less frequent occurrence, it is likely to be a reversal.

   This type of triangle is not known for its reliability, and the trend that started may not continue. The next two types are seen as more trustworthy.

2. *Ascending*. The ascending triangle has equal highs but higher lows. In an uptrend, it often turns out to be a continuation pattern and, in a downtrend, a reversal. However, it is more commonly seen as a continuation pattern.

3. *Descending*. The descending triangle is an ascending one in reverse. It has equal lows, but lower highs. In an uptrend it tends to be a reversal and, in a downtrend, a continuation, which is more common.

Triple top and bottom

The triple top has three approximately equal peaks in an up trend and is considered a strong bearish reversal pattern. As each peak forms in the eventual triple top, volume should expand, but less on the second peak than on the first, and least on the third. If the volume does otherwise, it does not abnegate the pattern.

There may be more than three peaks, in which case the pattern is not a triple top but a form of *rectangle* (see page 96).

The triple bottom is an upside down triple top. As a bullish reversal pattern, it is considered strong.

Wedge

The wedge has boundary lines that slope both up or both down into an apex. The symmetrical *triangle* (see page 97) is comparable except in that it has a top line that slants down and a bottom line that is up.

A rising wedge has rising peaks and faster rising troughs that converge. On the same principle, a falling wedge has falling troughs and faster falling peaks. Completion rarely takes longer than three months.

If the wedge is slanted against the trend, it indicates likely continuation. If it follows the trend, it suggests reversal.

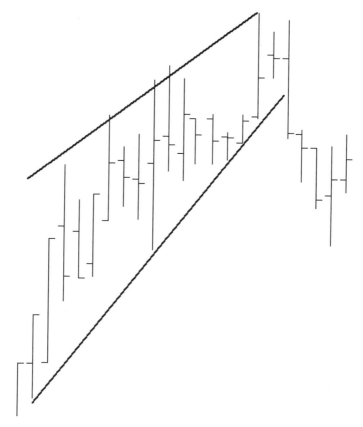

Figure C11   Wedge

Candlesticks

Counterattack line

The counterattack line is considered a weaker alternative to **_piercing_** (see page 101) or **_dark cloud cover_** (see next entry). A bullish line arises where a white candle follows a black one and closes at the same level. In a bearish one, a black candle follows a white one.

Dark cloud cover

This is when a black **_real body_** (see page 102) opens above the high of a preceding tall white one, and closes ideally below its centre.

Dark cloud cover sends out a bearish signal after a rally and can indicate a **_short selling_** (see page 159) opportunity. The opposite pattern is **_piercing_** (see page 101).

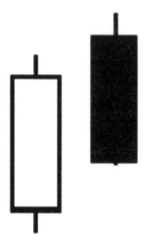

Figure C12   Dark cloud cover

Doji

The doji is where the share price closes at the same price, or almost, as that at which it opened. It is a horizontal line representing the ***real body*** (see page 102) that crosses a ***shadow*** (see page 102). The doji shows that supply is in equilibrium with demand, and indicates substantial indecision.

The pattern arises in markets that are either trendless or about to become so, according to technicians. The less frequent the doji, the more significance is attributed to it. After a share price rally, a doji suggests that you should sell the shares because the bull trend is tired. But after a share price decline, it does not so easily indicate that you should buy.

If the upper and lower shadows are both long, you have a long-legged doji. When the open-close line is at the top of the shadow, or nearly so, it is a *drag-onfly* doji. When the open-close line is at the bottom of the shadow, it is a *graveyard* doji.

A weaker variation on the doji is the ***spinning top*** (see page 102).

Figure C13   Doji

Engulfing pattern

If a white *real body* (see page 102) follows a black real body and is longer at either end, it *wraps* round it. This is a bullish engulfing pattern. Conversely, if a black real body wraps round a white real body, it is a bearish engulfing pattern. These are considered reversal signals.

Hammer

The hammer is an *umbrella* (see page 103) at or near the bottom of a share price or market downturn.

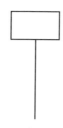

Figure C14   Hammer

Hanging man

The hanging man is an *umbrella* (see page 103) at a new high following an uptrend.

Harami

This is a *spinning top* (see page 102) that arises after a taller candle. Harami is based on the Japanese word for 'pregnant'. The tall candle is the symbolic mother and the spinning top is its baby.

   If a *doji* (see page 100) rather than a spinning top follows the tall candle, it is a harami cross. In either case, the pattern is said to signal a possible trend change.

High wave candle

If a small *real body* (see page 102), either black or white, has very long upper and lower *shadows* (see page 102), it is a high wave candle. The close will hardly have changed from the open despite a significant gap between the high and low. The pattern indicates great indecision.

Piercing

This is when a white *real body* (see next entry) opens lower than a preceding tall, black real body, but closes ideally above its centre. It *pierces* the black one, and is a bullish pattern following a market decline. The opposite is ***dark cloud cover*** (see page 99).

Real body

The real body is a vertical rectangle extending from the opening to the closing share price. For more detail, see the **candlesticks** entry in subsection Charts (page 83).

Figure C15　Real body

Shadow

This consists of the vertical lines above and below the ***real body*** (see page 102). For more detail, see the **candlesticks** entry in subsection Charts (page 83).

Spinning top

The spinning top is a small ***real body*** (see page 102) with small difference between the opening and closing price. It may have ***shadows*** (see page 102).

　　The pattern demonstrates that the bulls, if the real body is white, or the bears, if it is black, are taking only limited control. It is an indicator of indecision, but less so than the ***doji*** (see page 100), which has been called its half-sister.

Star

The star is a small ***real body*** (see page 102) separated from both a previous and a subsequent real body by two separate ***windows*** (see page 103). It signifies indecision and a possible reversal. Here are some versions.

1.　*Shooting star.* The shooting star appears in an upturn and indicates a likely reversal. It is a small real body and it has a long upper ***shadow*** (see page

102), which indicates that the market cannot support the continued rising price. The pattern resembles an upside down *hammer* (see page 101).

2. *Evening star.* The evening star indicates likely reversal. It has a long white body, followed by a *spinning top* (see previous entry) that is both higher and shorter, and then by a long but lower black real body that overlaps heavily with the original white one. The three candles are separated by two windows.

    If the middle candle is a *doji* (see page 100) rather than a spinning top, the pattern is called an 'evening doji'.

3. *Morning star.* The morning star signals a likely bullish reversal after a downturn. It is a black candle, followed by a spinning top and then a long white candle that overlaps heavily with the earlier black one. The three candles are separated by two windows.

4. *Doji star.* The doji star is a window followed by a *doji* (see page 100). The pattern follows a long share price move, and suggests a watershed in the market.

Three white soldiers

Three white soldiers are three long, successively rising white candles, each closing at or near its high. It is a bullish pattern. The reverse is three black crows.

Tweezers

Tweezers are matching highs or lows in sequence. It is a reversal pattern.

Umbrella

The umbrella is a *spinning top* (see page 102), with a lower shadow that is at least twice as long as the *real body* (see page 102) but with little or no upper *shadow* (see page 102). See also *hammer* (page 101) and *hanging man* (page 101).

Windows

The window is a candlesticks equivalent to the *gap* (see page 92). It tends to be a continuation pattern.

The window arises only between shadows. It is not in itself enough to make a window if the *real bodies* (see page 102) have a distance between them.

It will form an area of *support* when the share price is rising or of *resistance* when the share price is declining (see 'Support and resistance', page 299). The share price must break through the entire window if it is to breach support or resistance.

Reversal signals

Introduction

The reversal signal weakens, but does not break, the trend. It is not as strong as a reversal pattern, and not to be confused with it. It needs to be shown on a chart such as a bar chart that records the highs and lows. A line chart is unsuitable.

Closing price reversal

For a closing price reversal in an up trend, there must be a single day when the high is above the previous high and, similarly, the low is higher than its predecessor. In a down trend, there should be a day with a lower high and a lower low. In addition, the close must always be below the previous close.

Hook reversal

The hook reversal is a form of *inside day* (see next entry). In an up trend, the share price must open near the high and close near the low. In a down trend, it should open near the low and close near the high. In either case, the *range* (see page 88) must be inside the previous day's.

Inside day

The inside day arises when the *range* (see page 88) is entirely inside the framework of yesterday's range. If the high or low goes so far as to match its predecessor, you will have half an inside day. Technicians view it as a weaker version of the full signal.

The full signal typically arises after a strong trend. It is a sign that the trend is weakening, and indicates that neither buyers nor sellers have been able to seize control. The trend may continue, but it is likely to change, according to technicians.

Island reversal

The island reversal is a sequence of gaps. In a rising trend, a first gap appears between the previous day's high and the new day's low. The day's *range* (see page 88) above it is the *island.* The second gap appears on the way down between the previous day's low and the new day's high. In a declining trend, the sequence is in reverse.

The island reversal may be completed in a day or longer, and is accompanied by high trading volume. Traders who placed their position after the first gap in the direction of the trend are, on reversal, left in a losing position. When the island includes several trading periods, it is known as the island cluster reversal.

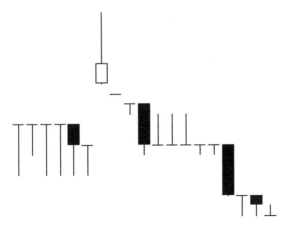

Figure C16   Island reversal

Key reversal

A key reversal occurs after a strong price trend. It is a reversal signal, but it may go so far as to represent a price reversal. At the end of an up trend, the price should make a new high and close well off that high, usually on very strong volume. A common misconception is that a key reversal must also be an outside day, but this is not a requirement. In fact, a key reversal after an uptrend need not even finish with lower prices. A key reversal at a bottom works on the same principle in reverse as at a top. It occurs with a sharp new low and a close well off that low, also on a high low.

One-day reversal

To form this signal, the share price rises sharply and continually during the day, on high trading volume. It may have opened higher than the previous night's close, leaving a *gap* (see page 92). Before close, the price reverses to its starting point on the day. The one-day reversal is expected after the share price has risen or fallen significantly.

Two-day reversal

This is an extended version of the one-day reversal. On the first day, the share price moves to a new high, and closes at or near this level. On the second day, it opens at a similar level but, by close, it will have retraced the entire first day's advance.

Open/close reversal

In an up trend, the open/close reversal arises when the high is above the previous high, and the low is higher than its predecessor. The open must be near the high, and the close must be near the low but above the close of the previous trading period.

In a down trend, the principle applies in reverse. The high must be lower than its predecessor, and the low must be lower. The opening must be near the low and the close near the high but below the previous close.

The signal indicates a change in control between buyers and sellers, which is detectable only from the relative position of the open and close. Technicians who only consider the trading price will miss this signal.

Outside day

The outside day is where the day's range is outside the previous day's range. The high must be above the previous high and the low beneath the previous low. If one of these is matching its predecessor, you have half an outside day, which is a weaker version.

The signal shows that the balance between buyers and sellers has moved widely during the day. The signal often follows a strong trend, and indicates uncertainty, according to technicians. It is stronger if backed by high volume. The opposite is *inside day* (see page 104).

Pivot point reversal

If the trend is up, the pivot point reversal arises under two conditions. First, there must be a trading day with a high above that of the two days either side of it. Second, the latest trading day should close below the low of the preceding day with the tallest high. It may come immediately after it, or some days later.

If the trend is down, the conditions apply in reverse. There must be a trading day with a low below that of the two days either side of it. The close of the latest day should be above the high of the day with the lowest low. Technical traders may use this signal to time market entries or exits.

Derivatives

Introduction

Derivatives are products that are *derivative* of traded financial instruments and tradable in their own right. They are highly geared, which means that you will put up as collateral only a small proportion of the value of your trade.

As a trader, you can use derivatives to hedge an existing position or to speculate. You can make money from falling as well as rising markets. In this section, you will find out how these products work, and some trading strategies.

Black-Scholes model

This is the favoured model for valuing **options** (see page 111) and **covered warrants** (see page 115). It sets a price after taking into account the derivative's intrinsic value, its time value and the fact that it does not pay **dividends** (see page 210).

The Black-Scholes model assumes efficient markets, no jumps in volatility, and a constant risk-free state, as well as no transaction costs, and no early exercising of the derivatives. The price of the underlying share or other financial instrument is assumed to be log normally distributed with constant mean and volatility.

The assumptions are not all justified, and some users have tweaked the model. But Black-Scholes is considered useful as a broad valuation yardstick.

Contracts for difference

The CFD (contract for difference) is a contract between two parties to exchange the difference between the opening and closing price of a contract, as at the contract's close, multiplied by the specified number of shares. It is available on most UK and US stocks, as well as in European markets, although the range offered by brokers can vary. CFDs were historically only used by institutions but, in recent years, private investors have become significantly more involved.

If you buy a CFD, you will not own the underlying share, but you will be entitled to *dividend* (see page 210) payments and, again depending on your broker, will have up to full access to corporate action, including *rights issues* (see page 247), *takeover* activity (see page 281) and similar. There are CFDs based on indices, currencies and commodities.

The institutions that trade CFDs most are *hedge funds* (see page 158), and *spread betting* (see page 114) firms that are hedging bets into which they have entered with private investors. The private investors who trade CFDs directly tend to be sophisticated. They can trade CFDs through spread betting firms which operate as market makers, or, more cheaply, through brokers.

The CFD is highly geared, and you will trade it on *margin* (see page 110), which is typically 10 per cent, but may be higher for CFDs on stocks outside the FTSE-100. It works on a sliding scale: the smaller the stock size, the greater the initial margin required.

You will pay no *stamp duty* (see page 128) on CFD purchases. You are liable for *capital gains tax* (see page 132) on profits beyond your annual exemption level (£8,200 in the tax year 2004/5), but you may offset losses against future liabilities and so you may not have lost the money for good. CFDs are a short-term investment and it is not economical to hold them unless they are significantly increasing in value. After you have held a CFD for about 60 days, the amount that you will have saved on stamp duty will be cancelled out by your interest payments.

Exercise price

The exercise price is the specific price at which a derivative may be bought or sold. It is also known as the 'strike price'.

Futures

The futures market deals in contracts. The contract is an agreement between two parties to buy and sell the underlying instrument in a specific quantity on a pre-arranged date at an agreed price.

The contract can be for commodities such as corn, steel, beef or cocoa. It is a paper investment and traders will never have to take delivery of the underlying product.

Alternatively, the contract may be for a financial instrument such as interest rates or stock market *indices* (see page 264). Futures traders put up *margin* (see page 110) on their trades. Most use a *stop loss* (see page 193) to lock in their profits or minimise losses as far as possible.

Spread betting (see page 114) is a user-friendly way for private investors to take a position based on financial futures but it can be expensive.

Futures trading

Here are a few futures trading strategies in use:

Calendar spread – see the box on *options trading* on page 112.

Carousel – way to trade any number of futures contracts simultaneously. Spinning of the carousel marks the passing of time, and the inner horse represents a new crop or production, and the outer horse the old. The trader lets the profitable relationship between horses run, but cuts the losses.

Tarantula trading – trading a number of futures contracts, long and short, which compensate for each other, and have the same delivery date. The contracts are the legs of the tarantula. When any long contract shows a loss, the spider's leg is broken, but it will heal if the contract turns to profit. The same concept can be used in options trading.

Three-dimensional chess – when you set up futures contracts with a variety of delivery dates. You close one out on a central chess board, then set up similar contracts with a longer delivery date on a longer chess board, or with a shorter delivery date on a shorter board.

Greek letters

Greek letters are used to express ratios in the ***Black-Scholes model*** (see page 107) for assessing the fair value of *options* (see page 111) or *covered warrants* (see page 115). The most important is the Delta, which measures the derivative's sensitivity to changes in the price of the underlying share.

The Gamma measures the Delta's sensitivity to share price changes. The Theta assesses how much value the ***premium*** (see page 113) loses as time progresses. The Vega measures the derivative's price sensitivity to volatility, and the Rho its price sensitivity to interest rates.

Leeson, Nick

Nick Leeson is the rogue trader who at the age of 28 destroyed investment bank Barings by gambling on derivatives. Starting out as a settlement clerk at Barings, he was by 1993 a star trader and general manager in the bank's Singapore office. His trading strategies were largely based on **arbitrage** (see page 276).

In January 1995, Barings started writing put and call **options** (see page 111) on the Nikkei 225 index at the same exercise price. This created a **straddle** (see the 'Options trading' box on page 112) where Barings as options writer would keep the premiums only if the index stayed within the 19,000–21,000 trading range.

On 17 January, Kobe and Osaka were hit by a huge earthquake and the Nikkei 225 fell below the 19,000 level, putting Barings' profits at risk. On 23 January, the index was down to 17,950.

Leeson started buying March and June 95 **futures** (see page 108) contracts, which were a bet on an improvement in the market. But the Nikkei 225 deteriorated further and eventually Barings had lost over £800 million, which was more than its capital.

The Bank of England did not bail out Barings as some had expected and, eventually, Dutch insurer ING acquired the bust bank. Nick Leeson was jailed, and he wrote a book about his experiences, *Rogue Trader*, which was later made into a film.

Margin

Margin is a cash sum that you deposit with your broker. If you trade futures, it is simply a deposit to show your good faith and on which your broker can draw should you incur losses. If you trade contracts for difference, or (mainly applicable in the US) shares, margin means something different. It is a cash down payment on your investment, and the rest of the money required is borrowed from your broker, with interest charged slightly above the Bank of England's base rate (if you are taking a short position, the broker will pay you interest).

Initial margin is the amount you first put up before trading and is typically 10–25 per cent of the sum to be traded.

Every day, any profits will be added to the balance on your margin account, and if your funds are reduced below a certain level, you will need to top up your margin account. This process is known as 'variation margin'.

Margin enables geared trading, which means that your gain or loss will be bigger than the amount that you have put up.

Options

Options are derivatives that you can use either to **hedge** (see 'hedging', page 157) your market position, or to speculate. They are highly geared, and so rise and fall dramatically compared to the underlying shares. You can quickly make a large gain, or a large loss.

If you trade options, the most that you can lose is your premium, which is 100 per cent of the money you have put up. But if you write options, you can lose more. There are options on equities, which are the most popular with private investors because share prices are easily followed. There are also options on indices, and commodities such as energy and grains.

If you have a traditional option, you must exercise it (buy or sell the underlying security) to establish a profit. A US-style option can be exercised on any day up to and including the expiry date, but the European-style option only on the expiry date. Traded options, which came to the UK in 1978, are more flexible as they can be traded as well as exercised, and are more popular.

There are two types of traded option. The first is a *call option,* which gives you the right but not the obligation to *buy* the underlying security at the **exercise price** (see page 108). The second kind is a *put option,* which gives you as options buyer the right but not the obligation to *sell* the security at the exercise price.

As a buyer of a call or put option, you are on the other side of the fence from its writer. In a call option, the writer must sell the shares at the strike price if the buyer requires it. For a put option, the writer may have to buy the shares at the strike price.

As compensation for taking this risk, the writer receives a **premium** (see page 113) from you as buyer, which is the market price that you will pay for an option. You may pay only part of the premium, otherwise known as **margin** (see page 110), up front. If you buy an option, you will make money if the price of the underlying share or index moves in the right direction beyond the premium you paid. But, if the price does not move beyond the premium, the option writer will pocket the premium.

When you buy a *call option,* you will choose from various exercise prices. If the exercise price is lower than the underlying security's current market price, the option is *in the money*, and the difference between the exercise price and the current market price is its value. If the exercise price is higher than the current market price, the call option is *out of the money*, and the premium will be lower.

When you buy a *put option,* you also choose from a range of exercise prices. If the exercise price is higher than the share price, the option is *in the money*. If the exercise price is lower than the option, it is *out of the money.*

As an option moves more into the money, the premium rises. As the option moves more out of the money, it becomes cheaper. When the exercise price equals the current market price, the option is *at the money*.

It is possible to exercise traded options, which would require owning (or acquiring) the underlying shares so that you can sell them in the market to realise your own option gain. But it is more usual – and often more profitable – to trade them, selling them in the market and so cashing in on any profit. Every buyer of an option is matched by a seller, but neither side has the odds intrinsically in its favour.

Taking trading costs into account, more than one in five people who play the traded options market make money, according to the market consensus. To beat the odds, you will need to be a comfortable risk-taker who is prepared to watch the market very closely. Options are a very liquid market, which means that you can usually buy or sell without difficulty.

Options trading

For the options specialist, there is a large number of specialist option types and trading strategies. Some are included below.

Bull spread – simultaneous buying and selling two call options with different exercise prices but the same maturity date. The aim is to gain from an expected rise.

Boston – buyer avoids paying for premium until exercise date.

Butterfly spread – ordinary butterfly is when you sell two call options at the same exercise price and simultaneously buy two calls at different exercise prices. The aim is to profit from price stability but to limit risk exposure.

Calendar spread – aims to profit from price differences in options (or futures) of the same series but with different maturities.

Cliquet option – enables locking into profits at a given time.

Chooser option – enables holder to choose at a given time whether to hold a particular option.

Collar – risk confined to collar or band. In the foreign exchange market is a cylinder – buying an option and simultaneously writing one for same amount but at a different exercise price.

Combination option – strategy involving two options originally dealt as one. A *straddle* (see below in this box) is an example.

Compound option – option on an option.

Condor spread – this is to buy one call option, sell two others, and buy a fourth, each at a different exercise price. It spreads risk. Also known as a 'top hat spread'.

Contingent option – holder pays a premium only if option is exercised.

Delayed start option – setting of exercise price is deferred until agreed date.

Instalment option – premium paid in instalments.

Ladder option – option holder can lock regularly into profits.

Lookback option – holder can trade the underlying instrument on expiry at most favourable price over contract period.

Moving strike option – exercise price reset during contract period in accordance with movement of underlying instrument.

Rainbow option – linked to correlated underlying assets.

Straddle – when you simultaneously buy or sell a call and put option with the same expiry date and usually the same exercise price. This strategy is for when you expect the underlying instrument to move sharply, but you are unsure in which direction.

Strangle – when you simultaneously buy (or sell) a call and put, out of the money, with different exercise prices but the same expiry date.

Synthetic call/put – this is a synthetic instrument which copies the behaviour of a call or put option.

Turbo charging – when you buy two options that are similar but with different exercise prices. If the options move into profit, you stand to make more than if you had bought one option. If they move into loss, you stand to lose more.

Premium

The premium is the market price for a derivative. It is how much you pay for the right to buy or sell the underlying asset at a fixed price in the future.

Put-call ratio

The put-call ratio is the ratio of trading volume in *put options* against *call options* (see 'Options', page 111). When the put-call ratio is significantly lower than 1, buyers of call options are usually out in force, and sentiment is bullish. The reverse is also true. When the put-call ratio is much higher than 1, there are many buyers of put options, and sentiment is bearish.

Spread betting

Spread betting enables you to place a bet with a financial bookmaker on the direction of a share price, *index* (see 'Indices', page 264), and interest rates or similar. It is a way to take a *short position* (see 'Short selling', page 159), which is impractical for private investors in the stock market because of the way the rolling settlement system works.

You will usually bet on *futures* (see page 108) or *options* (see page 111), which anticipate and so move slightly in advance of the underlying financial instrument. The bookmaker quotes you a two-way price, and you will place your bet on *margin* (see page 110).

Before you make a profit you must cover the spread, which is the difference between the buying and selling price and a main source of the firm's profit. If you bet on large, liquid stocks or markets, the spread narrows. You will pay no *stamp duty* (see page 128) on purchases. Your profits will be free of *capital gains tax* (see page 132), but most spread bets lose money rather than make it.

A *stop loss* (see page 193) is available, but it can be difficult to apply it in time as the underlying financial instrument's price may move too fast. There is the more attractive alternative of a *guaranteed* stop loss (not usually available on traded options), that the bookmaker will apply automatically at a set level, at the expense of a wider spread.

In general, spread betting attracts a large number of gamblers, but some sophisticated traders. *Contracts for difference* (see page 108) bought from a broker will often offer better value for money, although the minimum trading size may be larger.

There are a number of courses and seminars in spread betting. They can be ridiculously expensive, and not all the trainers have good credentials. Events have shown that the Financial Services Authority uses its teeth in regulating spread betting firms. In late December 2004, it fined Cantor Index £70,000 for failing to give adequate risk warnings in a September 2003 promotional campaign.

Triple witching hour

The triple witching hour arises four set times a year when contracts for stock index futures, stock index options, and stock options expire simultaneously. It causes market volatility.

Warrants

Traditional warrants

Traditional warrants are tradable securities that enable you to buy a specified number of *new* shares in a company at a specified exercise price at a given time, or within a given period. Do not confuse these with **options** (see page 111), which enable you to buy *existing* shares.

Companies like to issue traditional warrants because they do not need to include them on the balance sheet. Warrants are not part of a company's share capital and so have no voting rights.

Warrants tend to rise and fall in value with the underlying shares, sometimes exaggerating the movements. You will pay **capital gains tax** (see page 132) on any profits.

Covered warrants

A covered warrant is a highly geared derivative that gives the holder the right, but not the obligation, to buy or sell a share (or other asset) at the end of, or during, a given period. The product was introduced into the UK only in late 2002, after some years of popularity in continental Europe, including Germany, Italy and Switzerland.

Covered warrants are issued by a party other than the issuer of the underlying stock. Unlike with a traditional warrant, new shares may not be issued. The warrant is *covered* because the issuer covers its position by simultaneously buying the underlying financial instrument in the market.

Every covered warrant has a limited period until maturity, generally 6 to 12 months, but potentially up to 5 years. The period tends to be shorter than for the traditional warrant.

To trade covered warrants, you must find a stockbroker that deals in them. Before you deal, your broker will ask you to complete a derivatives risk warning notice and a suitability questionnaire to say that you understand the risks involved.

Because market makers compete in a highly transparent market, the **spread** (see page 275) on covered warrants is quite tight, and the dealing commission is as payable on shares.

Your broker will obtain a price on current warrants either through issuing investment banks, or through an alternative quote-driven market provided by retail service providers, which represent the issuers. The banks issue covered warrants for such reasons as that traditional warrants are unavailable, or there is a restriction on the transfer of the underlying shares.

The covered warrant is priced on fair value, unlike its traditional counterpart where the pricing criterion is supply and demand. The covered warrant has a wider range of structures and a more liquid market.

As time passes, the time value of the covered warrants decreases and this is reflected in a declining *premium* (see page 113).

The trader can buy calls or puts in covered warrants which are fundamentally similar to those used in *options* (see page 111). To spread the risk, the trader can invest in a *basket* of covered warrants, which covers a sector.

Trades in covered warrants must be reported within three minutes. Electronic settlement takes place within three days through **CREST** (see page 263), and is normally for cash. No *stamp duty* (see page 128) is payable, but there is liability for capital gains tax. The owner receives no *dividend* (see page 210) from the underlying share.

If a trade in covered warrants moves against the trader, he or she will lose at most 100 per cent of his or her premium, plus dealing costs, which puts a limit on the risk. If as a trader you fail to exercise an *in the money option* (see page 111, 'Options', for an explanation) on a covered warrant before expiry, it will be automatically done on your behalf.

Equities and stock picking

Introduction

Equities are important to the private investor and are well covered in the press. In this section, we will look at some important aspects and definitions. See also Section Y on the cost of capital, which includes equities.

Bellwether stocks

A US term for *blue chip* (see page 117) stocks.

Biotechnology companies

Biotechnology companies are a high-risk investment. Fewer than 10 per cent of their products reach clinical development. If a company has a number of products in its pipeline, some with a large market, the failure risk is lower. Once production has leapt early hurdles, the success rate improves.

Blue chips

This is a generic term for large, reputable companies that lead the market and are traded in large quantities by institutional investors. In the UK, the 100 companies included in the *FTSE-100* index (see page 265) are so described.

the**share**centre:

investing shouldn't be a chore - and we're here to make sure it isn't

At The Share Centre we believe buying Tesco shares should be as easy as buying Tesco's beans. That's why we've made The Share Centre the place to get the information, advice, choice and fair value you need to share in the wealth of the stock market.

We recognise that investing in the stock market isn't right for everyone; after all, it's well understood that share prices, their value and the income from them can go down as well as up and that you might not get back what you originally invested. So if you're not sure whether it's appropriate or you we'd recommend you seek independent financial advice.

But when investing in the stock market is the right thing for you to do, that doesn't mean it has to be a chore. True, you do need to invest more than just your money. Making time to understand core principles, doing your research and monitoring your shares is time well spent. And you've already made a good step in this direction by reading this book. But we can help you go further. We'll share our know-how and experience by giving you practical advice to help you choose the investments that are right for you - and give you that advice free of charge.

Register at www.share.com and you've access to a wealth of support, advice and information. From guides in the Learn section to help you with picking individual shares, to the Research section with its 'Fund Picker' and access to comprehensive information on individual companies, and much more besides.

Plus, open an account and you've a value for money way to buy and sell shares, funds, ETFs, Gilts ... in fact a whole range of UK and overseas investments to help you achieve your investment aims. And there's a range of account services to choose from too, from a day-to-day share dealing account to ISAs and Self-Invested Pensions for you, and Child Trust Funds and the Junior Investment Account for your kids.

So when it comes to investing made easy, choose The Share Centre. To find out more, or for your free introductory guide to investing, call us on 0870 400 0260.

The Share Centre is a member of the London Stock Exchange and is authorised and regulated by the Financial Services Authority under reference number 146768.
The Share Centre P O Box 2000 Aylesbury Bucks HP21 8ZB. Registered in England No. 2461949.
Registered office: Oxford House, Oxford Road, Aylesbury, Bucks HP21 8SZ.

the**share**centre:

where you'll find the help and advice you need to share in the wealth of the stock market.

Visit www.share.com or call 0870 400 0260

The Share Centre is a member of the London Stock Exchange and is authorised and regulated by the Financial Services Authority under reference number 146768.
The Share Centre P O Box 2000 Aylesbury Bucks HP21 8ZB. Registered in England No. 2461949. Registered office: Oxford House Oxford Road Aylesbury Bucks HP21 8SZ.

Traditionally, blue chips have been regarded as safe investments, although they can sometimes be volatile, particularly in the high-tech sector. Blue chip stocks generally pay dividends and are regarded favourably by investors.

Bottom fishing

Bottom fishing is the search for bargain stocks whose prices have fallen so low that they now represent good value, even if the company's short-term prospects are not great.

Bottom up

The bottom up investor focuses as a priority on the fundamentals of individual companies first and only secondarily on industry and economic trends. US fund manager *Peter Lynch* (see page 125) famously works this way. The opposite approach is *top down* (see page 130*)*.

Buffett, Warren

Warren Buffett is chairman of US insurance group Berkshire Hathaway, and is said to be worth over US $30 billion from his investing. He is mainly a value investor, and was heavily influenced by *Benjamin Graham* (see page 122).

He invests in long established companies with a strong franchise, and the ability to generate earnings. He considers such ratios as return on equity, profit margin and gearing. He looks for a company to have an intrinsic value of 25 per cent or more above its market capitalisation.

As a long-term investor, Buffett sees himself as an owner in his chosen companies and is concerned with how they succeed as a business. He does not much consider market conditions, timing, or stock supply and demand.

Bulls and bears

The terms 'bull' and 'bear' describe how investors expect the stock market to perform. Bulls are optimistic about the stock market or individual stocks, and bears are pessimistic. The terms may have arisen because bulls toss people up, while bears knock them down. The consensus market view will be reflected in trading activity and to a large extent becomes a self-fulfilling prophecy.

Burn rate

The burn rate, also known as the 'cash burn rate', is the speed at which a company uses up cash. The term is often, but not exclusively, applied to biotechnology companies.

Business-to-business

This describes a business model where the company provides goods or services for another company rather than for a consumer. In the case of internet companies, this business model exploits the internet's order-taking and service facilities without using a middleman, and is considered to have high potential.

Business-to-consumer

This describes a business model where the company provides goods or services directly to the public. Within e-commerce, it is the least proven model. This type of *internet company* (see page 124) must buy items from producers and store them, and so it pays middlemen for inventory space and for extra administration. Market leaders such as Amazon, the online bookseller, are best placed to survive.

Buyback

This is when a company buys back its own shares from the shareholders. The move might be seen as positive for investors in that it will reduce the number of shares in issue and so increase the *earnings per share* (see page 211). It is also a way for investors to sell their shares without incurring such costs as broker's fees that would apply if they sold in the open market. But a buyback is only possible when a company has a surplus of cash, and it may suggest that it has nothing better to do with it.

Cockroach theory

The cockroach theory is that, if bullish or bearish news arises, further developments will reinforce the message. The underlying premise is that cockroaches come not singly but in groups (see 'Momentum investing', page 125).

Consumer-to-consumer

This is the business model for companies that match one consumer with another. In the case of internet companies, it is considered to have high potential because it takes in revenue but does not hold inventory.

As a consumer-to-consumer business, US-based online auctioneer eBay has been profitable since it went public in the autumn of 1998, bucking the loss-making trend of most quoted internet companies in their early years.

Cyclical companies

Shares in cyclical companies rise and fall quickly with economic conditions. House builders, resource companies, or paper and car manufacturers are in this category. For example, when the economy is strong, house builders will benefit from the accompanying housing boom, but in weaker economic conditions, demand for housing can go down. Resource companies often do well in spring and summer but not at Christmas.

EPIC code

This is a three or four letter symbol for individual stocks. To obtain a price quote from your online broker, you may be asked to key in the EPIC code on its website. Most brokers will offer a search facility to enable you to look up the EPIC code if you do not know it by entering the company name.

Ex-dividend Day

Ex-dividend Day is the date on which a UK company pays a *dividend* (see page 210). As the date approaches, the share price will rise slightly in anticipation of the payout. When the dividend has been distributed the shares become *ex-dividend*, and the price will slip back a little.

Eyeballs

This refers to the number of visits to a website. In the dot com boom of 1999 and early 2000, technology analysts measured eyeballs for internet companies. But, as experience has shown, frequency of visits to a website is not always correlated with revenue.

Graham, Benjamin

Benjamin Graham was a US-based mathematician and classics enthusiast who first developed the concept of value investing in the 1920s. He said that a value investor should select shares as if buying the entire underlying company. Among other criteria, the company should have small gearing and a low P/E ratio, and the dividend yield should be at least two thirds of the company's AAA bond yield.

He also specified that the company should have a market capitalisation of two thirds or less of its quick assets (current assets, excluding stock, less current liabilities). After it has risen to 100 per cent of these, the investor should sell the shares. See definitions of *gearing* (page 309), *P/E ratio* (page 218), *dividend yield* (page 210) and *market capitalisation* (page 217).

The criteria set by Graham are tougher now than in his day and, in a bull market, often impossible. He explains his methods in detail in his classic books, *The Intelligent Investor* and *Investment Analysis*.

Greater fool theory

This theory suggests that, if you overpay for a stock during a speculative bubble, the price will rise still further because a *greater fool* will pay more. The downside of the theory is that the fools eventually stop buying and the share price plummets as everybody rushes for the exit.

Growth investing

The strategy is to buy stocks that are growing fast, either before, or soon after, the market has recognised their potential. A *selling strategy* is also important (see 'Stop loss', page 193).

The March 2000 crash in high-tech stocks drew attention to the risks of buying stocks with a high turnover and no earnings, or not much of either.

Some fund managers select stocks on the principle of GARP (growth at reasonable price) which combines growth and value. A useful ratio for this is *PEG* (see page 219).

Two great growth investors are *Peter Lynch* (see page 125) and *T Rowe Price* (see page 127).

High yield investing

The strategy is to buy and hold high yield stocks. The yield is the net dividend as a percentage of the share price. High yield investors buy stocks that have fallen out of favour, reflected in a yield that has risen proportionately to a decline in the share price. The market is likely to have overreacted and the shares could recover, making a capital gain. Until that happens, the yield should be handsome.

The risk is that a low stock price may not indicate value. The share price may fall still lower, particularly if the company's problems are long-term. This has happened at various times with *blue chip* (see page 117) companies such as Marks & Spencer, Shell, and British Telecom, although companies of this strength and size tend to recover.

If a stock plummets in value, it is not much compensation to have a high yield, although high yield investors have learnt to take a longer view. High yield investment methods such as the *O'Higgins system* (see page 125) involve periodically selling dud stocks in your portfolio, as well as reinvesting dividends.

Infrastructure companies

Infrastructure companies provide the internet sector with services ranging from software to web design. They have more reliable revenues than other *internet companies* (see page 122) and so had a better survival rate following the March 2000 collapse of high-tech companies.

International equities

Trading in international equities from the UK became easier after exchange controls were abolished in 1979.

You can now trade US or continental European equities through many UK brokers, in some cases as cheaply as trading UK stocks. To invest elsewhere in the world, you may need to use local brokers, which could create hurdles.

If you trade shares in emerging markets such as China, Poland, Turkey or Russia, the risks are high but so are the potential rewards. There may be liquidity or settlement issues.

To spread the risk of investing outside the UK, you can buy **unit trusts** (see page 288), including in emerging markets.

If you invest in companies listed as **American Depositary Receipts (ADRs)** (see page 241) in New York or **Global Depositary Receipts** (see page 244) in London, the risks are less. The reassurance factor is that the company will have been required to meet international standards of transparency, accounting and other aspects of **corporate governance** (see Section O, page 225). It is likely to be a large company.

However, the 2004 decline of US-quoted Russian oil giant Yukos, listed in the form of ADRs on the New York Stock Exchange, shows that very real risk remains. Yukos was regarded as the model Westernised Russian stock until it was hit with fraud claims.

Internet companies

Internet companies are any that have their *main* business on the internet. In the early years, they typically have limited turnover and no profits.

The best business models are **business-to-business** (see page 121), **consumer-to-consumer** (see page 121) and **infrastructure companies** (see page 123). The unproven models are **business-to-consumer** (see page 121) and **online content** (see page 126).

Analysts do not normally use **discounted cash flow analysis** (see page 305) to evaluate internet companies because their future revenues are unpredictable. In late 1999 and early 2000, some analysts saw **real option pricing** (see page 127) as a useful valuation method.

In the absence of profits, the **earnings per share** (see page 211) do not exist, and analysts have often used the **price/sales ratio** (see page 219) instead. Another criterion is **eyeballs** (see page 122).

January effect

This is the relative out-performance of stocks in January. Over decades, it has manifested itself in UK and US markets.

Lynch, Peter

Peter Lynch is a master growth investor, who managed Fidelity's Magellan Fund in the US for 13 years. He has a **bottom up** (see page 120) investment strategy.

He has focused on companies with both high earnings growth and a winning business formula. The business model is more important than the strength of management. Lynch has invested for the long term, selling only on stagnation of growth.

A typical Lynch-style investment might be in a company with earnings that have temporarily declined, and a share price lower than net asset value, but with an improving financial status. Companies with slow or average earnings growth and **cyclical companies** (see page 121) are to be avoided.

Momentum investing

The momentum investor focuses on timing, aiming to take advantage of upward or downward trends in the share price.

The theory is that the stock price will continue to head in the same direction once it has started to move because of the momentum behind it, driven by the presence of a large number of investors in the market who will buy a stock that is moving up.

The buying trigger may be a change in analysts' forecasts, or in relative market strength. Momentum addicts will continue to buy as long as everybody else does but will sell when the turnover slackens. The trick is to do the same.

A key component is volume of shares traded. If a share goes higher and higher on declining volume, it is a bit like Tom and Jerry running poised for that precious second after they have run over the cliff and before they fall, as a fund manager put it to me.

O'Higgins system

The O'Higgins system is the best known of the **high yield investing** (see page 123) methods. Michael O'Higgins, a fund manager based in Albany, New York, popularised the system, which is based on investing in selected large blue chip stocks in the Dow Jones Industrial Index in the US.

To apply the system, open a cheap, execution-only account with a stockbroker. Invest in either the 10 highest yielding stocks in the Dow Jones, or in the five of these with the lowest closing prices. Hold qualifying stocks for the long term, reviewing your portfolio once a year, replacing stocks only if new ones qualify. Reinvest all dividends.

The system has a track record. In 1973–91, the five highest yielders with the lowest share prices in the Dow Jones outperformed that index for 15 out of the 19 years. Since then, the system has worked less well.

Online content companies

These companies specialise in collecting and producing online content. The business model is not yet properly proven. People who will pay for newspapers or TV will not always pay for similar material on the web.

The online content companies may rely more on advertising and user list rentals than subscriptions. Many are loss-making. Yahoo!, the US internet search engine, is a frequently cited exception.

Ordinary shares

To own ordinary shares in a company is to have a stake in it. The shareholders are entitled to vote at annual general meetings.

Pari passu

When new shares in a company carry equal rights to those of its shares issued earlier, they are *pari passu*. It means *of equal rank*.

Penny shares

Penny shares are low priced. There is no defining price boundary but, in the UK, penny shares are seen as costing up to about 50p or £1.00, depending on your view, and in the US, perhaps up to US $5.00. They tend to be shares with a small market capitalisation.

There is often one main *market maker* (see page 270) in a penny stock, and others may follow its lead. The *spread* (see page 275) tends to be wide and investors can deal only in limited sizes, perhaps 5,000 or 2,000 shares. If investors try to sell many shares, the market maker may drop the bid price significantly as a deterrent.

A penny stock moves mainly on news and rumours. If the market gets hooked, the share price may soar higher than fundamentals justify. If company or market news is adverse, the share price may fall sharply. But the company is more likely to get taken over than go bust.

Because they are so speculative, penny stocks should occupy only up to 15 per cent of an investor's equity portfolio. Even then, it is safer to spread the risk over several penny shares, including growth and recovery situations.

Successful penny share investors tend to pick their own stocks. Avoid the specialist penny dealers. They try to offload shares in dubious or troubled companies that they have bought up cheap. *Stockbrokers* (see page 128) interested in small companies can give advice, but at this end of the market it can be geared towards generating commission.

Preference shares

Preference shares carry a fixed *dividend* (see page 210) which is paid before dividends are paid to holders of *ordinary shares* (see page 126). They have priority over ordinary shares if the company has gone into liquidation. They own part of the company but have no voting rights.

There are various types of preference share. Cumulative preference shares accumulate dividend arrears and carry them forward, but non-cumulative shares receive dividends only if the company pays them. Convertible preference shares may be switched after a fixed term into ordinary shares, and redeemable shares pay the investor the nominal value of the shares on a specified date. Zero coupon preference shares pay no dividend.

Price, T Rowe

T Rowe Price was one of the great US fund managers from the 1930s to the 1950s. He was a growth investor with a *top down* (see page 130) investment strategy.

After choosing a suitable sector, Price sought companies with a competitive advantage, including strong management and patents and sound research. He favoured a rising *earnings per share* (see page 211), a high and a rising *profit margin* (see page 220), and a sound *balance sheet* (see page 203).

Price would sell stocks in a bear market or if growth prospects had subsided. Should a stock that he owned rise to a higher price than he would be willing to pay for it, Price would sell 25 per cent. If the stock rose still higher, he sold more.

Real option pricing

Real option pricing is a technique of valuing a share based on the underlying company's potential reaction to a range of scenarios.

In the run up to the March 2000 stock market decline, real option pricing was often used to value high-tech stocks. It gave too many over-optimistic recommendations based on unreliable information fed into the models.

Real time prices

Real time prices are valid at the time of publication. They are available free of charge through some online brokers and through Teletext (www.teletext.co.uk).

Recovery stocks

These are out-of-favour stocks that show potential for returning to, or in the direction of, former glories. It could happen if the underlying company becomes a *takeover* (see page 281) target. See also the next entry, 'Shell company'.

Shell company

The shell company has low-priced shares and little or no business of its own. It is a form of *recovery stock* (see previous entry). Its share structure enables new management, perhaps already a substantial shareholder, to seize control.

Stamp duty

Stamp duty is a tax that the UK government levies at 0.5 per cent every time that you buy shares. It is also payable on property. It is a constant gripe that UK stamp duty is more expensive than in continental Europe. Stamp duty does not apply on purchases of North American or most European stocks. You will also avoid it if you trade contracts for difference or place spread bets.

Stock screeners

Stock screeners enable investors to set valuation perimeters such as for the *P/E ratio* (see page 218) or *dividend yield* (see page 210), and to view a list of stocks that fit.

Stockbroker

Stockbrokers buy or sell shares for investors. They vary in their approach, but the more personal the service, regardless of how good it is, the more you are likely to be charged for it. Stockbrokers are advisory, execution-only or discretionary. There are also the boiler rooms. Let us take a look at each:

Advisory

Advisory stockbrokers advise clients on which stocks to buy or sell, and when. Some specialise in certain types of stock, and levels of expertise vary enormously.

Online

The execution-only broker does not advise on which shares to buy but simply executes orders. By this limitation on its services, it reduces staff and other costs and passes the savings on to the customer. Execution-only services are provided both online and by telephone, and charges are typically a fraction of those associated with using an advisory or discretionary broker.

The cheapest online broking service offers a facility for you to buy or sell shares by e-mail. The firm will accumulate trades, and then place bulk orders. This is for occasional investors. The disadvantage is that you could be hit by price volatility between when you placed your order and when it was executed.

The browser-based broker provides a faster service. It offers investors a facility for executing a trade themselves via the internet. They may deal at a price shown on screen through a connection with the **London Stock Exchange** (see page 270).

The active trader broker provides software with a facility for fast trade execution, and will not ask for order confirmation, as some browser-based brokers do.

Clients of brokers that operate primarily online may find that, if trading becomes busy, long telephone waiting times can occur.

Discretionary

Discretionary brokers take full charge of an investor's portfolio, and to make this worthwhile, it needs to be substantial. They make buying and selling decisions on the investor's behalf for a fee. There may also be a trading commission, which gives the broker an incentive to review the portfolio, but it should not be so high as to encourage overtrading. The charges overall are lower than on unit trusts.

There are some good discretionary brokers and some bad ones. Following the March 2000 stock market decline, bad discretionary fund management produced unfortunate results. Even in early 2005, many discretionary portfolios invest 80 per cent of funds into equities, which are a high risk asset class, for retired clients who need defensive portfolios.

Some discretionary brokers overtrade portfolios. If the fund is completing 40–50 trades a year, this is the level at which the broker often receives commission. Investors should never leave everything to the broker, but should ask questions and request frequent statements.

Boiler rooms

Boiler rooms push dubious or non-existent shares or other investments on gullible members of the public by telephone and the internet. Even if the shares do exist, they are likely to be subject to restrictions which make it impossible for the purchaser subsequently to sell them. These outfits now operate mostly from outside the UK.

Clients of the boiler rooms will often lose all their money, and they have little recourse. Investors in firms unauthorised by the Financial Services Authority have no access to the **Financial Services Compensation Scheme** or, for making a complaint, to the **Financial Ombudsman Service** (see page 254 for both). Some jurisdictions make no effort to stop local businesses ripping off clients based outside the country.

Even when the investor has lost money on shares the game may not be over. An operation may cold-call the investor and offer to attempt to recover the cash invested in return for an upfront fee. In reality, it may be linked with the original fraudster, and the recovery operation a fraud.

The FSA publishes on its website (www.fsa.gov.uk) a warning list of unauthorised firms selling financial products into the UK, but it tends to be incomplete. The FSA consumer helpline receives 100 calls a month from the public about boiler rooms.

In the summer of 2004, the FSA conducted a survey of 105 victims who had called the helpline. It found that 87 per cent of them were male, 44 per cent were aged 35–55, and 42 per cent were over 55 years old. About 41 per cent of the callers had been investing for over 10 years, which, according to the FSA, dispelled the myth that it is only the novice investor who becomes a victim of investment scams.

Ten bagger

A ten bagger is a stock whose price rises tenfold. The word derives from baseball terminology. US fund manager **Peter Lynch** (see page 125) first applied it to stocks.

Top down

The top down investor focuses on economic and industry trends first, and the fundamentals of a company last. The opposite approach is **bottom up** (see page 120).

Value investing

Value investing is buying stocks at below fundamental value and selling when they become expensive. See **Benjamin, Graham,** page 122.

Fiscal and tax

Introduction

This section covers key fiscal and tax matters, as they arise in the press. Other coverage in these areas is included elsewhere in this book. For example, in Section I (page 161), I have included tax information on life insurance policies and pensions.

Bed and breakfasting

Bed and breakfasting was the practice of selling your shares or unit trusts (or similar) and buying them back a day later to establish a gain or a loss for *capital gains tax* (see page 132) purposes without losing your investment. This was often done on the last day of the tax year. In March 1998, it was abolished. The time gap between a sale and a repurchase now has to be over 30 days if the two are not to be matched.

You can still, however, do a bed-and-spouse, when you sell your shares and your spouse buys back a day later, which will establish a gain or loss for capital gains tax purposes. Another variation, not considered very profitable, is a bed-and-ISA.

Capital allowance

Capital allowances replace accounting deprecation for taxation purposes. They are a standard tax allowance that allows qualifying plant and machinery to be written down, normally at the rate of 25 per cent a year on a *reducing balance basis* (see 'Deferred taxation', page 133). Capital allowances are available (some at different rates) on other types of asset.

Capital gains tax

Capital gains tax is payable by individuals and trustees on realised profits from investments when your overall taxable gains exceed a set limit (£8,200 for individuals, £4,100 for trustees, in the tax year to 5 April 2005).

CAT standard

The CAT is a voluntary government benchmark for the *ISA* (see page 135) which the government introduced in December 1998. It also applies to *mortgages* (see page 234).

CAT stands for Charges, Access and Terms, and shows how the product has met all government standards in these areas. It does not guarantee performance or suitability. Companies may offer products with the CAT standard alongside them, and other products without it.

Child tax credit

Child tax credit is a means-tested allowance for parents and those who care for children. If your family has one child or more, and meets the qualifying criteria, you may be entitled to child tax credit. Currently, the payment includes an annual family element of £545 and a child element for each child that is worth £1,625. The available payments are tapered away as family income rises but the family element is available in full up to an annual income of £50,000, with some support up to £58,175 (higher amounts for the first year of the child's life).

Support for qualifying childcare may be available through the working tax credit, which is designed to help people on low incomes.

Corporation tax

A UK company or non-resident company trading in the UK will pay corporation tax on income and capital gains. Qualifying smaller companies pay liabilities nine months after their financial year-end, but large companies pay in quarterly instalments.

The main rate of corporation tax has been 30 per cent since 1 April 1999. For companies with profits between £300,000 and £1.5 million, there is marginal relief. For smaller companies with taxable annual profits of between £50,000 and £300,000, the *small companies' rate* is 19 per cent and, for companies with profits below £50,000, the rate is up to 19 per cent.

There is a 0 per cent rate applicable to the first £10,000 of taxable profits (all limits are divided by the number of associated companies under common control). But the nil rate is a bit of an illusion, according to John Whiting, tax partner, PriceWaterhouseCoopers. If, as a company, you have taxable profits below £10,000 and thus no corporation tax charge, but then distribute some of the profits as a dividend, you will be caught by the *non-corporate distribution rate*, which means that the company has a 19 per cent tax bill on such profits, equivalent to the 19 per cent small companies' rate.

Dividends (see page 210) received by companies from other UK companies are not subject to corporation tax. They are classed as **franked investment incom**e (see page 134).

Deferred taxation

Deferred tax recognises the timing differences between profits recognised for accounting purposes and tax purposes. It is an estimate of the future taxation liabilities of transactions recognised in past and present financial periods. It exists principally because of differences between accounting **depreciation** (see page 208) and capital allowances, as well as certain revaluations.

Deferred tax accounting redirects the tax payments to the period in which relevant income or expenditure was recorded.

Dividend income

Companies pay you dividends from profits on which they have already paid tax. To prevent double taxation, the dividends carry a 10 per cent tax credit on the grossed up amount. For example, if a company pays you a net dividend of 90p, you will receive a 10p tax credit, which is 10 per cent of 100p, the grossed up dividend. It is the equivalent of one ninth of the net amount. For tax purposes, your dividend income is the dividend received plus the tax credit, which in the example given totals 100p. With every dividend comes a voucher that shows the dividend paid and the amount of the related tax credit.

Individuals who are not higher rate tax payers pay no tax. This is because the 10 per cent rate of tax on gross dividend income is satisfied by the offset of the 10 per cent tax credit. Higher rate tax payers will pay a 32.5 per cent tax rate reduced by the tax credit to 22.5 per cent of the gross, equivalent to 25 per cent of the net cash dividend payment.

Dividend stripping

In the past, an investor would buy shares *cum* (ie, with) *dividend* just before the record date of the **dividend** (see page 210), hold them until the dividend was received and then sell *ex-dividend* (see 'XD', page 302).

In this way, the investor would register a capital loss because the ex-dividend share price would be lower than the cum-dividend one. But the dividend received would compensate, or nearly so. The capital loss could be offset against capital gains, which was the purpose of the exercise.

Dividend stripping is no longer tax-effective, but it is still referred to in the press.

Double tax relief

If a company or individual pays tax overseas on income or gains, there is normally double taxation relief available. This means that the UK tax bill will be reduced by the tax paid overseas.

Enterprise Investment Scheme

The Enterprise Investment Scheme (EIS) was introduced in the November 1993 budget to replace the Business Expansion Scheme.

Under the scheme, some unlisted small companies offer you as an investor 20 per cent income tax relief for up to £200,000 a year (2004/5) invested in new ordinary shares. In addition, you will receive capital gains tax exemption. You need to hold the shares and meet the qualifying conditions for three years for the tax relief.

You can also defer unlimited capital gains tax arising from disposal of other assets by reinvesting your gains in EIS companies. This tax is deferred until the shares are sold. You may also obtain income tax relief by way of election for capital losses suffered.

To qualify for the income tax and capital gains tax exemption as an EIS investor, you must be unconnected with the company in which you plan to invest. You cannot be an employee, a paid director, or a more-than-30 per cent shareholder. The companies in which you invest must be UK-based, unquoted, and carrying on a qualifying business, or intended to do so. Some activities such as financing, law, property investment, hotels, gardening and farming are barred.

EIS companies are typically high-risk, and the tax perks do not always compensate for this. Always consider the investment case first. To spread the risk, consider investing also in *venture capital trusts* (see page 138), on which tax relief is somewhat similar, and in other investments.

Franked investment income

Franked investment income is the *dividend* (see page 210) that a UK company pays another company from its after-tax profits. It is treated as coming with a tax credit of one ninth, meaning that the receiving company need not pay corporation tax on UK dividends received, so there will be no double taxation.

Inheritance tax

Inheritance tax (IHT) is payable on your worldly goods after you have died, or after your assets have been transferred by way of gift to a discretionary trust.

The rate is 40 per cent on the net value of an estate or gift, after a nil rate band of £263,000 (2004/5 tax year). It affects you only if your estate, including the value of your home, is worth more than the exemption.

If so, consider IHT liability when writing your will. Assess the value of your estate by listing your assets and liabilities. If you leave your estate to your spouse, you will avoid any IHT liability provided that you are both domiciled in the UK but, under certain circumstances, it may be better to transfer some assets to your children on death to utilise one nil rate IHT band.

Otherwise, you can reduce your IHT liability by giving away assets. Gifts made more than seven years before your death will usually not be subject to IHT and, during the seven-year period, there are progressively reduced rates of tax from the start of the fourth year. This type of gift is called a 'potentially exempt transfer', given that any tax-efficiency, and its level, depends on for how long the donor will live.

Small gifts below £250 are generally exempt, and wedding gifts have additional exemption of between £1,000 and £5,000 depending on the relationship of the donor. There is an annual exemption of £3,000; all gifts or legacies to charities are exempt.

The costs of administering your estate and your funeral are tax deductible from your estate.

Interest and tax

The interest from your bank or building society account is taxed at source. That means that before it is paid into your account, tax at the lower rate of 20 per cent is deducted – so if you are due £100 of interest, your account will be credited with £80. This deduction means that most people have no further tax to pay, but if your total taxable income exceeds the higher rate tax threshold, a 40 per cent rate applies, leaving you with a further £20 to pay.

If you have taxable income less than your tax allowances or only slightly higher, you can claim back at least some of this tax paid. For claiming back tax, the Inland Revenue helpline is 0845 077 6543.

ISA

The Individual Savings Account, known as ISA, is a wrapper in which you may invest flexibly and not pay tax on the proceeds. The ISA was introduced on 6 April 1999 to replace the *PEP* (see page 137) and *TESSA* (see page 138), and is guaranteed to run until April 2009. To open an ISA, you need to be 18 or over, and normally resident in the UK for tax purposes.

You do not pay capital gains tax on your ISA, but cannot uses losses to offset against gains elsewhere. You will pay no tax on the interest or dividends of your savings within the ISA, but you will pay charges. There is unlikely to be a tax benefit for a basic rate tax payer with a stocks and shares ISA, but he or she will gain a benefit from a cash ISA. No minimum holding period or subscription level applies.

There are two types of ISA: maxi ISAs, which must be managed by the same investment company, and mini ISAs, whose components may be managed by different investment companies. Every new tax year, you can have either one or the other.

In any tax year from 6 April 2001 to 5 April 2006, you could invest up to £7,000 in total, as well as any capital sum from a matured TESSA into a TOISA. It was proposed that this limit would be reduced to £5,000 but, at the time of going to press in February 2005, the likelihood is that it will be kept at £7,000 until 2009.

In a maxi ISA, you can invest up to the maximum £7,000. Of this you can put anything up to the full amount in stocks and shares, including collective investment schemes and gilt-edged stocks. You can include up to £3,000 in cash provided that you keep to the overall £7,000 limit. A possible combination would be £4,000 in stocks and shares and £3,000 in cash. In practice, most investors in a maxi ISA prefer to invest entirely in the stocks and shares element.

In a mini ISA, you can invest up to £4,000 in a stocks and shares mini ISA, again including collective investment schemes and gilts, and up to £3,000 in cash. In both types of ISA, it was possible to invest £1,000 in insurance, but this has been scrapped from April 2005, and the extra £1,000 has been added to the amount that may be invested in the stocks and shares element, as given in the figures above.

The ISA provider cannot reclaim the one ninth tax credit on **dividend income** (see page 133), and so this is effectively wasted. But interest on the funds of corporate bonds is received gross, which is an argument in favour of having this type of bond in your Stocks and Shares ISA.

You will pay no **capital gains tax** (see page 132) on investments sold from within an ISA, but you cannot use losses to offset gains elsewhere.

You can use an ISA to assist in the repayment of a **mortgage** (see page 234). You can transfer your ISA directly between two managers, although you may be charged by the new manager.

CAT ISAs

CAT ISAs meet the government **CAT standard** (see page 132) ie, in Charges, Access and Terms. In the Stocks and Shares ISA, the annual charges must not exceed 1 per cent, including **stamp duty** (see page 128), and the minimum saving is set at no more than £500 in a lump sum or £50 a month, although many advisers have improved on those standards.

In the CAT Cash ISA, no charges are permitted except when providing duplicate statements or replacing lost cards. The minimum transaction size is £10, and withdrawals are permitted within seven working days or less. The interest rate must never drop more than 2 per cent below the Bank of England's *base rate* (see 'Repo rate', page 153).

For the CAT Life Insurance ISA, charges must not exceed 3 per cent of the fund's value. The minimum premium is £250 a year or £50 a month. Surrender values must, over time, reflect the value of the underlying assets, and should after three years or longer repay the original investment. There are no surrender penalties.

The CAT standard is also applied to *mortgages* (see page 234).

PEP

The Personal Equity Plan is a wrapper for sheltering investments from both personal income and *capital gains taxes* (see page 132). From 6 April 1999, the PEP has no longer been sold and the *ISA* (see page 135) has superseded it. Investors may indefinitely retain any PEPs that they acquired earlier, but may wish to reconsider the types of funds held, given that global investment has become permissible.

Personal allowance

This is the amount of income that you can receive tax-free every year. You should receive this automatically.

In 2005/6, the basic personal allowance is £4,895. You may be entitled to a higher amount if you are 65 or older, and there is an extra allowance for the blind.

Self-assessment form

About 9 million individual tax payers have had to complete a tax return under a process known as self-assessment. The form is lengthy. Recently a shortened version has become available on a pilot basis to those below certain income thresholds.

Tax rates (for income tax)

Tax rates are levied on the amount over your tax-free *personal allowance* (see page 137). They are included in a series of tax bands based on taxable income.

In the 2004/5 tax year, you have a basic personal allowance of £4,745. After this amount, you will pay 10 per cent tax on taxable income up to £2,020, and 22 per cent on taxable income between £2,021 and £31,400. You will pay 40 per cent on taxable income over this level.

TESSA

The tax-exempt special savings account, better known as TESSA, was a five-year deposit account with a bank or building society from which interest was paid out, or accumulated, tax free. Any cash that you deposited in a TESSA would have been sheltered from tax. The product has not been on the market since 6 April 1999, and so every TESSA has matured.

You could have retained your TESSA until its term was up, and then, within six months, could have transferred the original capital into a TOISA (TESSA-only individual savings account), which is a separate *ISA* (see page 135) allowance of up to £9,000. Any investor who gave up a TESSA before the term was up would have lost the tax benefits of this transfer.

TOISA

See discussion in previous entry, TESSA.

Venture capital trust

Venture capital trusts (VCTs) are quoted companies that invest in small growth companies. They are similar in structure to conventional *investment trusts* (see page 284). There is very little trading in the shares, and *market makers* (see page 270) usually offer a wide spread.

The VCT must choose its investments within three years. It must hold at least 70 per cent of its investments in qualifying, unquoted companies trading in the UK.

Investors receive 40 per cent income tax relief on their investment in new ordinary shares in the VCT, to a maximum level of £200,000. (This 40 per cent relief has been available for 2004/5 and 2005/6; for other years, the rate is 20 per cent.) However, the maximum income tax relief in a year is such an amount as reduces the investor's income tax bill to nil.

There is no longer capital gains tax deferral on investment but the gains (and losses) you make on the VCT shares are exempt from capital gains tax generally. All VCT dividends received are exempt from income tax. The investment must be maintained for three years to qualify for the tax relief.

The annual charges on a VCT tend to be higher than for conventional investment trusts, but investors may spread the risk by investing in several at once. The least risky VCTs are large, do not invest too much in start-ups, and have relatively low charges and experienced management.

The VCT will plan an exit from its investments through a stock market listing or a takeover. If the company achieves a London Stock Exchange listing, it may remain a VCT investment for five years. If the VCT is taken over, its investors will take a cut of the payment.

VCTs may be bought directly, or though a stockbroker or financial adviser. They often encourage co-investment, which is best suited to sophisticated investors.

Global economy and foreign exchange

Introduction

The global economy underpins foreign exchange and other financial markets. It is given prominent coverage in the financial pages. See also Section M, which covers money markets.

Balance of payments

The balance of payments is a record of all transactions between a country and the rest of the world. It consists of the *current account* (see page 144) and the *capital account* (see page 141). They are supposed to balance, with any current account deficit offset by a surplus in the capital account. In practice, there is often an imbalance, and compensating items are introduced.

If a country's balance of payments deficit or surplus is both significant and lasting, it suggests that the currency is wrongly valued.

Base rate

This is the *Repo rate* (see page 153).

Basis point

This is a hundredth part of a single percentage point.

Bretton Woods

The Bretton Woods agreement was a *fixed rate exchange system* (see page 147) agreed in 1944 at a conference in Bretton Woods, New Hampshire.

Under the agreement, member countries each assumed a par value for their respective currencies against the dollar, with a fluctuation allowance of 1 per cent either side of par. The currencies were, in turn, *pegged* (see 'Pegged rate', page 152) to gold at US $35 per ounce on demand.

The newly created *International Monetary Fund* (see page 149) was to help out by lending both gold and foreign currencies to countries that might otherwise need to devalue their currencies.

In 1969, the IMF produced special drawing rights, a currency of its own valued against the US dollar and other major currencies, which enabled countries to settle debts with each other.

The Bretton Woods system stayed in operation until the early 1970s, when its Achilles heel, common to fixed rate exchange systems, became apparent: the banks did not have enough currency reserves to sustain the currency at the required levels.

Capital account

The capital account consists of a country's long-term investment income, and assets such as land or foreign shares as well as speculative money flows. See *Balance of payments* (see page 140) and *Current account* (see page 144).

Capital flight

Capital flight is when money is transferred out of a country, typically to avoid economic problems. Russia has experienced it in recent years.

Classical economics

This is an economic theory based on the ideas of *Adam Smith* (see page 155), which was prevalent in the 19th century. It holds that economic growth is best promoted by free trade.

Comparative advantage

This is the country's production of one product more efficiently than of another.

Consumer Prices Index

The Consumer Prices Index is the measure used by the UK government since December 2003 to set its 2 per cent *inflation* (see page 149) target. It provides

The global economy requires cash and trade efficiencies

Lloyds TSB's Corporate Transaction Services unit has taken an unusual step for a bank – reorganised itself around the needs of the customer. Colin Hemsley, head of Trade Sales, explains

Over the years, the leading trade finance banks have offered a range of services and products aimed at comforting trading companies (both importers and exporters) when undertaking risky ventures abroad. However, what they have not done – until now – is marry the trade and risk elements of overseas trade with the more usual cash management functions of a company.

In most companies, the treasury team is charged with cash management efficiency – i.e. making sure the cash accrued is placed in the right place at the right time to maximise the companies income and minimise the company's costs. Meanwhile, the export-import team is usually more concerned with the risks involved with overseas trade such as payment risk, foreign exchange risk and shipment risk.

Yet in recent years a growing number of companies have made treasury management the hub around which a company's entire trading value-chain circulates. This includes trade finance, given the fact all exports – whether commodities, components or finished products – end in a cash transaction. This makes the joining of cash and trade management an intuitively sensible marriage – although one only now making serious headway within company thinking.

Why the delay? Companies should blame their banks for offering services via a structure that suits the bank, and not the customer – often forcing their customers to follow suit. At Lloyds TSB Corporate, however, we have taken the lead in blending our cash and treasury functions. And while pleased to reorganise in a way that fully reflects our customers' needs, the central aim is to maximise their cash management efficiencies, thereby spreading liquidity enhancement throughout the company.

When I first sit down with the treasurer of a UK exporter, whatever the size of the business, I therefore try to gain a clear sense of their priorities as a business. Such priorities may include a combination of better management information, better risk management, maximisation of revenue and the reduction of cost.

Indeed, cost reduction is often the top priority, which usually requires matching cash reserves – or receivables – with debt positions. In the case of receivables, this means fast and efficient collection followed by placement of the cash where it will be of maximum benefit to the group. In the case of a company with more free cash than debts, however, the objective would be to concentrate these reserves in order to maximise interest receipts.

Many of these efficiencies are being driven by new technology – another area where Lloyds TSB has taken a lead. Web-based systems in particular are bringing a new and unprecedented degree of confidence to trade and cash transaction – as well as new efficiencies in combining the two. Indeed, it is the bank's firm belief that the coming generation of trade and cash services provision will be based around single browser portals provided by banks – accessed via a password-protected website. Efficiencies indeed!

 Corporate

advertisement feature

WHEN SIGNOR MARCONI WAS SENDING HIS FIRST BROADCAST WAS RECEPTION GETTING A GREAT WAS EXPORT FINANCING OUR

Every day we help thousands of companies pick up business from all over the world. We have connections with more than 1,200 correspondent banking groups worldwide, as well as our own UK regional and overseas offices. We can easily arrange back-to-back letters of credit, receivables or bill discounting, and many other financing options. All of which is sure to get a great reception. For more information please contact **itf@lloydstsb.co.uk**

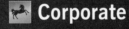 **Corporate**

THE BUSINESS. SINCE 1765.

www.lloydstsb.com/corporate/THEBUSINESS

Please remember we cannot guarantee security of messages sent by e-mail. Lloyds TSB Bank plc. Registered Office: 25 Gresham Street, London EC2V 7HN. Registered in England and Wales no. 2065. Lloyds TSB Scotland plc.
Registered Office: Henry Duncan House, 120 George Street, Edinburgh EH2 4LH. Registered in Scotland no. 95237. Authorised and regulated by the Financial Services Authority and signatories to the Banking Codes. Lloyds TSB Bank plc
and Lloyds TSB Scotland plc represent only the Scottish Widows and Lloyds TSB Marketing Group for life assurance, pensions and investment business.

annual inflation rates from 1996 onwards. Estimates are available from 1988, and indicative figures are available for 12 years earlier.

Previously, the CPI was called the 'UK Harmonised Index of Consumer Prices', which was set up to compare inflation rates across EU member states. It remains calculated on the same principle and, for international comparisons, is considered a better measure than the RPI-X, an offshoot of the ***Retail Prices Index*** (see page 154) previously used for government inflation targets.

The CPI excludes some items in the RPI-X, mainly connected with housing, which is partly why its annual rate is usually higher. It combines prices by a geometric mean rather than the arithmetic alternative used for the RPI. See the discussion on both measures in Part 1, Chapter 2.

Crawling peg

This allows a government to change its currency's exchange rate in proportion to movement in the ***pegged rate*** (see page 152).

Current account

The current account is the balance of a country's gains or losses from buying and selling physical goods and services overseas. It includes invisibles such as interest rates and ***dividends*** (see page 210). In conjunction with the ***capital account*** (see page 141), it makes up the ***balance of payments*** (see page 140).

At the time of writing, the UK has a current account deficit, but not a particularly large one.

Deflation

This is a continued reduction of price levels. A government may try to create deflation by reducing demand in the economy, perhaps through an increase in taxes or interest rates.

Disinflation

Disinflation is a reduction in the ***inflation*** (see page 149) rate.

Econometrics

This is the production of economic forecasting models and the testing of links between variables.

Economic and Monetary Union

Economic and Monetary Union (EMU), is a process by which EU member states move towards a single market, single currency and harmonised interest and tax rates.

EMU was initiated by the Delors Report, which led to the *Maastricht Treaty* (see page 150). Important to the process were the *ECU* (see next entry) and the *European Exchange Rate Mechanism* (see page 146).

ECU

The ECU is a notional 'basket' currency constructed from the merged currencies of all European Union members, weighted by size. In 1999, the *euro* (see next entry) replaced it.

Euro

The euro is the currency of the countries of the European Union. It came into use in business in 1999 and replaced the *ECU* (see entry above). Coins and notes were issued in 2002.

To join the euro, countries in the EU were required to be in line with convergence criteria in areas such as *inflation* (see page 149), interest rates, exchange rates and government borrowings.

The 11 countries that initially were qualified for and elected to join the euro were Austria, Belgium, Finland, France, Germany, Ireland, Italy, Luxembourg, the Netherlands, Portugal and Spain. In 2000, Greece joined the euro after having earlier failed to meet the criteria.

The exchange rates of the initial participating countries were fixed within narrow percentage bands against the new currency, which is part of *Economic and Monetary Union* (see page 145). The exchange rate mechanism used was ERM2 (see the next entry, *European Exchange rate Mechanism*), set up by the European Council on 1 January 1999.

On 1 May 2004, 10 new countries joined the EU: Cyprus, the Czech Republic, Estonia, Hungary, Latvia, Lithuania, Malta, Poland, the Slovak Republic and Slovenia. They were expected to adopt the euro in future under the terms of their accession.

An advantage of the euro is that it eliminates exchange rate risk in business across borders between EU member countries, and exchange transaction costs. The main disadvantage is that the European Central Bank sets the same short-term interest rates for all member countries, regardless of whether it suits them individually.

Denmark, Sweden and the UK have held back from joining the euro. The UK government has been planning to join since 1997. It has said it will do so if Government, Parliament and the people agree the move in a referendum.

European Exchange Rate Mechanism

The European Exchange Rate Mechanism (ERM) was set up in 1979. The aim was to reduce variability of exchange rates within the European Monetary System of the European Union, and prepare for a single currency.

Currencies of ERM members were fixed against each other, subject to a small amount of fluctuation in *ECUs* (see page 145). They floated against the currencies of non-member countries. If a currency moved too far outside the permitted perimeters, central banks and the European Monetary Cooperation Fund intervened.

Britain joined the ERM temporarily in October 1990. It left in September 1992 after speculators led by *George Soros* (see page 160) put the pound under pressure.

Since that year, Britain has adopted a floating exchange rate mechanism. It has not at this stage joined ERM2 (see *euro*, page 145).

Exchange controls

This is when governments try to control capital movements to and from a country with the aim of safeguarding the exchange rate.

Exchange rate

The exchange rate is what a foreign currency costs outside its country of origin. Currencies are usually expressed against the dollar. Sterling is the exception and it is usual to talk of dollars to the pound. Currencies may also be expressed against each other in cross rates, or against a basket of currencies represented by a trade-weighted index.

Factory gate prices

See 'Producer Prices Index' (page 153).

Federal Reserve

The Federal Reserve is America's Central Bank. It started in 1913, and consists of 12 regional banks. It advises on monetary policy, manages public debt, sets interest rates, controls the issue of banknotes, and launches bonds issues.

Fixed rate exchange system

This fixes a currency's valuation. Any participating country must play by the rules, even if it damages its economy.

In practice, fixed rate exchange systems do not work well. See **Bretton Woods** (page 141), **European Exchange Rate Mechanism** (page 146), **Gold Standard** (page 148), **Pegged rate** (page 152) and **Snake** (page 155).

Foreign Direct Investment

Foreign Direct Investment (FDI) is when a direct investor buys companies or properties abroad in the host country's currency.

Foreign exchange

The foreign exchange market involves fast buying and selling of currencies at rapidly fluctuating **exchange rates** (see page 146). The price is always expressed in two foreign currencies, usually against the US dollar. A currency may be valued against any other in cross rates or against a basket of trade-weighted currencies (see discussion in Part 1, Chapter 3).

The most popular currency internationally is the US dollar. It serves as an intermediary. One currency is not changed into another directly, but is first changed into dollars, and then dollars are changed into the required currency. The introduction of the **euro** (see page 145) at the start of 1999 has enabled EU member countries to trade with each other directly without exchanging their currencies. These two currencies, with sterling and the Yen, are the ones most covered in the financial pages, reflecting their importance in international trade.

The forex market, as it is known, is driven by governments and central banks and speculative flows, but also by trade from companies and tourists' requirements. Its size has grown significantly in recent years. In the late 1980s, daily global trading was around US $450 billion. In April 2004, it was US $1.9 trillion, according to the Bank of International Settlements. The market operates 24 hours a day across global time zones.

Forex transaction costs are low due to the scale of trading, and this is the most liquid of markets in the City of London. It has no physical location but it tends to be conducted from leading financial markets centres. London accounts for more than a third of the global forex market by trading volumes, which is the highest proportion in the world.

London's attraction as a location is that it is conveniently placed in the world time zones, and has easy access to Europe. New York is the next largest forex trader, and Tokyo comes third. The smaller centres include Frankfurt, Zurich, Paris, Hong Kong, Singapore and Toronto.

Foreign exchange dealers are the large commercial banks. They buy and sell currency on behalf of clients and they also take speculative positions for themselves. They make about a third of their profits from currency dealing.

The forex broker deals directly with dealers, and may make up a shortfall or accept a surplus position. If one bank deals with another in the same financial centre, it will be through a broker.

The dealer gives a foreign exchange quote on a bid/ask basis, and may be held to it for only seconds. The dealers are open for foreign exchange business 24 hours a day, which they achieve by running both a night and a day shift.

In 1992, electronic trading was introduced into the *spot market* (see page 155) for forex, and it has since moved into the *forward market* (see next entry). It poses competition for the broker.

For settlement on large trades, a system of netting operates in London. The two parties make or take one net payment for a currency deal on a given settlement date. There is a slight risk of default, particularly when trade is between vastly different time zones such as London and Tokyo.

At retail level, settlement of transactions will be over the counter. The forex office may or may not be part of a bank, and is likely to take a substantial commission. The customer pays for the convenience of changing money on the High Street.

Forward market

Forward contracts provide for the sale of a given amount of currency at a specified exchange rate at a specified time or within a given time period. The dealer arranges a contract directly with the customer.

Most forward deals are foreign exchange swaps with maturities, most for less than seven days and almost all for less than a year. The deals are often in dollars or sterling where a wide range of short-term instruments and securities is available.

Compare the *spot market* (see page 155).

Gold Standard

The Gold Standard is a *fixed rate exchange system* (see page 147) that the UK introduced in 1840. Many countries were following it by 1880.

The regime linked a country's money supply to the central bank's gold reserves. Coins or notes became interchangeable with gold. In theory, the Gold Standard meant stability of exchange rates, but it did not properly achieve this.

Gross Domestic Product – GDP

Gross Domestic Product (GDP) is the most popular measure of output used by economists. It is the combined market value of final goods and services produced in an economy over a given period.

GDP is announced quarterly, and its significance is in its growth rate. If GDP rises over 3 per cent in each of four quarters in succession, it sends a strong inflationary warning and the **Bank of England** (see page 195) will probably raise interest rates as a restraining measure. The figures are sometimes revised.

Gross National Product – GNP

Gross National Product (GNP) measures a country's wealth, or the total goods and services produced by companies owned by the country. It is the **Gross Domestic Product** (see previous entry) plus income earned by domestic residents from investments abroad. GNP excludes income earned by foreign investors in the domestic market.

Index of Production

The Index of Production measures the volume of production in manufacturing, mining and quarrying, and energy supply industries. It is a monthly time series. The index is measured at base year prices, and is a short-term economic indicator, as well as a component of the output measure of **GDP** (see page 149), and a contributor to EC indices.

Inflation

Inflation is a continued rise in price levels that diminishes the value of money.

Experts cannot agree on the cause. Some cite cost-push inflation, based on rising manufacturing costs, and others believe in demand-pull inflation, based on demand exceeding supply. See also **Monetarism** (page 151).

The Government inflation target from December 2003 has been measured by the **Consumer Prices Index** (see page 141). The previous measure was RPI-X, an offshoot of the **Retail Prices Index** (see page 154).

International Monetary Fund

The International Monetary Fund (IMF) is an organisation that lends money to member states to help them to overcome problems in the **balance of payments** (see page 140). It was established in 1946 as a result of the **Bretton Woods** (see page 141) agreement.

Countries receiving help from the IMF must in return introduce specified reforms, which may include government privatisations. The IMF has been criticised for proposing reforms that are both too strict and insufficiently tailored to the country's circumstances. It has denied this, and is constantly reforming its own processes.

Intervention

This is when the government or central bank trades a currency in order to change the exchange rate or market conditions. It may be aiming to help the treasury to balance its books.

The government may announce its intention in advance. Alternatively, it may operate secretly, using a little known bank to place the order.

If a government practises intervention without cutting interest rates, it is *sterilised* and it may not move markets so effectively.

Keynesian economics

This follows John Maynard Keynes, a pioneering economist who published his main ideas in the early to mid 19th century. He believed that aggregate demand in the economy was significant in deciding real output, and that governments could manipulate it, mainly through taxes, to reduce unemployment.

Leading indicator

A leading indicator is an economic signal that changes before the economy changes. In technical analysis, it means an indicator that signals an expected change in the share price.

Maastricht Treaty

The Maastricht Treaty gave rise to the European Union, and was officially known as the Treaty of the European Union. The Treaty was agreed in 1991, signed in 1992 and, following ratification from member states, became effective from 1 November 1993. It added justice and home affairs, and a common foreign and security policy to the already established European Community. These became the three pillars of the Union.

Maastricht defined the stages of *Economic and Monetary Union* (see page 145) that led to the single currency. A controversial aspect of the Treaty was its recognition of subsidiarity, by which the Union takes action only if it is more effective than action taken nationally, regionally or locally.

Malthus, Thomas Robert

Thomas Malthus was an early 19th century economist and the son of a country squire. He argued that population pressure was a main reason for poverty because the population grew geometrically, but the natural resources that supported it grew arithmetically, which put pressure on living standards. He proposed the introduction of a moral limit on the size of families.

Malthus's ideas were based on the **subsistence theory of wages** (see page 156). Using these, some queried the need for wage rises because they appeared to lead to a higher sexual appetite and poverty.

Marx, Karl

Karl Marx was a philosopher and scholar who said that a commodity's value was in direct proportion to the amount of work that went into producing it, and so the worker was entitled to the entire rewards of production. But the capitalist class stole the rewards from the worker, according to Marx. He forecast a revolution in which *socialisation* of the means of production and distribution would bring back to the workers the full fruits of their labour.

The failure of Communism is based on flaws in Marxian economics, which is considered too simple a model for a consumer economy.

Mill, John Stuart

John Stuart Mill was a 19th century economist who advocated utilitarianism, which favours actions promoting the happiness and well-being of the greatest number of people. He said that the distribution of wealth, unlike its production, could be organised as mankind wished.

Monetarism

Monetarism is a theory of economics. It holds that *money supply* (see next entry) and interest rates are the main influence on the business cycle. It attributes inflation to a money supply that has grown too quickly. The best known of the monetarists is Milton Friedman, an economist born in 1912 in Brooklyn, New York.

Money supply

Money supply represents the liquid assets available in the economy for buying goods or services. If it grows excessively, it will cause *inflation* (see page 149) but if it declines, it could cool the economy. To control the money supply is to keep inflation in check, according to monetarists.

The more narrowly the money supply is measured, the easier it is for the government to control it, but the less complete it is. M0 is a narrow measure of money, consisting of all coins, notes and bankers' operational balances held at the Bank of England, and M4 is a broad money aggregate which, in the long run, may be expected to grow at a similar rate to nominal spending and **GDP** (see page 149).

NAIRU

This is the Non-accelerating Rate of Unemployment. It is the rate at which *inflation* (see page 149) neither rises nor falls, and has been controversially described as the *natural* rate of unemployment.

National income

This is the total income earned by individuals in an economy within a specified period. It is **Gross National Product** (see page 149), less a **capital allowance** (see page 205) to replace old stock.

New classical economics

New classical economics holds that demand-led intervention by the government is ineffective. It takes the opposite view to **monetarism** (see page 151).

The school of thought is based on the *policy ineffectiveness* theory, which states that governments may have impact on the economy only if their policies were not anticipated.

Pegged rate

A currency rate is *pegged* when one country holds its currency's value constant against that of another country, with which it probably has close trading links.

The peg may be against a basket of currencies. If so, the government has some control as it can change the weighting of each component currency.

Phillips curve

The Phillips Curve was invented by Professor Alban Phillips, an academic economist prominent in the 1950s. It shows an inverse relationship between unemployment and *inflation* (see page 149). When one is high, the other is low.

From the late 1960s, both inflation and unemployment became high, and the curve did not work. Milton Friedman introduced a version of the Phillips Curve adjusted for inflation expenditure.

Most economists today do not believe that inflation and unemployment are linked.

Portfolio balance model

This states that exchange rates are linked to the expected return on the assets in which international capital flows invest. It is an alternative theory to *purchasing power parity* (see page 153).

Producer Prices Index

The PPI measures price changes in goods bought and sold by UK manufacturers. It is a key *inflation* (see page 149) measure, and is based on a weighted basket of goods. The output price indices (factory gate prices) measure change in the price of goods produced by manufacturers. The input prices measure change in the price of materials and fuels used by UK manufacturers for processing.

Purchasing Managers' Index

The Purchasing Managers' Index (PMI) is a seasonally adjusted index aimed at providing an overall view of the manufacturing economy. It is provided by NTC Research and the Chartered Institute of Purchasing and Supply. In compiling this weighted average index, account is taken of output, new orders, suppliers' delivery times, stocks of items bought and employment. The index is an indicator of business confidence.

Purchasing power parity

Purchasing power parity is the oldest theory of how currency exchange rates are formed. It holds that, because of arbitrage opportunities, exchange rates will converge to a level where purchasing power is the same internationally.

Governments take the theory seriously, but it is unreliable, particularly in the short term. An imbalance between exchange rates and *inflation* (see page 149) can last a long time because it is financed by speculators who trade currency exchange differentials.

Repo rate

The Repo rate is the technical term for the base rate. It is the rate of interest charged by the *Bank of England* (see page 195) to banks for *repurchase agreements* (see page 199). It is subject to alteration by the Monetary Policy Committee at monthly meetings in accordance with the government's 2 per cent annual *inflation* (see page 149) target based on the *Consumer Prices Index* (see page 141). It is known as the 'Official dealing rate', and was previously the 'Minimum lending rate'.

As the UK's core interest rate, the Repo rate influences banks' lending rates, including on *mortgages* (see page 234). The margin on these in relation to the Repo rate varies between products and financial institutions and is decided on a commercial basis.

Recession

This is when the **Gross Domestic Product** (see page 149) has been declining over a period, defined by some as over two quarters. There is no hard rule, but a recession is less extreme than a depression. The end of a recession is marked by a recovery.

Retail Prices Index

The Retail Prices Index (RPI) is a widely followed *inflation* (see page 149) indicator released monthly by the Office for National Statistics. It measures the price rises in a basket of goods, with prices collected locally and centrally, using a random sampling of locations. The figures are on a weighted basis, reflecting where people spend more.

The headline RPI has derivations. There is the RPI-X, which is the headline figure excluding mortgage rates. The RPI-Y is the RPI-X excluding VAT and other indirect taxes.

In December 2003, the RPI-X was replaced by the **Consumer Prices Index** (see page 141) as the measure of the government's replacement target. But the RPI and its derivations are still used for the indexation of pensions, state benefits and index-linked **gilts** (see 'Bonds', page 71). See Part 1, Chapter 2, for further discussion of the RPI-X and CPI.

Ricardo, David

David Ricardo was an early 18th century economist known for his theory that rent was 'that portion of the produce of the earth which is paid to the landlord for the use of the original and indestructible powers of the soil'. He argued that money was not significant in the payment of the rent, but that the landlord instead wanted a share in the produce of the land.

Ricardo believed that working men's wages were fixed by a capital fund available to entrepreneurs, divided by the total population. He argued against interference with the market forces that, in his view sensibly, created disincentives for the poor to procreate further.

Ricardo's notion that all wages derive from a capital fund is no longer accepted. Instead, it is acknowledged that banks and firms contribute to capital, and the entire *national income* (see page 152) enables payment of wages.

Savings ratio

This is savings as a percentage of disposable income. It is also known as the 'Savings rate'.

Smith, Adam

Adam Smith, born in 1723, is acclaimed as the founder of economics (see 'Classical economics', page 141). He is famous for his theory that, when a product is in short supply, prices will rise and, when it is plentiful, prices will fall, showing that markets guide economic activity and direct resources like an *invisible hand*.

According to Smith's theories, a free market is possible. His case is that producers make a profit by providing products without government intervention, and they reduce their prices to the lowest level to compete, which benefits the consumer.

Snake

The snake is a now defunct fixed rate exchange system, which the UK joined in 1972 for just six weeks. The system failed in its attempts to keep currency within 2.5 per cent of a band level, partly because of volatility in the oil price.

Spot market

The spot market is where you buy or sell a currency for immediate delivery and is normally settled in two working days. Business between New York and Toronto is cleared in one day as they are in the same time zone. Compare the *forward market* (see page 148).

If a spot transaction is small, it can be arranged face-to-face, as when a tourist changes money. Larger transactions are still arranged mainly on the telephone, but electronic broking plays an increasingly important role. (See 'Foreign exchange', page 147).

Stagflation

Stagflation is a combination of stagnation, with a high unemployment rate, and *inflation* (see page 149). The term was coined in the 1970s.

Strategists

Strategists are experts on the economy. They analyse the macroeconomic climate and make forecasts. They are often employed by investment banks.

Subsistence theory of wages

This holds that wages could never stay above subsistence level. If they rise temporarily, the apparent wealth will encourage having larger families, and so increase competition among workers, with the result that wages will decline again. The theory was the basis of the ideas of *Thomas Malthus* (see page 151).

Taylor rule

The Taylor rule is that, if growth and *inflation* (see page 149) are rising on target, they will, added together, be a likely target short-term interest rate. It was named after John Taylor, an economist who became US Treasury Under-Secretary in 2001. Central banks tend to follow the Taylor rule in making interest rate forecasts.

World Bank

The International Bank for Reconstruction and Development, known as the World Bank, provides long-term loans to developing countries at favourable interest rates. The loans are guaranteed by the governments of borrowing countries.

Like the *International Monetary Fund* (see page 149), the World Bank was set up in 1946 as a result of the *Bretton Woods* (see page 141) agreement. It has been criticised for inefficiency and for failing to take sufficient account of environmental and people factors in its projects. It denies the criticisms and is undergoing reform.

World Trade Organisation

The World Trade Organisation (WTO) develops and polices a planned multilateral trading system among its more than 120 member states. The WTO was established in Geneva in 1995 and it replaced the General Agreement on Tariffs and Trade (GATT).

Yield gap

The yield gap is the difference between the average yield on shares and the average current yield on long dated *gilts* (see 'Bonds', page 71). When the yield on shares is lower, it is called the 'Reverse yield gap'.

Hedging, short selling and hedge funds

Introduction

In this section, we look at the hedging of your portfolio, as well as short selling and hedge funds. Derivatives may be used for taking a short position and are covered in Section D.

Gold

Gold is a useful hedge against political, economic or market uncertainty. It tends to become more valuable during a war. You can buy gold bullion coins, which are tradable, and keep them in a bank or safe deposit. But gold does not give you an income and it costs 2 per cent a year in holding expenses. You should probably restrict it to up to 10 per cent of your investments.

An alternative way to buy gold is through investing in gold mining companies. The administration expenses are smaller than on direct gold purchases, and the potential gains are large.

Hedging

To hedge is to reduce the risk of adverse price movements in your core portfolio by taking an opposite position, perhaps using ***derivatives*** (see Section D, page 107).

For instance, an investor in a blue chip share portfolio may hedge it by buying a put option. If the portfolio rises in value, as expected, the investor will have lost the cost of the option premium and dealing expenses. But if the portfolio goes into a sharp decline beyond the level of the premium plus dealing costs, the investor will profit from the rising value of the put option.

Hedging can also mean to buy or sell derivatives as a temporary substitute for a planned cash transaction.

Hedge funds

A hedge fund is a specialist type of investment fund that is free to invest in high-risk or other financial instruments or markets. It may be either an entrepreneurial start-up operation or part of a larger group. In December 2004, surveys suggested that there were between 6,000 and 9,000 hedge funds globally. (See also 'Funds of funds' under 'Multi-manager funds', page 286 and 'Prime broker', page 159).

Hedge funds use diverse investment strategies, often in combination, the best known of which is *short selling* (see page 159). They are notorious for moving markets at sensitive times, including during the book build for a securities issue. Hedge funds are subject to fewer regulatory restrictions than ordinary investment funds.

A majority of hedge funds is based in the Cayman Islands where regulations are more relaxed than in, for example, Dublin or Luxembourg, which some funds favour for the European exposure. The fund management often chooses to be in London because of the commercial clout that derives from being regulated by the *Financial Services Authority* (see page 255). The administration may be based in another jurisdiction.

Among new contenders, Guernsey, Jersey and the Isle of Man have relaxed regulations to attract business, but have so far had limited success in cracking the competitive hedge fund market. They have attracted mainly administrators for local funds.

Hedge funds aim for absolute returns, regardless of market conditions. Failure, like success, can be huge. Long Term Capital Management was a hedge fund that experienced a high profile failure in 1998. Its theoretical liabilities were US $1.25 trillion.

In the US, hedge funds are traditionally set up as private partnerships limited to 100 investors, two-thirds of whom must individually be worth at least US $1 million. Hedge fund strategies have spread to mutual funds as a result of legislation in 1993 that made it easier for them to take short positions. *Market timing* (see page 259) scandal in mutual funds was part of the reason why the US Securities & Exchange Commission has started taking an aggressive approach to hedge funds and registration requirements.

By early 2005, hedge funds no longer had the buccaneering image that they had enjoyed in the heyday of speculator **George Soros** (see page 160). They are now attracting medium- to long-term investors who want to diversify their portfolios more. The funds have gained a deserved reputation for preserving investors' capital and achieving a real return, which is more than equities have done in recent years.

The UK's **Financial Services Authority** (see page 255) acknowledges this role, and the extra liquidity that hedge funds bring to capital markets, helping to arbitrage away mispricing. Hedge funds make the financial system more efficient but, because of their importance to the market, their opaqueness, complexity and leverage capacity, they are of regulatory concern from a financial stability perspective.

Prime broker

This type of broker is responsible for settlement, custody and reporting of trades for **hedge funds** (see previous entry).

Short interest

Short interest is how many shares have been **sold short** (see next entry, 'Short selling') and not yet repurchased. Your broker should give you the figure on request. If short interest is more than 5–6 per cent of shares in issue, a new short seller should not become active because the stock may not have too much further down to go. Rising short interest is seen as a bullish indicator in the near term because the shares that have been sold represent imminent buy orders.

Short selling

If you sell a stock short, you will sell a stock that you do not own with the aim of buying it back at a lower price before you settle.

Your profit will be any price decline less dealing costs. If the price has risen when you buy back, you will have lost to the extent of the price differential plus dealing costs. In this way, short sellers benefit from a declining but not a rising share price.

The practice has an unsavoury reputation because it is considered to profit from others' misfortunes, and there is sometimes a suggestion that it is based on insider knowledge. In its defence, short selling provides much needed liquidity to the market.

Short selling has been illegal at various times in France, Germany and the US. In 1733, it became illegal in the UK, but in 1860 the ban was revoked.

The London Stock Exchange's electronic settlement system prevents private investors, for practical purposes, from selling short. They can, however, take a short position through *contracts for difference* (see page 108) or financial *spread bets* (see page 114).

In 2002, concerns arose that Al-Qaeda terrorists may have raised funds by taking a short position on international stock markets before the planned 11 September 2001 attacks on the US. The case was never proven.

In April 2003, the *Financial Services Authority* (see page 255) announced its conclusions from an investigation into short selling. It found the practice acceptable, but called for more disclosure.

Soros, George

George Soros, born in 1930 in Hungary, is the world's best known *hedge fund* (see page 158) operator and short seller. He owns the Quantum Fund, a hedge fund registered in Curacao, Netherlands Antilles.

In his strategies for trading in financial markets, Soros has been heavily influenced by the ideas of philosopher Karl Popper, including his scepticism about the validity of any single human belief.

On 22 September 1992, Soros initiated his most famous transaction. The Quantum Fund took a US $10 billion short position in sterling in the belief that it was overvalued. Soros increased his position even as the British government raised interest rates to prop up the currency.

The Bank of England eventually withdrew the pound from the *European Exchange Rate Mechanism* (see page 146), and it plummeted in value. Soros made an estimated US $1 billion from his bet.

Paradoxically, Soros is a critic of financial speculation, believing that it has adversely affected the economic prowess of many undeveloped countries.

Insurance and pensions

Introduction

Insurance and pensions is a complicated subject. The personal finance pages in newspapers focus on individual products and help you to understand what is on offer. Some of the coverage is critical; much of it is complimentary.

If a scandal arises, the press will often follow it in detail. It happened with the Equitable Life collapse, and with endowment mis-selling scandals in the late 1980s and early 1990s, but which were recently subject to compensation.

In this section, I will explain the basics and provide you with a framework for understanding what you read in the press.

In the first entry, I will explain the range of insurance and pensions products. Further entries cover the London market, including Lloyd's of London, and protection and indemnity associations. The last entry is on reinsurance.

See also sections P and U, which cover personal finance products sold by insurance companies.

Choosing the right financial planner

Choosing a financial planner may be one of the most important decisions you make for yourself and your family. A planner can play a central role in helping you meet your life goals and achieve financial well-being. Consequently, take the time to select a financial planner who is competent and trustworthy, one on whom you can depend for professional advice and services. Your future depends on the choices you make.

Most people think that all financial planners are "certified", but this isn't true. Anyone can call themselves a "financial planner." Only those who have fulfilled the licence and renewal requirements of the Institute of Financial Planning can display the CFP marks. When selecting a financial planner, you need to feel confident that the person you choose to help you plan for your future is competent and ethical. The CFP licence provides that sense of security by allowing only those who meet stringent requirements the right to use the CFP licence marks.

When you work with a CFP professional, you are the focus of the financial planning relationship and your needs drive the financial planner's recommendations. CFP practitioners follow certain standards when providing financial planning based on the six-step financial planning process. This broad-based approach to financial advice distinguishes financial planning practitioners from other professional advisers who typically focus on only one area of a person's financial life.

When providing financial planning advice, a CFP professional will define the scope of the work they will do with you, explain and document the services they will provide, discuss the method of compensation and relay any other relevant information. They will work with you to determine your personal and financial goals, your tolerance for financial risk, and your time frame for achieving results. They are also required to gather all necessary financial information about you when developing your personal financial plan. Finding the right professional to address your financial planning needs isn't always easy.

It is important to take your time when choosing a financial planner, and before making a decision, become familiar with the planner's business style and understand the level of services they provide. Look for a measure of the planner's commitment to ethical behaviour and adherence to high professional standards. Look for a financial planner who will put you and your needs at the centre of every financial planning engagement. To verify that your planner is licensed by the Institute of Financial Planning, visit their website at www.financialplanning.org.uk

Institute of Financial Planning
Whitefriars
Lewins Mead
Bristol BS1 2NT

t: 0117 945 2470
f: 0117 929 2214
e: enquiries@financialplanning.org.uk
w: www.financialplanning.org.uk

advertisement feature

Insurance and pensions

Insurance is a service that offers financial compensation for something that may or may not arise. In an insurance transaction, one party, the insurer, undertakes to pay another party, the insured, money if a specified form of financial risk should arise. For this service, the insured pays the insurer a fee, known as a premium.

It is big business. The UK is the largest insurance market in Europe, and third largest in the world behind the US and Japan, accounting for 8.4 per cent of worldwide premium income. It employs 348,000 people, which is a third of all financial services jobs. UK insurance companies receive £30 billion a year in premium income from overseas business, which is nearly a quarter of the whole.

Of the 772 insurance companies authorised to carry on insurance business in the UK, almost 568 do only general business, as defined below, and 159 are authorised for long-term business (such as life insurance and pensions). There are 45 composite insurers, which are able to do both.

Insurers will have good and bad years. To remain solvent, which means keeping enough reserves to pay claims, can be a balancing act. The insurer invests premiums received to increase reserves, but investment performance depends on markets.

From 31 December 2004, the *Financial Services Authority* (see page 255) introduced requirements for insurers to have capital that matched the risk of the business that they wrote more closely than before. The FSA now regulates all mortgage and insurance business.

Let us now take a look at the different types of insurance under the headings, 1) General insurance; 2) Life and pensions; and 3) Health and protection.

1. General insurance

General insurance is defined by the Association of British Insurers (ABI) as insurance of non-life risks where the policy offers cover for a limited period, usually a year. It includes the following.

a) Transportation insurance

This includes marine, aviation and transit. Motor is the largest class of general insurance in the UK because cover is a legal requirement. The largest 10 motor insurers handle 82 per cent of the business.

b) Property insurance

The values at risk are high, and mortgage companies require property cover. For private properties, available cover includes buildings and contents insurance. The largest 10 property insurers account for 84 per cent of the market.

c) Pecuniary insurance

This covers the risk that an organisation may be required to pay out a large amount of money, or that its money may be unexpectedly diminished.

d) Liability insurance

This pays court awards or damages where a person is held legally liable, subject to policy limits. It includes employers' liability insurance, and public liability insurance, which can include products liability.

Liability insurance is mostly long tail. It means that the liability may be discovered and claims made many years after the loss was caused. Insurers have been dealing with claims for those who contracted asbestosis-related diseases some years ago and, so far, have paid £200–£300 million in compensation.

Among perceived liability risks are mobile phones, silica and toxic mould.

2. Life and pensions

In the long-term insurance market, consisting largely of life and pensions, the largest 10 companies account for 72 per cent of the market.

Life insurance

Life insurance policies are all based on a contract by which the insurance company must pay a sum, known as the sum assured, to an individual or individuals on death or after a specified period. If it is *assurance*, the policy covers an event that will happen, ie that we will die, and so there will be a definite payout. If it is *insurance*, it covers an event that is not certain, such as if you should fall down skiing, and the payout would come only if it happened. The two terms are now considered interchangeable, perhaps due to US influence.

The premium paid on a life insurance policy depends on the type of cover required and the risk profile of the life assured. Tax relief on premiums paid depends on when the policy was taken out. If it was after 13 March 1984, there is no relief. If an earlier policy was varied after that date, there is also no relief. But for polices taken out before this date, and where all policy and policyholder conditions are met, the premiums will qualify for 12.5 per cent tax relief, which must be deducted from the amount payable as premium.

Life insurance is divided into two types: a) protection insurance, which includes term and insurance and whole-of-life insurance; and b) investment-type insurance, which consists of endowment products. Let us look at each.

a) Protection insurance

Term insurance offers the cheapest form of life insurance. It pays out if you die within a specified period, either as a lump sum or as income, in either case tax free. If you survive the term, it pays nothing.

Today, *repayment mortgages* (see 'Mortgages', page 234) – the most popular kind – are often accompanied by term insurance. It enables the mortgage to be paid off if the family breadwinner should die during the policy's term. A popular choice is decreasing term insurance, when the sum assured – the amount payable if the insured dies – decreases with time to match the declining mortgage balance. The premium stays constant, and is slightly lower than for standard term insurance.

Whole-of-life insurance pays out on the death of the insured at any time and aims at protection, not investment. The cover is not limited to a period like term insurance, which is why it is more expensive. The way it usually works is that part of the premium paid is invested by the insurer to build up a pot of money. This is not as a savings vehicle, but to soften the blow of premium increases.

The money paid into a whole-of-life policy could be put into trust using standard trust documents provided by your insurance company, or by your solicitor, who could customise them. Properly structured, it would not form part of the life assured's estate for *inheritance tax* (see page 134) purposes, and the beneficiary could use the policy proceeds to pay any such tax.

A whole-of-life policy is likely to be unit-linked if it is purchased today, which means that the insurance company invests your premiums by buying units in funds. The amount payable on early surrender depends on the value of the investment within those funds. The amount payable on death is the guaranteed sum assured stated on the policy document.

New buyers today are much less likely to be offered a with-profits policy. Here the insurance company pools your premiums with those of others in a fund, which invests in assets. The investment return is smoothed by bonuses to protect the insured against volatility in the fund. Any annual bonuses are added permanently to the policy and there may be a terminal bonus on maturity. These bonuses are discretionary, and are not linked to the performance of the wider investment market. If the insurer runs into financial problems, it may reduce or suspend bonus payments, and may impose new exit penalties to discourage early surrender.

Gains on whole-of-life policies, as on *endowment* policies (see next entry) are free of any further tax charge, provided that the policies are qualifying. Generally, 'qualifying' means that the policy must be held for 10 years, or three-quarters of the policy term, whichever is less, and have premiums paid at least annually. Before this stage, however, returns on the life funds within the policies, inclusive of any bonuses, will have been taxed at source or at a 20 per cent corporation tax rate.

Death benefits are paid free of income and *capital gains tax* (see page 132). Provided that the proceeds are paid into a trust, or to beneficiaries who are not the policyholder, they will also be free of inheritance tax.

If a policy does not meet the qualifying rules, the gain will be taxed to income tax at the policyholders' marginal rate charged on the net gain, with a deemed tax credit of 20 per cent. It means that higher rate tax payers will have a further 20 per cent tax to pay, but basic rate tax payers will have no further liability.

b) Investment-type insurance

Endowments

Investment-type insurance is based around endowments, which have the same tax treatment on gains as whole-of-life policies (see previous entry), and are similarly either unit-linked or with-profits. An endowment policy will pay a fixed sum on death during the period of the policy; if the policyholder survives the term, the accumulated value of the policy will be paid out.

Sales of endowment products have dwindled drastically, partly due to the impact of mis-selling in the late 1980s and early 1990s. Financial salespeople, particularly in banks and building societies, frequently recommended interest-only mortgages with an endowment policy. The expectation was that once the term was over, the policy proceeds should at least repay the mortgage, but there were no guarantees of the required investment returns and the risks were not always made clear.

Declining stock markets and overall returns that were lower than expected led to a predicted shortfall in the value of the capital sum to be repaid at the end of term by some endowments purchased with an interest-only mortgage.

All mortgage endowment providers must regularly write to their customers to update them on the performance of their investments and the projected value of their policy. While the existence of a projected or actual shortfall is not, in itself, grounds for complaint, those letters set out how policyholders may complain if they believe that the nature of the endowment and its risks were not properly explained to them, and if they have suffered financially as a result of buying this sort of mortgage. If customers have proven their case, companies have been paying compensation, although the process can be lengthy.

For customers facing a shortfall on an endowment with an interest-only mortgage who have not been eligible for compensation, additional action has been advised. It may take the form of saving more money into another vehicle or the total or partial conversion of the interest-only mortgage into the repayment kind.

Investment bonds

The investment bond is a savings vehicle designed for lump sum investment and not for protection. It is a pooled investment, either with-profits or unit-linked, and is sold with a minimum life insurance element to ensure that it meets qualifying rules for tax purposes. Investors buy units in the life company's funds. Financial advisers receive commission of up to 7 per cent to sell this product, and so have often been known to recommend it above cheaper and more tax-efficient alternatives. Basic rate tax is charged to the fund, so basic rate tax payers have no further liability. Up to 5 per cent of capital invested may be withdrawn free of higher rate tax for up to 20 years, a claimed perk that the **Sandler Review** (see page 238) has recommended abolishing.

Pensions

Introduction

A pension is a single or regular payment into a savings vehicle designed to provide both income, which is subject to income tax, and tax-free cash on retirement. Most pensions are offered by insurance companies. As in insurance, there are unit-linked and with-profits funds. *Self-Invested Personal Pensions (SIPPs)* offer a far wider choice of investments and are particularly suitable for large funds.

Dividends (see page 210) received by the pension fund are no longer supplemented by recovery of the notional tax suffered. On retirement, the bulk of the fund must be used to buy an annuity, which provides an income for the rest of your life. See **Annuities** (page 169) for more on how this works.

The pension scheme offers generous tax relief on contributions up to a maximum annual allowance depending on your age, but this restriction on annual contributions will be significantly relaxed under new legislation in April 2006, which we will consider shortly.

There remains a £27 billion annual savings gap between the amount being saved and the amount of savings needed to fund a comfortable retirement, according to research commissioned by the ABI. The lack of enthusiasm for pensions is partly because they are complicated and so people underestimate the need to make provision for themselves, but also because of mis-selling and other scandals that have dogged this industry in recent decades.

Main types of pension

The main types of pension are state (basic and second), personal (including the stakeholder pension, which was introduced to address the shortfall in pension provision) and occupational. Let us now look at each.

State pension

The UK government provides a full basic state pension to women when they are aged between 60 and 65, depending on when they were born (to become 65 from 2010) and men at 65 who have paid enough *National Insurance* (see page

236) contributions. It was introduced into the UK in 1908, and the National Insurance Act 1946 made it universal.

At the time of writing it is worth £79.60 a week, or £127.25 a week for a married couple, amounts that are acknowledged as modest given the cost of living.

The state second pension was introduced in April 2002, and provides an additional state pension for low to moderate earners. It replaced the state earnings related pension scheme, or SERPS, which was an earnings-related part of the basic state pension.

If you are an employee, you can pay into the state second pension. Alternatively, you can opt out of it, and have partial rebates of your national insurance contributions paid into a personal pension instead.

Personal pension

A personal pension is available to those who are self-employed, or are not in a company pension scheme. It is in addition to the state pension. Income tax relief at the highest marginal rate is available on all payments into the plan.

Personal pensions vary enormously in the range of investment choices, their returns and their charges. Some have a penalty for stopping and restarting payments, but if not, charges may be higher. Plans issued before 2000 tend to be more expensive and less flexible than more recent ones, and to have heavy front-end loading, which refers to the concentration of charges in the early years of contributions to pay the salesperson's commissions and other start-up costs.

You can contribute up to £3,600 after tax a year to your personal pension (including if it is a *stakeholder* version – described in the next entry) and can have it concurrently with an occupational pension, provided that you earn less than £30,000 a year.

Between 29 April 1988 and 30 June 1994, many firms sold personal pensions to individuals who would have been better off staying in, or joining, their employer's scheme. It was a major scandal that led to compensation payments.

Stakeholder pension

The stakeholder pension is a cheap and flexible form of personal pension that meets government standards for fair value. It was introduced before the **Sandler Review** (see page 238) and it aims to help low earners and those who do not have access to a good value personal pension or occupational scheme.

The scheme is run by trustees or an authorised stakeholder manager, and you will often have a choice of the fund or funds in which your contributions are invested. From April 2005, a stakeholder pension has been able to charge up to 1.5 per cent a year in management fees for the first 10 years, and 1 per cent subsequently. The scheme accepts contributions starting from £20 a month. You may stop or start payments, or change pension provider without penalty.

You can use a stakeholder pension to leave (contract out of) the additional state pension. Every employer with five or more staff must provide them with access to a stakeholder pension or a suitable alternative. The employer may be exempt from this requirement if it already offers certain group pension plans or an occupational pension scheme.

Occupational pension

This is a company scheme that an employer makes available to members of its staff. The ratio of contribution between the company and its staff varies. The employer may match employees' contributions with its own, make none, or – as in many public sector schemes – all, of the contributions.

All contributions are subject to tax relief. Some of the schemes are administered by a life company. Others are administered by employers, in particular when they are large companies or in the public sector, and life companies are not involved. In all cases, employees may supplement their own payments by additional voluntary contributions (AVCs) or, alternatively, by personal pension contributions.

There are two main types of occupational pension scheme: final salary and money purchase.

In a *final salary* pension, which is the most popular type of *defined benefit* scheme, employees will receive a proportion of their final salary on retirement. Many companies are phasing out these schemes because they are expensive to maintain and there is an open-ended commitment to pay benefits irrespective of their cost to the business.

In a *money purchase* pension, also categorised as *defined contribution*, cash is invested in a fund to create for the employee, on retirement, a pot of money. The amount received depends on both how much was put in and the investment returns. It is the employee and not, as in a final salary scheme, the employer, who bears the risk.

Annuities

How they work

The annuity is a contract available from an insurance company. It converts your pension fund into income that you will be paid for the rest of your life. Until 6 April 2006, if your pension scheme is money purchase, whether personal or occupational, you must buy your annuity before you reach 75 years old.

If you retire and have a personal pension, you can typically take up to 25 per cent of the pension money saved as a tax-free sum, and use the rest to buy your annuity. Under the annuity arrangement, the insurer makes regular income payments to you based on the accumulated pension pot after any cash removal. The capital becomes the property of the insurance company.

The level of income paid by the fund depends on the annuity rate at the time of conversion. It is derived from two main variables: the long-term interest rate on government **bonds** (see page 71) and the average life expectancy of an individual aged the same as the purchaser. The shorter your life expectancy, the higher will be the interest rate.

The *open market option* enables you as buyer to look for the best annuity rate rather than necessarily the one offered by the company in which your pension fund was accumulated. Women have to pay more for an annuity than men because they live longer, but they can expect to receive payments for longer. An impaired annuity, with a bigger income, may be available to smokers or those with a reduced life expectancy.

The most usual type of annuity is single life, which ends only on your death. It will pay a guaranteed income until death, but the capital will have become the property of the insurance company. It is also possible to buy a joint life annuity, under which payments continue to your surviving partner after your death, but your starting income will be lower.

You can choose whether you want the income from your single or your joint annuity to stay level throughout, to increase each year, or to be guaranteed for a specific period. It may be linked to investments or indexed, and is taxed.

Critics note that because under present rules people must take out an annuity before the age of 75, the income may be affected by prevailing poor market conditions. However, annuities can be good value for anybody living longer than average.

Income drawdown

An initial alternative to a pension annuity is income drawdown. You could, for example, retire at 60 and receive an annually reviewed income from your remaining personal pension fund, delaying the purchase of your annuity until 75 years old. The advantage is that the capital of your investment will remain in place although you will be drawing income from it.

The arrangement is most suitable for those with a pension fund of at least £100,000, and other sources of income. You can switch from one drawdown provider to another.

Changes in pension legislation

From 6 April 2006, the government plans to simplify existing pension legislation. Anybody will be able to contribute up to 100 per cent of their earnings with a cap of £215,000 (rising to £255,000 after five years) to any pension scheme. An individual's combined pension funds will be subject to a lifetime limit of £1.5 million, rising to £1.8 million and, subsequently, by the **Retail Price Index** (see page 154). Above this cap, a punitive taxation treatment will arise, which can in some cases lead to an effective 55 per cent rate.

The **SIPP** (see page 167) already enables a choice of investment but this will be expanded to include **buy-to-let** (see page 231) properties and perhaps classic cars, art and fine wines. Income drawdown will become available after the age of 75 as an alternative to a traditional annuity. There will be far more opportunity to build your retirement income in a way that suits you.

3. Health and protection

Health and protection insurance enables you to pay for private medical treatment for short-term illness or injury. There is critical illness cover, income protection insurance, and long-term care insurance. Let us consider each type of cover.

a) Private medical insurance

This aims to cover the cost of private medical treatment of acute conditions, defined as illness or injury where treatment will lead to recovery. Premiums increase with age.

b) Critical illness

This pays a tax-free lump sum if you suffer from any illness or condition, or have any surgical procedure, covered by the policy. Sales of critical illness insurance have boomed recently.

The product is often sold alongside a repayment **mortgage** (see page 234) to single people as an alternative to life insurance where there are no dependants. If they became ill, it would help them to keep up mortgage payments. Parents may consider these policies because children's cover up to £15,000 per child is sometimes included.

The policies are not standardised, and customers should check carefully on what is covered. There is a common industry minimum coverage on key illnesses such as cancer and heart attacks.

c) Income protection

This pays a tax-free monthly income for an agreed period if you are unfit to work because of sickness or accident, resulting in a loss of earnings. The policy may replace some of your lost earnings, or cover some of your living expenses such as your **mortgage** (see page 234).

The definition of incapacity is crucial to the policy. It may cover your own occupation, or any similar occupation, or any job. It may cover activities of daily living, or just of working. After you have claimed, there will be a deferred period before you receive benefits.

d) Long-term care insurance

This covers the cost of long-term care in your home, or in a residential or nursing home. It includes a wide range of care services.

London market

Introduction

The London insurance market consists of international insurance and rein-surance business, almost entirely non-life. It has only about 3 per cent of worldwide non-life premiums, but it includes 10–15 per cent of industrial insurance business, and 40 per cent of the marine market, according to a Swiss Re report. London represents 25 per cent of internationally available reinsurance.

The London market is almost evenly split between the company market, which consists of insurance companies, and Lloyd's of London, which consists of syndicates.

The company market has the slightly smaller share. It became larger in the 1970s as foreign insurers opened City offices. Most London market companies are members of the International Underwriters Association, which is the world's largest representative organisation for international and wholesale insurance and reinsurance companies.

Lloyd's of London, with its slightly larger share of the London market, has insurers that operate only as Lloyd's syndicates. Every syndicate is an inde-pendent business unit run by a managing agent, which appoints the under-writers. The managing agent is a private or public company with a franchise to operate at Lloyd's.

There are about 150 London market brokers. Most of the larger ones at least are also Lloyd's brokers, for which the accreditation criteria are higher.

How the market works

The London market, whether the insurers are companies or Lloyd's syndicates, works as follows. A broker seeks insurers for specific risks, and must find a *lead* underwriter who will accept perhaps 25 per cent of the risk, and so establish the policy terms, and then find *following* underwriters who will subscribe on this basis. This risk syndication can be spread across anything from 1 or 2 to 10 or more companies or syndicates on each risk, with great vari-ations across different classes of business.

Some underwriters will take more risks than others, and the results may not be immediately accessible. The quality of underwriting may vary according to information received, advice taken and risk modelling, as well as the type and amount of business taken on, premiums payable and **reinsurance** (see page 175) terms. Market conditions also play a part.

The way the insurance cycle works is as follows. The unit price rises; in the industry jargon, rates become 'hard'. It brings overcapacity of insurers into the market, which reduces the price. Rates become 'soft', as at the time of writing has happened in personal insurances, private motor, and some commercial motor. Insurers need to be cautious not to cut rates beyond their means, which is what led to the high-profile collapse of Independent Insurance, a liability insurer, in June 2001.

Business in London tends to be conducted face-to-face, using paper records. Technology is a bugbear of the market, and this may have taken a toll. London's share of the global growth in non-life premiums has been declining on aggregate since the 1990s, and it has lost ground to rival insurance centres such as Bermuda.

However, the London market retains a high reputation, and it has access to a concentrated mass of quality back-up specialists, including lawyers, consultants and claims adjusters. It has the best expertise in interpretation of insurance clauses for settling claims.

The experts are in demand, not least because of what the **Financial Services Authority** (see page 255) has described as a *deal now, detail later* ethos, leaving brokers to sort out the wording once the cover has been written. At the time of writing, the industry is trying to produce a market-led solution that will satisfy the FSA.

Insurance brokers are under the regulatory spotlight for their commission practices. In late 2004, it became widely known that Elliot Spitzer, the New York State Attorney General, had been investigating alleged bid rigging and use of contingent commissions by US broker Marsh & McLennan.

Spitzer alleged that Marsh brokers had taken payoffs from insurance providers in exchange for introducing clients, and that corporate clients were accordingly denied best prices for policies required. In January 2005, the broking giant agreed to pay US $850 million to settle the charges, but neither admitted nor denied the allegations.

Spitzer has said that there will be other cases across the industry. About seven of the world's top brokers have made public statements that they have given up contingent commissions, or will do so. By early 2005, they were presenting revised business models, according to the British Insurance Brokers Association.

Lloyd's of London

Lloyd's of London is a 317-year old market. It started with *Edward Lloyd's Coffee House*, a 17th century coffee house where timely shipping news was made available. Almost a century later, customers broke away and established the *New Lloyd's Coffee House*, which focused on marine insurance. In 1774, as business increased, rooms were hired in the Royal Exchange, and the market was incorporated as the Society of Lloyd's and Corporation of Lloyd's under the Lloyd's Act of 1871.

Insurance is underwritten at Lloyd's by members of the Society, not the Society itself. The members – either private individuals (Names), limited partnerships or companies – come together in the groups known as 'syndicates' (see above) to underwrite, although the liability of a member to the insured is several, not joint with other members of the syndicate. The capital backing of a syndicate determines how much business it can write in a year; this is known as the 'syndicate's capacity'. In 2005, the capacity of all syndicates at Lloyd's was £13.7 billion.

Over the past three centuries, Lloyd's has traded successfully and developed an iron reputation for paying claims. Large underwriting losses in the late 1980s and the ensuing widespread litigation involving Names, their agents, auditors, Lloyd's and other parties led to a market-wide reconstruction and renewal settlement plan in 1986.

Lloyd's is now attracting good press coverage, and the problems of the late 1990s are no longer prominent. It is regulated by the **Financial Services Authority** (see page 255) and has licences to write business in over 190 countries and territories. In April 2004, Lloyd's announced annually accounted profits of £1.9 billion for 2003, up 127 per cent on 2002, based on a combined ratio (percentage of incurred losses and incurred underwriting expenses to earned premium) of just 90.7 per cent.

In November 2004, Lloyd's raised £500 million in new capital by issuing a 20-year bond. These moneys have strengthened Lloyd's central assets, which include the Central Fund, a fund available, at the discretion of the Council of Lloyd's, to meet policyholders' claims in the event of members being unable to meet their underwriting liabilities. The move enhanced the market's flexibility and financial stability.

Protection and indemnity associations

The London market has 39 protection and indemnity associations, known as the P&I clubs. It is the leading world centre for this type of insurance. The associations were set up to cover marine risk, but have subsequently been used by doctors and lawyers to provide professional indemnity cover.

The clubs provide much higher levels of cover than available commercially because they will buy substantial pooled *reinsurance* (see next entry). A club pays the initial insurance claims, and the pool pays the next layer.

In 2002, the clubs wrote gross premiums of about £865 million, out of an overall £25 billion written across by companies and Lloyd's syndicates in the London market.

Reinsurance

How it works

Insurers limit exposure to risk by passing their liability to a reinsurance company, a procedure known as 'reinsurance'. The insurer passing the liability is known as the 'ceding office'. It will pay a premium to the reinsurer, which is the company that accepts the cession. Any of the business that the insurer keeps rather than passing onto the reinsurer is known as 'retention'.

A reinsurance contract can be proportional or non-proportional. If it is proportional, both the premium received from the insured and the claims are split equally between the ceding office and the reinsurer. This is also known as 'participating reinsurance'. Property insurers prefer it because the sum insured is usually known, making proportional divisions practical.

The proportional reinsurance may be treaty or facultative. If it is surplus treaty, the reinsurer must accept any surplus risk above that retained by the ceding office. If it is quota share treaty, the ceding office must reinsure a stated portion of every risk. If it is facultative, the ceding office chooses whether to reinsure and, if so, how much, and the reinsurer similarly chooses how much to accept.

Non-proportional reinsurance is where losses are split disproportionately, if at all, between the ceding office and reinsurers. It is commonly excess-of-loss reinsurance, where the ceding office pays the initial layer of every claim. The reinsurers pay the balance up to a set figure, beyond which further excess-of-loss cover may apply.

Excess-of-loss cover may be arranged on a treaty or facultative basis. Liability insurers use this type of cover because the extent of any payout is based on the value of claims. Marine insurers sometimes use excess-of-loss and, at other times, proportional, reinsurance.

A variation on excess-of-loss is excess-of-loss-ratio, or stop loss, reinsurance. It does not insure individual events, but it prevents excessive fluctuation in the net claims ratio (the average of net claims to net premiums). For example, a company might be covered for 90 per cent of any excess beyond 60 per cent.

For excessively large risks, reinsurance pools can operate. They enable insurers to reinsure 100 per cent of their risk into a pool. Profits and losses will be shared equally between participants.

There are also specialist types of reinsurance, including financial rein-surance, which aim to spread the incidence of losses over a number of accounting periods and not just one. Subsequent comparable products include the securitisation of insurance risk, and insurance derivatives.

Impact of terrorism on reinsurance

Attacks by the IRA in the early 1990s threatened to make insurance cover for acts of terrorism unavailable. Following extensive discussions between the government and the insurance industry, Pool Re, a mutual reinsurance company, was created in 1993. It is owned by participants in UK commercial property insurance, and is backed by the Treasury. It covers all risks related to terrorism.

The 11 September 2001 terrorist attacks on New York, and the World Trade Center destruction, resulted in a loss now estimated at between US $35 and US $45 billion. The reinsurance industry bore much of the loss and it substantially increased the premiums that it charged insurers, who passed on the cost to their own customers.

Subsequently, insurers started looking more closely than before at their reinsurance arrangements, including the quality of their reinsurers. They are now less inclined to use these as a substitute for good under-writing. To assess a reinsurance programme through a reinsurance secu-rities committee is usual.

As part of the same reaction, *credit rating agencies* (see page 74) have lowered the ratings of some reinsurers, although they rate the sector outlook as stable. If a reinsurer's rating falls below a trigger level, the primary insurer may be permitted to void the contract or require collateral to be posted. The existence of this trigger limits the reinsurer's ability to attract new business.

Jollies and freebies

Introduction

To become a shareholder brings benefits. In this section, we will take a quick look.

Annual general meeting

Quoted companies must hold an annual general meeting (AGM) once a year. Shareholders named on the register have a right to attend and speak at the AGM, and must be given at least 21 days' notice of the time and place.

The directors may hold their AGM in an obscure place during unsocial hours to discourage attendees, or they may make it into an easily accessible jolly, offering free samples from their goods range.

At every AGM, the board of directors will discuss the company's performance. Shareholders may put questions to the chairman and directors and vote on such matters as the election of directors and the appointment of auditors. By attending the AGM, they can get a feel for how the company operates.

Investors who hold their shares within a nominee account will not be listed on the shareholder register and will therefore not be contacted directly by the company with details of its AGM. Instead, your broker will receive the information and can then make arrangements for you to attend. It is a good idea to notify your broker in advance if you would like to do this. Some brokers offer the service automatically while others offer it only on request.

Any meeting of shareholders besides the AGM is called an 'extraordinary general meeting'. Shareholders can compel the board to call an EGM if they are supported by at least 10 per cent of the company's share capital.

Shareholder perks

Shareholder perks are gifts or discounts that a company may give shareholders. Food, retail and leisure companies have a large consumer customer base and so are often generous.

Investors who hold their shares within a nominee account may not be eligible for shareholder perks. If this is the case, it may be worth considering holding the stock in certificated form so that you are entitled to the perks. The rules vary between companies and your broker will be able to provide further information.

Key technical indicators

Introduction

Technical analysts and traders use technical indicators to supplement price charts. Not everybody believes that the indicators enable better investment decisions but, in this section, I will explain how they work.

Accumulation/Distribution line

The Accumulation/Distribution line, developed by Mark Chaikin, is a trend-following indicator that closely links share price and volume movements. It does not include buy and sell perimeters.

The Accumulation/Distribution line rises if the stocks close above the mid-point of the day's trading range, and it falls if the closing price is below the average of the day's high and low.

Advance/decline line

The advance/decline line, also known as a 'breadth of market' indicator, plots the difference between how many stocks advanced and how many declined. Unlike an index, it presents a picture undistorted by movements in leading stocks.

If the advance/decline line fails to corroborate a rising index, it indicates that the rise is driven by only a few large stocks and so is unlikely to be sustained.

The indicator stops working effectively at market bottoms.

Bollinger bands

Bollinger bands were invented by John Bollinger, a trader of options and warrants in the late 1970s, when he became especially interested in volatility.

They are a form of *envelope* (see page 182) with bands plotted at levels of *standard deviation* (see page 313) above and below a *moving average* (see page 183).

When the share price is static, Bollinger bands tighten, and when it is volatile they bulge. When the share price moves outside the bands, the trend is seen as likely to continue. Unlike other envelopes, Bollinger bands are not used alone to provide buy and sell signals.

Bollinger bands are normally constructed on closing prices, but occasionally on weighted closing prices, or typical closing prices (high + low + closing price, divided by three).

Commodity Channel Index

The Commodity Channel Index, developed by Donald Lambert, is based on the premise that heavy irrational buying in the market is likely to continue.

To calculate the Index, find the differential between the underlying share price and its *moving average* (see page 183). Divide the result by the average differential between the two numbers over the period of the moving average.

When the line is above 100, the market is overbought, but is accepted as still rising until proved otherwise.

Coppock indicator

The Coppock indicator was invented by Edwin Coppock, a Texan investment adviser, and was introduced in the US magazine *Barron's* in 1962. It has a reputation for reliability that in recent years has slipped a little.

The indicator has the sole aim of helping long-term investors to time an accumulation of shares at the start of a bull market. It was designed for the Dow Jones Industrial Average, although is often applied more broadly.

In creating his indicator, Coppock had observed that crowds were driven by emotions and tended to overreact. He believed that the same principle applied to trading shares. Coppock asked local church officials how long the average person needed to grieve after bereavement. They said that it was 11 to 14 months. He calculated his indicator as the monthly closing value of the index as a percentage of the same index 11 and 14 months earlier.

The monthly calculations will be positive or negative. Add them together, and you will have a 10-month weighted *moving average* (see page 183) of the combined total. You can plot it beneath a bar or line chart as an oscillator that swings either side of a zero line.

When the Coppock signal rises from below the zero line, it is a signal to enter the market with a long position. There was never any sell signal because Coppock did not foresee the need for US institutions to liquidate their portfolios.

Technicians may use the Coppock indicator in conjunction with, for instance, the *Advance/decline line* (see page 179), which signals when the market appears oversold.

Dead cross

The dead cross is a bearish signal arising when *two **moving averages*** (see page 183) cross as they move downwards. The triple dead cross is when *three* moving averages cross in the decline. It is considered less effective.

Directional Movement

The Directional Movement System, designed by J Welles Wilder, aims to indicate whether the market is in a trend or not, but not when you should enter or exit it. Let us look at the system's component parts.

The Directional Indicator (DI) is the directional movement (DM), whether positive or negative, divided by the *true range* and expressed as a percentage.

The DM is the part of today's range that is above or below yesterday's. If the majority of today's range is above yesterday's, it is known as +DM, or if the majority is below, it is –DM.

The true range is the high of today's trading range less yesterday's close, or yesterday's close less today's low, or, if greater, today's high less today's low.

On any given day, DM will either be positive, negative, or none, and so correspondingly will be DI, expressed as +DI when positive and –DI when negative. The Directional Indicator should be averaged out over a period, which is usually 14 days.

The bigger the difference between the up directional movement, represented by DI+, and the down directional movement, represented by DI–, the more directional is the movement.

To express the level of directional movement, J Welles Wilder developed the Directional Movement Index (DX). It is the difference between +DI and –DI, divided by the sum of +DI and –DI. The higher the index, the more directionality the market has, either up or down.

The Average Directional Index, abbreviated to ADX, is a 14-day average of DX.

Divergence

Divergence arises when two charts, such as a price chart and a ***momentum oscillator*** (see page 183), give conflicting signals. It warns of a potential reversal.

In his classic *Trading for a Living*, author and trader Dr Alexander Elder divides divergence into three signals.

Class A is the strongest. It is when the price makes a lower low than before, but the oscillator makes a higher low, creating a bullish divergence, or the price makes a higher high but the oscillator makes a lower high, creating a bearish divergence.

A Class B divergence arises when the price makes a move equal to its previous high or low, but the oscillator makes a higher low or lower high.

Class C, the third and weakest divergence, is when the price makes a new high or low but the oscillator makes an equal high or low.

Envelopes

The envelope is a trend-following indicator. It consists of a ***moving average*** (see page 183) of the closing price with two bands a given percentage either side of it. The upper and lower bands are the overbought and oversold lines. See also ***Bollinger bands*** (page 180).

Golden cross

The Golden cross is when two ***moving averages*** (see page 183) cross as they both move upwards. It is considered a bullish indicator.

The triple golden cross is when three moving averages (typically 5, 10 and 20 day) cross upwards, and is considered less effective.

Larry Williams %R

The Larry Williams %R focuses on momentum. It measures the latest closing price against its price range over a set period. It is calculated in a similar way to *Stochastics* (see page 187).

Overbought and oversold lines are used, but the indicator is plotted in reverse. If the reading has moved from 20 to 0, the share is overbought. If the reading has moved from 80 to 100, it is oversold.

The signals can be volatile and so misleading because the indicator lacks internal smoothing.

Meisels' Indicator

Meisels' Indicator, invented by Canadian broker Ron Meisels, is simple and has enjoyed a following.

The indicator is calculated over a 10-day period. It is up one point every day that the index closes higher, and down similarly every day that the index closes lower. If, for instance, the stock market closes up for seven days and down for three, the indicator will read +4.

The indicator has its own overbought and oversold lines. If the indicator is +6 or higher, it shows that the market is overbought. If the indicator is –6 or lower, the market is oversold.

Momentum

Momentum is the most basic of the *momentum oscillators* (see next entry).

It is based on the close today, less the close *n* days ago, which is a variation on the way the *Rate of Change oscillator* (see page 187) is calculated.

Momentum is typically drawn elsewhere than on the price chart. It has a single line, swinging between overbought and oversold lines.

Momentum oscillator

The momentum oscillator measures both the rate of change and the direction of the share price. As a *leading indicator* (see page 150), it attempts to give advance warning of a share price change. The main momentum oscillators are *Momentum* (see previous entry), *Rate of Change oscillator* (see page 187), *Relative Strength Index* (see page 187) and *Stochastics* (see page 187).

Technical traders can use the momentum oscillator most often for trading in ranging markets which, by definition, do not move in trends but instead fluctuate between overbought and oversold lines. They also use it to time an entry into a trending market, taking signals only with the trend. The trader buys when the trend starts and will hold throughout or, if buying later during the trend, will do so on weakness.

The trader can take reversal signals from the momentum oscillator to exit a trade from a trending market, but should have corroboration from a trend-following indicator, according to technicians.

Moving average

The moving average shows changes in the average share price over a given period. It is a trend-following indicator, and so lags the action. Technicians avoid using it in a trading range on the basis that it gives false signals. They prefer to use it in fast trends with minimum price fluctuation.

It is usual to calculate a moving average on the closing price. Alternatively, you may use the average price in the range (calculated as the high and the low added, and the total divided by two).

The three main categories of moving average are simple, weighted and exponential weighted.

The simple moving average is the most popular kind. It is the sum of closing prices (ie, the total added together) for a stock over the selected period, divided by the number of days included.

The weighted moving average gives more weight to recent share prices, and so is linearly weighted. To calculate a 20-day moving average, the price on the 15th day is multiplied by 15 and on the 20th day by 20, and so on. The sum of the prices over the period of the moving average is divided by the sum of the multiples.

The exponential moving average, like the weighted version, attributes more significance to recent prices. It includes price information outside the period of the moving average.

The length of the moving average is linked to cycles, and is typically 5, 10, 20 or 40 days. If it covers, for example, 10 consecutive days, it is a 10-day moving average.

If short-term, the moving average will be fast and react sensitively to the price. It will get you in trades early but is prone to give false signals. The long-term moving average is less likely to give premature signals, but they may also come very late. For a balanced picture, some traders keep track of two moving averages, each of a different length.

When the share price crosses from below to above the moving average, technicians see it as a signal that traders should go long. If the trend turns down, the price will typically take the lead and cross below the moving average, which they see as a signal to take a *short position* (see 'Golden cross', page 182 and 'Dead cross', page 181).

Moving average convergence/divergence (MACD)

The moving average convergence/divergence indicator or MACD (pronounced MacD) is a ***trend-following indicator*** (see page 189), and it keeps you permanently in the market. Technicians also use it as a ***momentum oscillator*** (see page 183).

To create the MACD indicator, take the difference between a 12-period and a 26-period exponential ***moving average*** (see previous entry) of the closing price to form the basic MACD line, which is plotted as a *solid* line on the chart.

You will also need a slow line, known as the signal line, which is a nine-period exponential moving average of the MACD line and is plotted as a *dotted* line on the chart.

The MACD line and the signal line may swing either side of a zero line, and there are no overbought/oversold boundaries. Signals come late. If the MACD line crosses from beneath to above the signal line, it is the signal to take a long position. If it crosses from above to below a signal line, the signal is to take a short position.

MACD Histogram

The MACD histogram represents the difference between the MACD line and the signal line used in the MACD indicator. The more they diverge, a process that is considered trend-driven, the larger the histogram will become.

When the MACD is above the signal line signifying an uptrend, the histogram is above the zero line. When the MACD is below the signal line, signifying a down trend, the histogram is below zero.

The MACD histogram gives its signals earlier than the MACD indicator. It changes according to how close the lines come together, but the MACD relies on the lines crossing each other.

Moving average oscillator

The *moving average* (see page 183) oscillator represents the difference between a short and long moving average. It is designed to show when a trend is gaining or losing momentum. When two moving averages move apart, it signals the gain and, when they converge, the loss.

When two moving averages cross, the difference between them is zero. The moving average oscillator reflects this point at its own zero line. When the short moving average moves above a long one, it is seen as a buy signal and the oscillator rises above the zero line into positive territory.

When it is used as a *momentum oscillator* (see page 183), the moving average oscillator will have an overbought limit above the zero line and an oversold limit below it. The levels are not defined but should capture some of the extremes.

On balance volume

On balance volume (OBV) was designed by US stock market guru *Joseph Granville* (see page 291) to show the balance between supply and demand.

To calculate OBV, volume is added up on a cumulative basis when a stock price closes higher than on the previous day, and is subtracted when the stock price closes lower. On days when the stock price closes unchanged, no change to volume is recorded.

If the share price is in an uptrend, or a downtrend, this will be stronger if OBV shows a similar pattern, according to Granville's theory. If it does not, it is seen as a warning sign. The indicator's absolute value has no importance.

OBV may rise ahead of the price. If so, this indicates accumulation in preparation for a price rise, according to Granville's theory. If it falls, it indicates distribution ahead of a price decline.

See also 'Volume accumulation oscillator' (page 189).

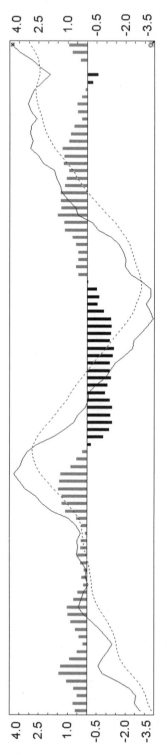

Figure K1 Moving average convergence/divergence indicator

Parabolic system

The Parabolic system, developed by J Welles Wilder, is a trading system with *Stop and reverse points* (see page 189) used to determine entry and exit points. It is designed for use only in a trend, which should ideally be fast moving, and applies in any trading time frame.

The indicator has *stop losses* (see page 193) based on price and time. They take the form of a parabolic sequence. On a bar chart, they are dots above bars in a short position or below bars in a long position.

The stops will move partly as the price changes, and partly without it, based on the expectation that the price will be moving in a trend. If the price hits a stop loss *below* bars, it requires you to close a long position, and you should immediately open a short position. If the price hits a stop *above* bars, you should close a short position and open a long one.

Rate of Change oscillator

Rate of Change, known as ROC, is a *momentum oscillator* (see page 183). It measures the rate at which the price changes. It is based on the price close today divided by the close n days ago. It is a variation on *momentum* (see page 183).

Relative Strength Index

The Relative Strength Index, known as RSI, is a sensitive *momentum oscillator* (see page 183) created by J Welles Wilder Jr. It assesses the closing price against the previous closing price, rather than, like *Stochastics* (see next entry), against the recent range. The result is smoothed to create an index that fluctuates between 1 and 100. Traders disagree on its value.

Do not confuse RSI with *relative strength* (see page 221).

Stochastics

Stochastics, which Dr George Lane helped to develop in the 1960s, is a popular *momentum oscillator* (see page 183). It assesses the closing price against the recent range rather than, like the *Relative Strength Index* (see previous entry), against the previous closing price.

There are two types of stochastic chart: fast and slow. On the fast stochastic chart, the last closing price is shown as a percentage of the price range over a chosen period. The oscillator is plotted as two lines. The first is the %K line, which is dashed, and represents the price action. The second is the %D line, which is solid and is a three-day moving average of the first. The second line is less sensitive and is considered more important.

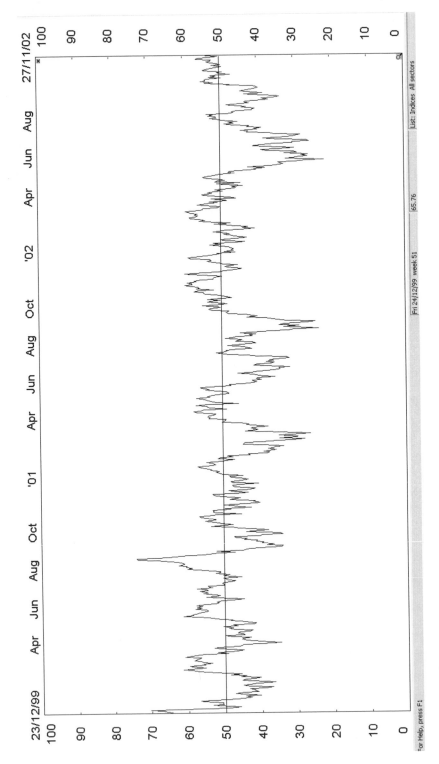

For Help, press F1 Fri 24/12/99 week 51 65.76 List: Indices All sectors

Figure K2 RSI

More recently, the less sensitive slow stochastic chart has been developed, and analysts prefer it to the fast version except in short-term trading. In Slow Stochastic, the %D of Fast Stochastic becomes %K, the main line, and its three-day moving average is %D.

The Stochastic line is given a 1–100 scale. There are standard 70:30 over-bought and oversold lines.

Trading strategies and signals can be complex. Seasoned Stochastics traders will refer to the 'Right Hand', the 'Stochastic Pop' and the 'Shoulder'.

Stop and reverse points

Stop and reverse points (SARs) are a trading system that keeps you in the market.

SARs are plotted as dotted lines that define a trend. When a stop is hit, it is a signal to close the position and to open the opposite position.

A popular version is the *parabolic system* (see page 187).

Trend-following indicator

The trend-following indicator smoothes price data and it represents the trend as a line, using the same scale as the price. It lags the price action. For easy comparison, the indicator is usually placed below the chart. *Moving averages* (see page 183) are the most widely used example.

Technicians use the trend-following indicator to show where a trend starts and ends. In a trading range, they will ignore it because it creates false signals, and instead use a *momentum oscillator* (see page 183).

Volume accumulation oscillator

The volume accumulation oscillator, created by Mark Chaikin, shows cumulative volume adjusted by the gap between the closing price and the mean of the day's range.

In reacting to volume in relation to price, the oscillator is more sensitive than *on balance volume* (see page 185).

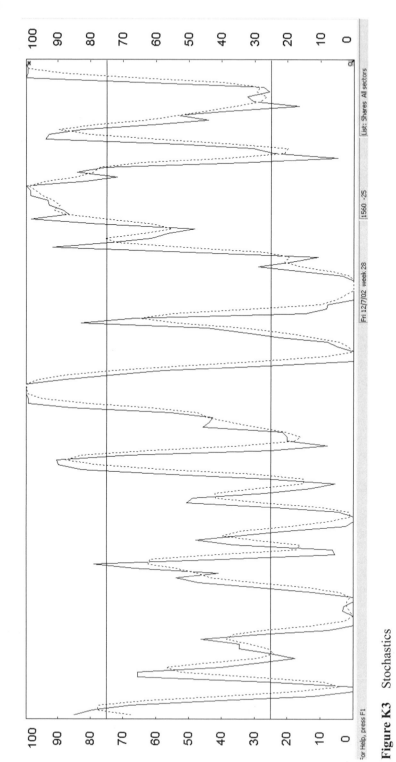

Figure K3   Stochastics

Loss control and money management

Introduction

Loss control and money management are crucial for successful securities trading. This section explains how they work. See also Section H, which covers hedge funds, short selling and hedging.

Limit order

A limit order is when you place an order with your broker specifying, as a buyer, the highest price that you will pay for a stock or, as a seller, the lowest price for which you will sell it. If the order is not fulfilled at the price that you have specified, it will be cancelled.

In practice, only some brokers will accept a limit order. If so, they may cancel it if it is not fulfilled on the day, or may operate the less flexible fill-or-kill strategy, by which they execute the order immediately at the price specified, or cancel it.

See also *market-if-touched order* (next entry), *stop limit order* (page 193), and *time stop order* (page 194).

Market-if-touched order

The market-if-touched order is similar to a *limit order* (see previous entry) but less demanding. It triggers a market order if the price limit is touched, even if this level will not have been sustained by the time that you place the order.

Financial fraud prevention

the power of financial management in business

It's businesses and consumers that pay the price for financial fraud through taxes, insurance premiums and higher prices. One recent estimate puts the weekly price of fraud at **£22** per household in the UK.

For a practical business strategy on fraud prevention visit the CIMA website at **www.cimaglobal.com/fraud**

Money management

Many believe that money management is the most important skill for traders. Expert investor Gibbons Burke has described it as like sex – everyone does it but not many like to talk about it and some do it better than others.

Money management is essentially about how much of your capital you should speculate on a given trade, the timing of your trades, and the price you pay. When you buy, you should control what you pay by placing a *limit order* (see page 191). As a rule of thumb, if you expect to be correct in your trades as often as you are wrong, you should trade positions where the minimum potential gain is three times the potential loss. If you expect to be correct in your trades more often, lower risk/reward ratios are acceptable.

It is a basic rule of money management that you should not risk too much of your capital on any single trade. This way you could, in a worst case scenario, enter a succession of losing trades without wiping out your position. You could perhaps commit 10 per cent of your savings to trading generally and, as an ideal, between 1 and 2 per cent of this capital to every individual trade.

In practice, if you are starting from a small base, you may need to commit a larger proportion of your savings to make your trades meaningful in size, but be careful. I have known traders risk 25 per cent of available capital on single trades and be wiped out after only a few successive losses.

You should cut your losses quickly, using a *stop loss* (see page 193), and run your profits. If you get this right, you can trade successfully even if, for instance, only 40 per cent of your trades make a profit. Taken as a whole, the large gains from your winners should surpass the losses from the larger number of stocks that performed adversely.

Stop limit order

The stop limit order combines a *limit order* (see page 191) on a purchase with a *stop loss* (see next entry) on a sale.

If the share price declines by the stop loss percentage, your broker will automatically sell your shares. A limit order for the repurchase of the shares then becomes active. It will be at a lower level than at which you had sold.

Stop loss

A stop loss is a point at a given percentage below the present price of a security which, when hit, is your cue to sell automatically. If you apply a stop loss, you will be following an axiom of money management that you should cut your losses. It is better to sell at a small loss today than at a large one in a few months' time. On equities, the stop should be at least 15 per cent to avoid a requirement to sell out on temporary dips. On small volatile stocks, you could set it at 30 per cent or more for the same reason.

A *standard* stop loss is set at a percentage below the price that you paid for the stock. A *trailing* stop loss moves higher as the price of your stock rises. If you initially bought your shares for 100p and set your stop at 85p, a rally to 115p would have you trail the stop to 100p, thus locking in your profit (as long as the stock does not gap sharply lower). If your initial position was short, the stop would be placed above the price at which the stock was sold.

Some traders set two trailing stop losses and, if the stock hits the lower stop, it is simply a warning. Traders who find that they are relying too much on stop losses may sometimes profitably switch to buying **put options** (see 'Options', page 111).

Time stop order

The time stop order requires you to sell a stock if it has failed to reach your price target by a specified date.

Money markets

Introduction

Money markets link borrowers with lenders of large amounts of unsecured money for short term loans. This section explains how they work. See also Section G, which covers the global economy and foreign exchange.

Bank of England

The Bank of England is the UK's central bank. In 1694, it was set up as a private company and, as a result of the Bank of England Act, 1946, it came into public ownership. In its 300-year history, the Bank has seen its functions evolve. Since it was founded, it has been the Government's banker and, since the late 18th century, it has been a bank for bankers.

The Bank manages the UK's exchange and gold reserves and the Government's stock register. It has had a monopoly on the issue of banknotes in England and Wales since the early 20th century. The Bank is often an intermediary and may partake in money markets on the government's behalf. It can influence the economy, and particularly *inflation* (see page 149).

In 1987 the Labour Government, when newly in power, gave the Bank the power to decide the *repo rate* (see page 153), an area in which it had previously only implemented policy. At its monthly meeting, the Bank's Monetary Policy Committee decides on whether the base rate should be changed, with the aim of meeting the 2 per cent annual inflation target set by the Chancellor of the Exchequer.

As *lender of last resort*, the Bank supplies funds through *open market operations* to banks that need further liquidity. It buys securities daily, both outright and on a repo basis (see **Repurchase agreement,** page 199). The Bank cooperates closely with the Treasury and the **Financial Services Authority** (see page 255), which is the banking regulator, and it participates in many international forums.

In January 2005, the Bank confirmed that it had established a surveillance team to obtain intelligence through usual market channels for the overall purpose of encouraging financial stability.

Base rate

See 'Repo rate' (page 153).

Bill of exchange

The bill of exchange is an IOU where the drawer undertakes unconditionally to pay the drawee a specified sum at a specified date, usually after three months. It is in the form of paper offered at a discount to face value. The discount, annualised out, is the equivalent to an annual interest rate, in synchronisation with others in the market. The bill is usually endorsed by an accepting house or by a bank.

Call money

This is money borrowed overnight, or where the lender has the right to retrieve it at short notice. It takes the form of cash.

Capital market

This is a market for buying and selling long-term money. The equivalent for short-term money is a money market.

Certificate of deposit

The certificate of deposit (CD) is a document certifying that the holder has deposited money with a bank or building society. It is issued for up to five years in large sums of money, usually at least £50,000. The buyer will pay less than the CD's face value, which at the end of the term the bank will pay the holder in full. The face value amounts to the sum deposited, plus an equivalent annual yield.

It is a flexible feature of the CD that it is tradable before it matures, although it cannot be cashed in early. If the CD is traded, pro rata interest is added to its purchase value. This liquidity comes at a price to holders, and interest rates are not quite as high as are available elsewhere. The banks that borrow the money benefit from this, and also from the lack of need to repay the loan until maturity.

Commercial paper

Commercial paper is an unsecured short term loan. It is sold at a discount. It originated in the US in the late 19th century to enable companies to borrow money more cheaply than from the banks.

In the UK, corporate borrowers offering commercial paper must have balance sheet capital of £25 million, and be publicly quoted on a stock exchange. There is a minimum denomination of £100,000. Borrowers must promise to repay the loan, with interest, at face value at the end of its term.

The paper has a life of up to a year, but it can be rolled over. The loan is a bearer note, which means that a physical certificate is required for ownership, and whoever holds it on the paper's maturity receives the payment.

Interest in commercial paper in the UK has dropped back from its height in the 1980s after *credit rating agencies* (see page 74) lowered ratings on several issuers and there were some high-profile bankruptcies.

Discount house

The discount house was an entity that existed for the purpose of buying various bills and either holding or reselling them. It financed its purchases by borrowing at a lower rate than earned as interest on the instruments held. But the loans were on call, which meant that the banks could retrieve them on demand. Such action could leave the discount house with insufficient cash.

To cover this, the discount houses entered into an arrangement with the *Bank of England* (see page 195). They agreed to make sufficient bids to cover the Government's weekly treasury bill tender. In return, the Bank would buy *treasury bills* (see page 200), *bills of exchange* (see page 196), and *local authority loans* (see page 198) from the discount houses.

In a phased period from March 1997, discount houses ceased to exist as separate entities.

Discount rate

This is the interest rate at which banks will discount *bills of exchange* (see page 196) for other banks. There is a maximum three months' maturity.

Euribor

The rate at which one prime bank offers euro inter-bank term deposits to another.

European Central Bank

The European Central Bank (ECB), established in June 1998 and based in Frankfurt, is run on a decentralised basis by the central banks of members of the

European Monetary Union, for which (as for Economic and Monetary Union) EMU is an acronym. The ECB is the sole issuer of the euro. Its president, vice-president and four other board members are from EMU member countries, and each has an eight-year, non-renewable term.

From the start of 1999, the ECB has been responsible for EMU members' monetary policy. In its first six years it has achieved its main aim, outlined in the *Maastricht Treaty* (see page 150), of ensuring price stability. It defines this as an annual rise in the Harmonised Index of Consumer Prices of below 2 per cent, which it undertook to achieve only in the medium term.

Given the increased importance of financial markets, the ECB sees its major challenge as that of guiding inflation *expectations*. Forecasts over the next 5 to 10 years are consistent with the ECB's definition of price stability.

Federal Reserve System

This is the Central Bank of the US, which was founded by Congress in 1913. The Fed aims to keep the financial system stable. It conducts monetary policy, regulates banking institutions, and provides services to the US government and other parties. It has an influential board of seven members, appointed by the President, and 12 regional offices.

Interbank market

The Interbank market is the money market in which banks lend to each other, usually for a fixed short-term period. See *LIBOR* (page 198).

LIBID

The London Interbank Bid Rate, known as LIBID, is the interest rate that a bank pays on another bank's deposit.

LIBOR

The London Interbank Offered Rate, known as LIBOR, is the offer rate at which banks will lend money to each other in London's money markets. It gives the best indication of short-term rates.

Local authority loans

Local authority loans are non-tradable instruments issued in the money markets. The market is stronger in the US than in the UK.

Lombard rate

This is an interest rate used by the German Bundesbank that sets a ceiling on money market rates. It is used as an emergency lending rate against high quality securities, including *bills of exchange* (see page 196).

Money broker

The money broker links lenders with borrowers in the money markets. The broker receives only a small commission on transactions and so depends on a high turnover of deals. The more volatile the markets, the easier the broker will find his or her work.

Money market dealer

The money market dealer is a bank or other financial institution that trades with other dealers, mostly on the telephone. The dealer's *spread* (see page 275) on transactions is only a fraction of a percentage point, but dealing is profitable because there is so much of it.

Repurchase agreement

A repurchase agreement is where an investor agrees to buy securities from a dealer for a stated period and to sell them back on a future date at a specified higher price. The difference between the buying and selling price, expressed as a discount, is the interest payable over the period.

The 'repo', as it is known, can use any type of security, although it tends to be government bonds. It can be for any period. The 'overnight repo' has a term of a day and is the most frequently used type. A 'term repo' has a term of more than a day. An 'open repo' has an unspecified repurchase date and can be ended by either side at any time.

The Bank of England (see page 195) enters into the repo with the *money market dealers* (see previous entry), enabling them to borrow money cheaply and stay liquid.

A 'reverse repo' is when the investor agrees to sell a security to the dealer and later to buy it back. In matched book trades, some dealers organise a repo in one security and a reverse repo in another, both with expiry on the same day, in anticipation that the price differential will move in their favour.

Repo rate

See page 153.

Sweep account

A sweep account is where a bank or broker sweeps up any money not committed to investments or other financial outlay and puts it in money market funds to earn the highest possible short-term return. This type of account is usually owned by high net worth individuals.

Treasury bill

The treasury bill, also known as the T-bill, is the instrument traded most in the money markets. It is a government-backed short-term loan with a maturity of one year or less. It is issued at a discount, and its attractiveness depends on the discount rate and the yield.

If the government issues treasury bills to private companies and investors, they pay with cash withdrawn from banks. If the government issues the bills directly to banks, the cash used for payment stays in the banking system and so does not affect the broad *money supply* (see page 151).

Wholesale markets

This is a term synonymous with money markets.

Numbers and accounting

Introduction

To understand company announcements and analysts' comments, you need some awareness of accounting and ratio analysis. This section will guide you through the basics. It will not make you an expert but it will give you enough knowledge to make reading the financial news much easier.

Acid test

See 'Quick ratio', page 221.

Accruals

The accruals concept is at the heart of financial reporting, requiring a company to recognise costs as they are actually incurred in the business rather than when the cash is paid out. Accruals appear in the balance sheet when a company has used a good or a service but has not been invoiced for the cost, and are an estimate of the likely amount. Similarly revenue should be recognised in the profit & loss account when it is earned, which may not always be when it is invoiced.

Acquisition accounting

Acquisition accounting is used when one company takes over another. The target company's *assets* (see page 202) are consolidated in the group accounts at fair value, and any extra paid over this amount is **goodwill** (see page 214). The acquired entity's results are included only from the date of acquisition. Until recently, the alternative has been **merger accounting** (see page 217).

Advance revenue

Advance revenue occurs when a company receives cash for a sale before it has fulfilled its obligations in relation to that sale. This revenue cannot be recognised until all obligations have been fulfilled, and a deferred income balance is recognised as a liability.

Amortisation

Amortisation arises when the value of an intangible asset is reduced on the balance sheet by annual charges to the **profit & loss account** (see page 220), spreading the cost of the asset over the period in which it is used. The process is similar to **depreciation** (see page 208), which is applied to tangible assets.

Assets

Assets are the items a company owns and uses in carrying out its business. They are included on the **balance sheet** (see page 203) and are categorised as either non-current (fixed) or current.

Non-current assets are those that the company acquires to use over a period of more than one year in carrying out its business. They may be tangible or intangible.

Tangible fixed assets include items such building or machinery. They are valued initially at historical cost less depreciation, which may not actually represent what they are worth in the real world.

Intangible assets include such items as **brands** (see page 203), patents, licences, development costs and purchased **goodwill** (see page 214). With the exception of goodwill, they are usually **amortised** (see 'Amortisation', page 202) over their economic life, which is up to 20 years, and extendable if the assets retain value.

Current assets are generally made up of cash and cash equivalents, debtors (or accounts receivable) and stock (or inventory). They have in common that they are convertible into cash within a year. The most reliable current asset is cash, given that debtors can refuse to pay and stock can lose value.

Auditor's report

The auditor's report is required for all except very small companies. The company's auditor must state here whether the accounts have been properly prepared and information was made available, with satisfactory explanations where required, and whether the audit was properly conducted. The auditor will also state whether the financial statements give a good representation of the company's underlying performance and position. This is summed up by stating whether the accounts show a true and fair view.

The auditor should carry out particular procedures that may bring any fraud to light, but is not specifically required to detect fraud. However, where there are uncertainties these should be reported.

Balance sheet

The balance sheet is one of the three main financial statements in the company report and accounts. It is a snapshot of the company's position at a given point in time. The assets and liabilities on the sheet are a combination of those shown at historical cost and those requiring fair valuing each period. Let us take a look at the items included.

On the top half of the balance sheet are the company's *assets* (see page 202), those items the company owns. These are offset against the company's *liabilities* (see page 216), which are what it owes.

Total assets less total liabilities equal the net assets of the company. Current assets less current liabilities make net current assets, which is the amount available to pay bills within the year.

Issued share capital and *reserves* (see page 222) make up shareholders' funds. These, together with any minority interests, are equal to total capital employed. The key rule of the balance sheet is that a company's assets equal its liabilities plus its shareholders' funds. In this way, the balance sheet balances.

Brands

Brands often have a value, in which case they may be included as an intangible asset on the balance sheet. The useful life of the brand and its real ability to generate future benefits for the company must be assessed. The cost of the brand should be charged to the profit & loss account over its useful life as *amortisation* (see page 202). In some cases brands may be considered to have an indefinite life, in which case they must be annually tested for impairment.

When two companies have brands on their balance sheet, it can be hard to make an accounting comparison. This is because the brand valuations are highly subjective.

Balance sheet (International Financial Reporting Standards (IFRS)-style)

ASSETS

Non-current assets
Property, plant and equipment | x
Intangible assets | x
Investments in associates | x
Available for sale financial assets | x
Derivative financial instruments | x

Total non-current assets | x

Current assets
Inventory | x
Accounts receivable | x
Investments | x
Cash and cash equivalents | x

Total current assets | x

Total assets | x

LIABILITIES

Non-current liabilities
Accounts receivable payable in more than one year | (x)
Provisions | (x)

Current liabilities
Accounts receivable payable within one year | (x)

Net current assets | x

Total assets less current liabilities | x

Net assets | x

EQUITY

Capital and reserves
Issued share capital | x
Share premium account | x
Revaluation reserve | x
Retained profit | x

Minority interests | x

Total equity | x

Capital allowance

Capital allowances describe the deduction given by the Inland Revenue for tax purposes in relation to the cost incurred by the company from buying tangible fixed assets. They arise because *depreciation* (see page 208) charged on fixed assets is not a tax-deductible expense and is therefore added back to a company's profits to determine profits that are chargeable to corporation tax.

The method of capital allowances ensures that all companies receive a standard deduction based on the cost of an asset, irrespective of the period over which a company depreciates the asset in its financial statements.

Capitalising development costs

Development costs were historically charged to the *profit & loss account* (see page 220) immediately. However, companies must now capitalise the development costs as an intangible asset in the balance sheet as soon as they meet certain criteria. These criteria include ensuring that the development costs are clearly defined and identifiable, that the company has the resources to complete the project and that it will be able to either use or sell the asset once it has been completed for the benefit of the company.

The costs of development are *amortised* once the asset comes into use (see 'Amortisation', page 202) and so hit the profit & loss account gradually over the period that the company is expected to benefit from the asset. All research – as opposed to development – cannot be capitalised and must be charged immediately to the profit & loss account.

Cash flow statement

The cash flow statement presents movements in cash and other assets that are similar to cash (cash equivalents). All cash flows are split between operating, investing and financing items. It is arguably the part of the accounts that investors and users find most useful as it is easy to understand and not impacted by subjective judgements or assumptions.

The statement starts with cash flow from operating activities. It may present this in a direct way as cash received from customers, less cash paid to suppliers, employees and others. More usually, it will present this in an indirect, more complicated way, reconciling profit before tax to operating cash flow. If so, it will start with the profit before tax, and add back *depreciation* (see page 208), as this is not a cash flow. Any increase in debtors is subtracted as it means less cash for the company while the debts are outstanding. Any decrease in stocks or increase in creditors is added back, as it means more cash.

Net cash from operating activities on the cash flow statement will be preferably about the same as or, better still, higher than, the operating profit on the *profit & loss account* (see page 220).

Next comes the investing cash flows section. This includes cash flows relating to the purchase or sale of long-term assets. It will also include cash payments and receipts relating to the purchase or disposal of debt or equity in other companies. Interest payments and receipts and dividends will also appear in this section.

Finally we have the financing section. These cash flows relate to the way in which the company obtains cash to finance its operations.

Cash flow statement (IFRS-style)

	£,000
Cash flows from operating activities	
Cash generated from operations	x
Interest paid	x
Income tax paid	x
Net cash generated from operating activities	x
Cash flows from investing activities	
Purchase of property, plant and equipment (PPE)	x
Proceeds of sale of PPE	x
Interest received	x
Dividends received	x
Net cash used in investing activities	x
Cash flows from financing activities	
Proceeds from issue of ordinary shares	(x)
Proceeds from borrowings	(x)
Repayments of borrowings	(x)
Dividends paid to minority interests	(x)
Net cash used in financing activities	(x)
Increase or decrease in cash and bank overdrafts	
Cash and bank overdrafts at beginning of year	x
Exchange gains or losses on cash and bank overdrafts	x
Cash and bank overdrafts at end of the year	x

Chairman's statement

The chairman's statement at the front of the report and accounts – often written by his public relations team – will always represent the company in its best light. It will focus on the company's trading performance, its strategy and its prospects.

This statement is not subject to any auditing or accounting legislation, or even governed by a code of best practice. Despite this, the chairman should have considered his or her reputation in preparing the statement.

Comparability

Comparability is one of the fundamental characteristics used to prepare financial statements. It is a wide-ranging concept requiring that companies prepare their accounts in a consistent manner year on year and ensure that they are comparable with other companies in their sector and over time.

Contingent liabilities

When a prospective event is uncertain and, if it should happen, a liability will arise but the amount payable is hard to assess, it will not be included in the accounts. It is instead disclosed in the notes to the accounts, under the heading 'Contingent Liabilities'.

Cost of sales

Cost of sales is included second from the top on the *profit & loss account* (see page 220). These are the costs that a company incurs directly in relation to the sales. They include production overheads, raw materials, employees and product development. They also include *stock changes* (see 'Stock valuation', page 223), and *depreciation* (see page 208), both of which can vary depending on the accounting method used.

If the cost of sales has risen proportionately higher than sales, this will reduce the *profit margin* (see page 220), and is a warning sign.

Creative accounting

This is the frowned-on manipulation of *financial statements* (see page 213) and ratios to present a company in a more flattering light. It is seen as a problem everywhere, but is particularly prevalent in some emerging markets.

Warren Buffett, the world's most successful investor, has used this riddle to explain creative accounting. How many legs does a dog have if you call a tail a leg? Answer: four, because a tail is not a leg.

Current ratio

The current ratio measures a company's liquidity. It equals the current assets, divided by current liabilities, and so indicates the company's ability to pay its short-term debts from assets expected to be realised as cash in the short term. The figures are taken from the ***balance sheet*** (see page 203).

In a financially healthy company, the current ratio will usually be at least 2, indicating that current assets cover current liabilities twice. But if it is much higher, it may indicate that the company is not making its capital work for it in the most efficient way. A low ratio, perhaps less than 1, may indicate that the company will have difficulty in meeting its immediate liabilities. But what is appropriate depends significantly on the circumstances of the company and on the industry in which it operates.

Debtors' days' ratio

The debtors' days ratio tells you the number of days that it takes the company to collect money from its customers. If the ratio is rising, it shows that the company is taking longer to collect its money. The ratio is calculated as follows:

$$\frac{\text{Trade debtors} \times 365}{\text{Turnover} \times 1.75}$$

The calculation is somewhat crude and cannot be overly relied on. Errors will arise if, for example, the company's sales do not occur evenly throughout the financial period or if not all the company's sales attract a VAT rate of 17.5 per cent.

Depreciation

Depreciation is the amount by which the value of a fixed ***asset*** (see page 202) is gradually reduced as the asset is used by the business over its useful life. Depreciation is deducted annually as a charge within the ***profit & loss account*** (see page 220). For intangible assets, ***amortisation*** (see page 202) is used instead.

There are a number of ways to calculate depreciation. They vary between companies, and will have a different impact on reported profits. The depreciation policy used has no impact on tax allowances, however, which are given as ***capital allowances*** (see page 205) at a rate defined in law. Companies should use a consistent method unless there is a good economic reason for changing. The company must disclose in the accounts any change in the method of depreciation. The two most common methods are as follows.

Straight line method

The straight line method of depreciation spreads the cost of the asset equally over its expected useful economic life. It is the most popular method in the UK as it is easiest to calculate.

If, for example, a company plans to depreciate an asset valued at £10,000 over 10 years, it will reduce its value by £1,000 annually.

Reducing balance method

Under this method, the carrying value of the asset in the **balance sheet** (see page 203) at the balance sheet date is reduced by a percentage of its carrying amount at the previous balance sheet date. It gives rise to the highest depreciation level in the early years of an asset's life.

Table N1 compares the straight line and reducing balance methods of an asset costing £100 over four years, assuming a depreciation rate of 25 per cent per annum.

Table N1   Asset costing methods compared

Time	Straight Line		Reducing Balance	
	Carrying amount	Depreciation charged	Carrying amount	Depreciation charged
Start of year 1	100	0	100	0
End of year 1	75	25	75	25
End of year 2	50	25	56.3	18.7
End of year 3	25	25	42.2	14.1
End of year 4	0	25	31.6	10.6

Other, much less common, methods of depreciation are as follows.

Sum-of-the-digits method

This method evokes protests from accountants that they have never seen it in use. It remains, however, available, and has the distinguishing feature that it gives rise to a depreciation charge that is higher in the early years of an asset's life.

If, for example, an asset's useful working life is three years, you will add up the digits 3, 2 and 1 – representing the remaining years at annual stages – to make 6.

You will divide the number of years left in the asset's useful working life by this figure at each of your annual stages, and multiply the result by the asset value to give you a depreciation percentage. For example, in year one, the depreciation is 3/6 of asset value, and in year 2, it is 2/6.

Usage-based method

This method is based on how much the asset is used. It is often applied, for example, in the case of machinery.

Annuity method

The annuity method takes account of the cost of capital tied up in the asset.

Directors' report

The directors' report is part of the *financial statements* (see page 213). It helps the reader to interpret the numbers, and it provides extra non-financial information.

It includes a business review, which is limited to avoid revealing too much to competitors, but may still say a fair bit.

Details of post-balance sheet events, the company's research and development programme, its major shareholders, its employee policies, its *dividend* (see next entry) policy, and any share buyback are provided.

Dividend

This is the payment that a company makes to shareholders from available profit and is normally in the form of cash. UK companies will usually pay any annual dividend in two parts: an interim and a final dividend. Because of the way companies are constituted, final dividends declared on results for the year require shareholder's approval to become legally binding on the company, but interim dividends need only be declared by the directors.

A company will not pay out all its profit as dividends, but will retain some to help finance future corporate growth, keeping it within retained earnings. A company that has made a loss can, and will often try to, pay a dividend so long as it has sufficient profits from previous years to fund this.

Dividend cover

Dividend cover represents the number of times a company's net earnings cover its *dividend* (see previous entry). It must be at least once if the company is to pay the dividend from current earnings without using reserves.

Dividend yield

This is the percentage return on your investment in a share. It is the gross *dividend* (see page 210) divided by the share price, and multiplied by 100. It may be called simply the 'yield', and is discussed in Part A, Chapter 1. See also Section E, 'High yield investing' (page 123).

Double entry bookkeeping

Double entry bookkeeping is the underlying method of accounting for transactions and is the foundation of modern accounting. The method was invented at the end of the 15th century and first used in Italy.

Any amount entered on the right side of one account, known as a credit, must be balanced by the same amount on the left side of another account, known as a debit. The balance sheet has *assets* (see page 202), or debit balances, that are equal to liabilities plus the capital and reserves, or credit balances.

Earning per share (EPS)

This is a measure of the company's performance. Broadly speaking it equals the profit attributable to the ordinary shareholders (ie, profit before ordinary dividends) divided by the number of ordinary shares in issue during the year.

Listed companies are required to disclose two measures of EPS, basic and diluted, on the front of the *profit & loss account* (see page 220). The diluted EPS figure adjusts the basic EPS figure to show what the result would have been had all potential ordinary shares (such as employee share options and convertible debt) been converted into shares.

Companies can provide an adjusted EPS figure, but only in the notes to the accounts and not on the face of the profit & loss account. It may better support the company's view of its progress than the normally rather lower basic EPS. The adjusted figure may show earnings before such charges as *depreciation* (see page 208), *amortisation* (see page 202), *exceptional items* (see page 211) and any other items that the directors do not like the look of.

Earnings yield

This is *earnings per share* (see previous entry), divided by the share price. It is the reverse of the *P/E ratio* (see page 218).

Equity accounting

Equity accounting is when a group includes only its own share of an associate or joint venture's (see 'Group accounting', page 214) entire net assets in the group accounts. The consolidated *cash flow statement* (see page 205) includes *dividends* (see page 210) received from associates and joint ventures separately.

Exceptional items

Historically, these were significant or unusual items of income or, more usually, expense, that arose in a particular period and that the company wished to highlight to investors. *International Financial Reporting Standards* (see page

215) ruled out the disclosure of exceptional items although a company may, in the notes to its accounts, refer to one-off items that should be considered when determining the company's performance.

Exchange rate accounting

In the current global environment companies will conduct business in many different countries and currencies. The **exchange rate** (see page 146), and how exchange differences are accounted for, can have a direct impact on reported profits.

For **profit & loss account** (see page 220) transactions, the exchange rate used should be that at the transaction date or, if fluctuations have not been too great, an average rate for the period.

On the **balance sheet** (see page 203), monetary items are valued at the year-end closing rate, with exchange gains and losses taken onto the profit & loss account.

Factoring

This is when the company sells cash to be collected from trade debtors to another party, the debt factor. It is a form of financing, and the cash received from the debt factor will be less than the face value of the trade debts sold (usually around 80 per cent).

The debt factor may or may not have *recourse*. This is the right to recover from the company any debts that are not ultimately recovered by the debt factor.

Where the debt factor has recourse, the company may have to continue to show the trade debts on its balance sheet and the proceeds from the debt factor as a liability. This will affect the company's **gearing** (see page 309) ratio, which is its level of borrowing.

There are many different types of factoring arrangement, and those used may be detailed in the notes to a company's accounts. Factoring can improve the company's cash flow and save it the cost of managing its debtors.

Fair values

Companies have traditionally used historical cost as the main way of valuing their **assets** (see page 202) and **liabilities** (see page 216) in the **balance sheet** (see page 203). Increasingly they are required to reconsider these costs and to restate assets and liabilities at the fair value, or the current value at the date that the information is reported. This results in movements through the **profit & loss account** (see page 220) as the assumptions underpinning the fair values will change from one period to the next.

Financial instruments

All financial *assets* (see page 202) and *liabilities* (see page 216) are recognised on the balance sheet. This includes complex instruments such as *derivatives* (see page 107) as well as more straightforward items such as cash, debtors and creditors.

Many of these are re-measured to fair value at each balance sheet date. For financial assets the only exceptions are originated loans and held-to-maturity investments, which are carried at amortised cost.

Trading assets, which are acquired mainly to generate short-term gains or a dealer's margin, are initially recognised at cost and, every subsequent balance sheet date, remarked to fair value with the changes taken to the *profit & loss account* (see page 220). This generates significant additional volatility.

There are some exclusions from the normal accounting rules, usually because they are covered in other standards. Among these are financial guarantee contracts, rights and obligations under leases, and some interests in subsidiaries, associates and joint ventures.

Financial statements

Most UK quoted companies issue their publicly available financial information in two stages. There will be an interim statement after the first six months. Shortly after the full year, the company publishes full-year figures, known as preliminaries.

Following the preliminaries, the company will then publish the full audited annual report and accounts including the required financial statements and notes to the accounts. The most important of these are a *profit & loss account* (see page 220), the *cash flow statement* (see page 205), and the *balance sheet* (see page 203).

Although an analysis of the financial statements is a key tool in assessing the investment potential of a company, it must be borne in mind that they present a picture of the company's past performance. The market's perception of the future cash flows and profitability of the company, however, will drive the market value of the company.

To get hold of the annual report, telephone a company's registrar, and ask it to send you a copy, or ask the company directly. You can often download the accounts of a large company from its website.

Going concern

A key assumption of financial reporting is that the company is a going concern. This means that the financial statements are prepared on the basis that the company will continue in business for the foreseeable future.

Goodwill

This is the difference between the price paid for another business and the fair value of net assets acquired. This represents the value of a business that exists above simply the assets quantified in the balance sheet, and includes such intangible elements as reputation, order book and good relations with customers, experienced employees, beneficial contracts and similar.

It arises from a business combination accounted for using acquisition accounting, which under *International Financial Reporting Standards* (see page 215) is the only option. See also Merger accounting, page 217. Goodwill is treated as an intangible asset, but we do not have to amortise it. Instead, it is tested for *impairment* (see page 214) every 12 months

Group accounting

If a company has more than 50 per cent of shares in another, the latter is a subsidiary. Subsidiaries will also arise where one company controls another through means other than holding the majority of the share capital. The group prepares consolidated accounts, which combine the subsidiary's accounts with the parent's, as well as separate accounts for the parent company. The subsidiary is treated as an investment in the parent company's accounts, but not in the consolidated *balance sheet* (see page 203).

Where a company does not control another company, but can exercise significant influence, often through holding between 20 and 50 per cent of the shares, it is an associate. Associates will also be equity accounted, as high-lighted above.

If a company owns less than 20 per cent of shares in another company, it is normally an investment and is carried in the balance sheet at its fair value.

A joint venture is as an entity in which the reporting company holds an interest on a long-term basis and controls jointly with one or more other ventures. It can be represented in the accounts using either *equity accounting* (see page 211) or proportional consolidation.

Impairment

Sometimes the value of assets on the *balance sheet* (see page 203) is found to not actually represent their real value to the company. Where a company believes that the value may be less than that on the balance sheet it must conduct impairment tests. An impairment test involves comparing the reported value with the potential discounted future cash flows from either using or selling the asset. Where there is an impairment loss this will become a charge in the *profit & loss account* (see page 220).

Certain assets such as goodwill and intangible assets with indefinite lives must be tested for impairment every 12 months, whether or not there is any indication of impairment.

A company is required to disclose a lot of detail about how the impairment test has actually been conducted and the assumptions used.

Interest cover

Interest cover is a ratio. It is calculated as profit before the deduction of interest payable and tax, divided by interest payable. It gives an indication of a company's ability to service debt.

International Financial Reporting Standards (IFRS)

These are harmonised accounting standards intended to bring about global comparability in accounting treatments. From 1 January 2005, they came into force for all listed companies in the European Union and, in the next few years, will be adopted in 90 countries. Unlisted companies in the UK currently have a choice over whether to adopt IFRS from 2005 or to continue to use the UK standards.

The UK accounting standards board has stated that it will follow the international standards and bring out requirements that reflect the same rules so all companies will face the same challenges in converting in the coming years.

Under IFRS, company accounts are likely to be longer with greater disclosure that may give away more commercially sensitive information than before. Any material error discovered during the conversion process will need to be corrected. In the past there was a concept of fundamental errors, meaning that only very large errors would have been reported. Regulators hope that the new standards will contribute to fewer accounting scandals.

As part of IFRS, hybrid securities such as preference shares may be classified as debt rather than, like before, as equity. This is because there is a focus on the substance of the transaction, which may resemble a debt instrument. *Derivatives* (see Section D, page 107) must be brought on to the balance sheet at fair value and are accounted for by marking to market through the *profit & loss account* (see page 220), which can lead to extra volatility.

A further change is that the cost of stock options based on an estimation made at the date of grant will be expensed to the profit & loss account as the benefit is earned. Previously, little or none of this value was recognised as a charge through the profit & loss account.

Intrinsic value

This is the present value of a stock's future *dividends* (see page 210). In the context of share options, it is the difference between the market price at date of grant and the option exercise price.

Lease accounting

Leasing arrangements occur when a company has the right to use an asset which it does not legally own. In this way it avoids paying out the upfront capital cost. It arises when the lessee hires equipment from the lessor, who continues to own the asset in legal terms. We must, however, consider carefully whether the risks and rewards of ownership have actually passed to the lessee.

If the risks and rewards have passed to the lessee, the lessor accounts for the finance lease (any long-term lease) as a loan, and the amounts due from the lessee as a debtor. The lessee must include an asset on its *balance sheet* (see page 203), in accordance with the accounting principle of *substance over form* (see page 224), and it will be depreciated over its life, which is the shorter of the lease term and its anticipated useful life. The rule also applies to an asset bought under a HP agreement, even though the company does not own it until it has paid off all the instalments. Over the life of the lease, the cost to the lessee is recognised in the *profit & loss account* (see page 220) as *depreciation* (see page 208) of the asset and a financing charge on the *liability* (see next entry). The lease payments are split between interest and a reduction of the lease liability.

Operating leases, unlike finance leases, are usually short term. They do not provide the benefits of ownership, given that the risks and rewards of ownership have not been passed, and are not assets on the balance sheet of the lessee. Instead, their lease rental payments are charged to the profit & loss account as an operating cost.

The distinction between finance and operating leases is not always clear-cut. There are now a number of qualitative factors that have to be taken into account in determining whether the asset held is one or other kind of lease, including the length of the lease term, the proportion of the asset's cost covered by the lease payments, whether the asset is specialist in nature, and whether there are any options to buy at favourable rates at the end of the term.

Companies prefer to classify leases as an operating lease. It means that the gearing is lower because no liability is on the balance sheet, and interest cover is higher because none of the lease payments is classified as an interest charge.

Liabilities

Liabilities are what a company owes. They are included on a *balance sheet* (see page 203), where they are deducted from *assets* (see page 202) to form net assets.

Current liabilities are payments that may have to be made within one year. Among these are accrued expenses, such as salaries that have been earned but not yet paid, and bank overdrafts. Trade creditors are another current liability. Companies will aim to balance the need for strong relationships with their suppliers with the desire for longer credit terms so that they free up cash for other purposes. See *trade creditors ratio* (see page 224).

Non-current liabilities will include medium- and long-term debts. They will include provisions, which represent legal or constructive obligations resulting in probable future costs arising from past transactions or events.

Market capitalisation

This is the market value of a company. It is the current share price, multiplied by the number of shares in issue.

The market capitalisation divided by the share price will give you the number of ordinary shares in issue. There may be other classes of share that are excluded and, if so, they would have to be added to give the full figure.

Materiality

Materiality is a concept used by companies in the preparation of their accounts. An item is considered to be material if misstatements will impact the decisions of users of the accounts. It is considered both in measurable terms and in terms of the nature of the particular item.

Anything material, and so potentially affecting users' decisions, must be disclosed in a company's accounts.

Merger accounting

This way of accounting for a business merger between two companies has been abolished by the *International Financial Reporting Standards* (see page 215). Under merger accounting, the results of the combined *assets* (see page 202) are represented as if the businesses had never been separate. The newly combined assets and *liabilities* (see page 216) are not reassessed at fair value, and *goodwill* (see page 214) is not acknowledged. All business combinations now must be treated as acquisitions.

Minority interests

Minority interests may be present in a company's consolidated financial statements. They arise where a company has a subsidiary but does not own 100 per cent of the shares in it. On the *balance sheet* (see page 203), the minority interest represents the minority's share of the net assets of the subsidiary.

In such cases, the net assets are allocated between shareholders' funds and minority interests. It means that assets less liabilities are equal to the parent's shareholders' funds plus minority interests.

Net asset value per share

Net asset value per share is a useful yardstick for evaluating property companies or *investment trusts* (see page 284). It is the share price divided by *net assets* (see next entry) per share.

If the share price is at a discount to net asset value, this indicates that the stock is valued low. This may be for a good reason, or it may indicate a bargain.

Net assets

Net assets are total *assets* (see page 202) less total *liabilities* (see page 216). This will always be equal to the capital employed. It is a key measure often used in bank covenants.

Nominal value

This is the face value of a security, as distinct from its share price. It is also known as 'par value'.

Orphan assets

These are reserves held by life insurance companies consisting of unclaimed life policies and surplus funds of lapsed policies.

Par value

This is the same as 'nominal value' (see above).

P/E ratio (price/earnings)

The price/earnings ratio is the *market capitalisation* (see page 217) of the company divided by the profit attributable to ordinary shareholders in its last *financial statements* (see page 213). Another way to calculate it is as the share price divided by *earnings per share* (see page 211). This ratio shows how many years it will take the company, at the rate of earnings used, to earn the equivalent to its full value. See also the discussion of the P/E ratio as part of the share price tables in Part A, Chapter 1.

The P/E ratio varies, depending on how the earnings per share are calculated and how recent a share price is used. Analysts sometimes use historic earnings, and sometimes prospective, based on either their own or on consensus forecasts. Like should be compared with like.

PEG ratio

The price/earnings growth (PEG) ratio is the company's *P/E ratio* (see previous entry) divided by the average annual growth rate of its *earnings per share* (see page 211). As a valuation tool, the PEG ratio was popularised in the UK by private client investment guru Jim Slater, and the Motley Fool website.

The PEG ratio works best for small growth companies. If it is significantly less than 1, it could mean that the stock is good value. But the ratio is vulnerable to *creative accounting* (see page 207) because the earnings per share can be manipulated.

Preliminaries

The preliminaries consist of the full-year figures that a company publishes shortly after the full year. The full audited *financial statements* (see page 213) are published soon afterwards. Timing depends on the company and how quickly it will have released preliminaries.

Price/research ratio

The price/research ratio (PPR) is the *market capitalisation* (see page 217) of the company divided by its corporate research expenses for the previous year. The ratio is useful for valuing technology companies that have high research expenses.

US fund manager Kenneth Fisher uses the PRR ratio as a cross-check on the *price/sales ratio* (see next entry).

Price/sales ratio

The price/sales ratio (PSR) is the stock price divided by sales, expressed as a percentage. The lower the figure, the greater is the value of the stock.

Analysts have used the PSR ratio to value *internet companies* (see page 124), since their lack of profits has made earnings-related ratios less useful. But they use it also for profitable companies. As fund manager Kenneth Fisher has pointed out, sales are more stable than earnings. A low PSR ratio has proved likely to be accompanied by a low *P/E ratio* (see page 218).

Profit

Profit is essentially the difference between a company's income and expenditure in a particular period.

There are different measures of profit. For example, gross profit is sales (or revenue) less *cost of sales* (see page 207) only. Operating profit is arrived at after also deducting distribution costs and administrative expenses.

'Trading profit' is a term used sometimes, but its meaning is debatable. It is not subject to any formal definition in the context of external financial reporting, and does not usually appear on the face of the *profit & loss account* (see next entry).

Profit & loss account

The profit & loss account, or income statement, records the company's profits or losses, and how they were reached, over the previous financial year. It is one of the three main financial statements in a company's annual report and accounts, the others being the *balance sheet* (see page 203) and the *cash flow statement* (see page 205).

At the top of the profit & loss account is *turnover (or revenue)* (see page 224), which is all of the ordinary income received by the company. *Cost of sales* (see page 207), including production overheads, *depreciation* (see page 208), and stock changes (see Stock valuation, page 223), is deducted with other expenses on a net basis from turnover. The profit & loss account will state what the total operating profit figure is. In UK accounts, the charge for tax is typically less than the pre-tax profit multiplied by the tax rate. It includes *corporation tax* and *deferred taxation* (see pages 132 and 133).

Corporation tax is paid on the company's income and capital gains, usually nine months after the company's year-end. Deferred taxation acknowledges liabilities or assets in relation to timing differences existing up to the balance sheet date. Following UK standards currently, the company will need to provide for deferred taxation on the profit & loss account only 'to the extent that a liability or asset will crystallise'. However, under IFRS this will change so that deferred tax is recognised on all differences between the accounting balance sheet and the tax base of the asset or liability.

Profit margin

The profit margin is net, or gross, *profit* (see page 219), divided by *turnover (or revenue)* (see page 224) and expressed as a percentage.

Compare the profit margin, consistently calculated, with that for the same company in past years, or for peer companies. Outside the same sector, the profit margin may vary too much for effective comparison. For instance, it is much higher in *biotechnology companies* (see page 117) than in food retailers.

Consolidated income statement (IFRS style)

Turnover	x
Cost of sales	(x)
Gross profit	x
Administration costs	(x)
Distribution costs	(x)
Other operating income	x
Operating profit	x
Finance costs	(x)
Share of (loss)/profit from associate	x
Profit before tax	x
Taxation	x
Profit for the year	x
Attributable to:	
Equity holders of the Company	x
Minority interests	x

Quick ratio

Also known as the 'acid test ratio', this is a measure of liquidity. It is calculated as current **assets** (see page 202) less stock, divided by current **liabilities** (see page 216). This is similar to the **current ratio** (see page 208), but stock is excluded from the numerator.

Relative strength

Relative strength is how well a stock has performed against the market, or its sector. To calculate it against the market, divide the share price daily or weekly by the **FTSE All-Share index** (see page 265) at the time. Plot the result on a chart against price.

If everything else is right about the stock, good relative strength confirms that you should buy. Shares that outperformed the market consistently have often continued to do so. The reverse is also true, and weak relative strength is a bearish sign.

Do not confuse relative strength with the **Relative Strength Index** (see page 187).

Reserves

Reserves are part of **shareholders' funds** (see page 223) on the **balance sheet** (see page 203). They will include the reserve containing retained profit. The **profit & loss account** (see page 220) is the only distributable reserve. The others cannot be depleted to pay **dividends** (see page 210), but they can be used in **scrip issues** (see page 248). They include the share premium account, which contains the premium to the nominal value at which shares were issued; the revaluation reserve, which contains unrealised profits; and the capital revaluation reserve, which includes changes in the valuation of non-current **assets** (see page 202).

Technical reserves

These are funds held by insurance companies against possible claims.

Return on capital employed

The return on capital employed (ROCE) is a measure of management performance. It is calculated as **profit** (see page 219) before interest and tax, divided by year-end **assets** (see page 202) less **liabilities** (see page 216), expressed as a percentage. Analysts favour a rising ROCE that is higher than in peer companies.

Return on equity

The return on equity measures how effectively the company is using shareholders' money. It is defined as net **profits** (see page 219), divided by **assets** (see page 202) less **liabilities** (see page 216), and expressed as a percentage.

Segment reporting

Segment reporting shows an entity's financial position and performance according to the segments in which it operates. Listed companies and those in the process of listing must make segment disclosures. Non-listed entities may present segment information and, if so, it must be compliant with **International Financial Reporting Standards** (see page 215).

Segments are labelled 'primary' or 'secondary'. Generally, business segments are primary and geographical are secondary, but this would be reversed if the geographical segments were more important.

Share capital

Share capital can be issued or authorised. Issued share capital consists only of those shares that have been issued to shareholders, and is part of **shareholders'** *funds* (see next entry). Authorised share capital is the total number of shares available for issue.

The total amount of share capital includes ***ordinary shares*** (see page 126) and, if available, ***preference shares*** (see page 127). Less commonly, there may be non-voting shares, which have limited or no voting rights, and ***warrants*** (see page 115).

Shareholders' funds

These represent the net assets of the company attributable to the company's shareholders. Where there are ***minority interests*** (see page 217), shareholders' funds are arrived at by deducting from net assets the amount attributable to the minority. From the other side of the ***balance sheet*** (see page 203), the same shareholders' funds are expressed as issued ***share capital*** (see previous entry) and reserves, less minority interests.

Special dividend

A special dividend is a non-recurring ***dividend*** (see page 210). It is exceptional either in date of issue or in size.

Statement of total recognised gains and losses

This links the ***profit & loss account*** (see page 220) to the ***balance sheet*** (see page 203).

It shows any gains or losses including a likely very small proportion that are unrealised and cannot be included on the profit & loss account. These may include gains relating to the revaluation of non-current ***assets*** (see page 202) and the effects of currency movements.

Stock valuation

Over a period companies will be buying and using up stock resulting in changes to the stock level held in the ***balance sheet*** (see page 203). Therefore, stock balance is calculated as opening stock plus purchases minus closing stock. The net impact of the using up of stock and purchases of new stock will become part of ***cost of sales*** (see page 207) in the ***profit & loss account*** (see page 220) and will affect taxable profit.

How a stock is valued clearly influences the charge to the cost of sales in any period. Companies are required to use either a weighted average valuation basis for cost of sales or to value using the first-in first-out (FIFO) method.

Stock turn ratio

This is stock turnover divided by average stock. You may calculate average stock as opening stock plus closing stock, divided by two.

If the stock turn ratio is increasing year on year, this suggests that the company is finding it easier to sell stock, or reducing its stock holding.

Substance over form

Substance over form is the fundamental principle that underpins the preparation of all financial statements under both the UK standards and the *International Financial Reporting Standards* (see page 215). It stipulates that a company's accounts should reflect the commercial reality, and not just the legal form. The US has more of a rules-based approach where legal form may be more important.

Trade creditors ratio

This shows how many days the company takes to pay its trade creditors. It is calculated as the number of trade creditors divided by *turnover (or revenue)* (see next entry), with the total multiplied by 365.

If creditor days are increasing, it means that the company is gaining longer access to interest-free cash, which is to its benefit.

Turnover (or revenue)

Turnover (or revenue) represents a company's sales, and is the first item recorded on the *profit & loss account* (see page 220). New accounting rules were recently introduced in the UK to ensure that all companies calculate revenue on a consistent basis. Difficulties can arise, for example, when a sales contract contains multiple elements or when payment is deferred.

If turnover has risen year on year, it is a good sign, but not enough on its own to constitute a buying signal. If it is accompanied by diminishing profits, this may be temporary.

In the notes to the accounts, there is a breakdown of turnover by each class of business and geographical segment. It shows from where the company is generating most of its revenues, and the scope for the trend to continue. (See 'Segment reporting', page 222).

Working capital

Working capital is net current assets. This is current *assets* (see page 202) less current *liabilities* (see page 216). (See 'Balance sheet', page 203).

OFR and corporate governance

Introduction

Global accounting scandals such as Enron and Parmalat have highlighted the need for strong corporate governance. This section explains aspects of it, including the Operating and Financial Review. See also Section R, which covers Regulation and compliance.

Basel Accord

The Basel Accord is a measure of capital adequacy in banks set up as a standard minimum by the Basel Committee on Banking Supervision (www.bis.org), an organisation that regulates international banking.

The Basel Committee was set up in 1975. It consists of regulators and central bank officials from the 10 economies known as the G-10 (plus from Spain and Luxembourg). G-10 consists of Canada, Belgium, France, Germany, Italy, Japan, the Netherlands, Sweden, Switzerland and the US.

Basel 1 was introduced in 1988. It required banks to keep a minimum 8 per cent level of regulatory capital as a proportion of assets weighted by credit risk, and has since been amended a few times, including in 1996 so that it also covered market risk. The level was lower than required in many countries. Almost all solvent banks hold more than the minimum capital.

Basel 2 was introduced in the first of three draft consultation papers in 1999, and the final version was published in June 2004. There are different implementation schedules for separate parts of Basel 2, but the aim is that it will be implemented by the end of 2006. In the UK, it will proceed by way of Capital Adequacy Directive, or CAD 3, an EU Directive. It retains a minimum 8 per cent capital-to-assets ratio, and the buffer capital in the banking system must not be permitted to fall below levels required under Basel 1. But banks will be able to use a more advanced way of measuring their risks and, if so, will have lower capital charges than banks using simpler ways. In practice, only a few major banks are expected to take advantage of this.

A perceived benefit of Basel 2 is that as a result of greater risk aversion, institutions will be able to price more keenly. But critics say that it is too complicated and expensive to implement and monitor, and that the large banks may benefit more than the smaller ones. Banks may be reluctant to lend to small businesses because they represent a greater credit risk, and the strict requirements for covering risk might inculcate a false sense of security.

Corporate governance – a history of UK developments

Corporate governance is about how a company conducts its corporate affairs and responds to stakeholders, employees and society. It aims more to prevent losses than to create profits. Sir Adrian Cadbury defined it as 'the system by which companies are directed and controlled'.

In the UK, the perception is that more companies pay lip service to corporate governance than take it seriously. The concept has developed from market input and not, as in the US, from legislation.

In 1991, the Cadbury Committee was established following corporate collapses such as Polly Peck. It produced a code of best practices applicable to UK listed companies and was backed by the Financial Reporting Council (FRC), the London Stock Exchange and the accounting profession. In 1995, the Greenbury Committee was set up and, in July of that year, produced a code on directors' remuneration.

In 1998, the Hampel Committee proposed a Combined Code, which, following consultation by the London Stock Exchange, was published in July with a new edition of the Listing Rules. This set out the main guidelines for UK corporate governance. In 2001, Paul Myners reported on how institutional investors could better serve the long-term good of markets.

Higgs and Smith

In 2002, the Department of Trade and Industry and the FRC started developing Combined Code guidance on audit committees. It was a reaction to US corporate governance scandals at Enron and WorldCom. The FRC established a group under Sir Robert Smith that liaised with Sir Derek Higgs, who had been asked by the Government to review the role of non-executive directors.

The Higgs and Smith reports were published together in January 2003. Higgs said, among other things, that at least half the board members, excluding the chairman, should be non-executive directors, and that non-executive directors should meet at least once a year without the chairman or executive directors being present.

Critics among non-executive directors said that the Higgs report did not encourage investors to be sufficiently flexible in their attitude to corporate governance, and that it lacked an integrated vision of the board, requiring, for instance, non-executive directors to be assessed regularly, but not the same of executive directors.

Higgs suggested an expanded Combined Code, incorporating the amendments in respect of Audit Committees suggested by Smith, and the FRC started consultation.

Revised Combined Code

In July 2003, the Revised Combined Code was published. It made the Combined Code more principles-based, but most of the changes were in the detail. It applies to reporting years starting in or after November 2003.

The chairman and chief executive should have separate roles, according to the Code. Non-executive directors should be independent and appointments to the board made on merit. All listed companies should have a nomination committee, whose members are mostly independent, non-executive directors. Before a chairman is appointed, his or her time commitment should be assessed, and no individual should chair more than one FTSE-100 company.

Executive directors should take not more than one non-executive directorship in a FTSE-100 company and should not chair one, according to the Code. The chairman must ensure that directors receive timely information, and the Code revisions strengthen the requirement to enter into dialogue with shareholders. Disclosure in the annual report is compulsory.

The board should formally evaluate its own performance and the chairman should act on the results, which is the only new element in the Code revisions. Directors on first appointment should receive a tailored induction.

A requirement for pay to be linked to corporate and individual performance is the area of the Revised Code that addresses a major concern of financial journalists. It takes a sharp-eyed reporter only a few minutes to thumb through the relevant part of an annual report and accounts and to find that a chief executive officer is earning an inflated salary. The procedure for paying directors must be formal and transparent and they must not help to decide on their own pay, according to the Code.

In financial reporting, the board is required by the Code to present a balanced and understandable assessment of the company's position and prospects. A system of internal controls should be maintained and reviewed annually. The audit committee must make recommendations on appointments and removals of external auditors. Its membership should consist only of independent directors.

Model Code

The Model Code is an appendix to the listing rules, implemented by the *Financial Services Authority* (see page 255). It is a code of conduct imposing restrictions beyond the law. The Code aims to stop directors or employees of listed companies, and linked parties, from abusing, or placing themselves under suspicion of abusing, unpublished *price-sensitive information* (see page 70). It applies especially in periods shortly before results are reported.

Operating and Financial Review

The Operating and Financial Review contains a detailed analysis of the company's recent performance and statistics. This is included with the audited financial statements, and has been a legal requirement for all UK listed companies for financial years starting on or after 1 April 2005.

The OFR must provide a balanced and comprehensive view of, a) how the company is developing, its performance, and its position at the end of the year; and b) trends and factors affecting the company.

The aim was to create transparency, according to Patricia Hewitt, Secretary of State for Trade and Industry. But critics say that the requirements may feel too onerous. Directors have admitted difficulties with the more judgemental style of reporting required, using more qualitative and quantitative information than before.

Sarbanes-Oxley Act

The US Congress ushered in the Sarbanes-Oxley Act, 2002 after Enron, a US energy company, went bankrupt in December 2001 and was accused of share ramping and fraud.

The Act applies to any company that either owns a US subsidiary, or issues securities in the US. Almost half the companies in the UK's FTSE-100 index have a US listing.

Under Sarbanes-Oxley, accountants cannot mix auditing with certain activities, including actuarial or legal services, and bookkeeping. Auditors are supervised by a body that is answerable to the *Securities & Exchange Commission* (see page 260). Significant extra disclosure is required in the report and accounts, as well as ethical guidelines for senior financial officers. Guidelines are required on analysts' conflicts of interest.

The Act increases corporate responsibility for any fraudulent actions taken. The chief executive and chief financial officer must sign off financial statements to confirm compliance with the provisions of the Securities & Exchange Act, 1934. If the statements turn out to be incorrect, the signatories could be held criminally liable, even if they had not intended deceit. They face a maximum US $5 million fine or 20 years imprisonment, or both, for every violation.

Any employee attempting or conspiring to commit an offence faces the same penalties. To assist the process of justice, whistleblowers are protected.

Shareholder activism

Shareholder activism is when shareholders use their position to influence the behaviour of companies in which they have invested. It is weak in the UK, partly due to conflicts of interests. Some investment banks are believed not to want to get involved because it would interfere with lucrative merger and acquisition work.

Fund managers tend to apply shareholder activism in a tick box manner. They benefit from the more active work of a few big players. The UK Government has indicated that it may introduce regulation for shareholder activism, but it is currently voluntary. It is possible to mandate it to consultants.

Personal finance and property

Introduction

Personal finance is part of everybody's life. Over a lifetime, most people save and borrow money, buy or rent a property, take out a mortgage and use a bank account.

This section covers some main areas, but you should read it in conjunction with Section I, which covers Insurance and reinsurance, and should refer to Section F, which covers Fiscal and tax.

Advance fee fraud

An advance fee fraud is a loan offer that is presented as conditional on payment of an upfront fee. The promoters take the fee but do not pay the loan. When the crooks have stolen enough money, they disappear and later re-emerge under another name.

The promoters sometimes claim to be banks based in Guernsey, Jersey or the Isle of Man. Their only presence is on the internet. It takes at least a few weeks for the regulatory authorities on the islands to get the sites barred by internet service providers.

A well-known variation is the Nigerian 419 fraud, which is named after the appropriate part of the Nigerian criminal code. The fraud often originates from, but is not confined to, the West African criminal fraternity. In some cases, local government officials may be involved.

In the 419 fraud, the criminals pose as government officials and target businesspeople worldwide through e-mails and letters. The writer may claim that the Nigerian government is waiting to pay US $36 million for a contract just completed, and the recipient will be paid US $10 million if he or she will confidentially supply a foreign bank account through which to transfer the funds.

There are variations but the theme is the same. The letters are often full of incorrect grammar and spelling, designed to suggest that the writer is a poorly educated person without the ability to defraud the recipient.

If a targeted individual takes the bait, as many have done, the fraudster will coax from him or her one 'urgent' arrangement fee after another. He or she will plead poverty and eventually ask the victim to pay for the transferring of funds out of Nigeria. Victims are asked to wire over their cash. If they prove resistant, they are invited to travel to Nigeria to conclude a deal.

If the victims meet the fraudsters in the country, they will face demands for further fees before they are given a false cheque. Once a victim has understood that he or she has been fleeced, the same crooks, or their accomplices, may pose as Nigerian police. They may offer to investigate the scam in return for a fee.

Appointed Representative

Appointed Representatives sell financial services. They may be linked to one provider and advise on products within its range, which could be just the products of the provider itself, or include those of other providers. Alternatively, they may be authorised in their own right and sell a range of products on a multi-tied basis.

Until December 2004, and up to six months later, Appointed Representatives worked for one financial services company and only offered its products. They had a historical reputation for high pressure selling and ignorance about rival products.

Buy-to-let

Buy-to-let is when you buy a property for renting out and for potential increase in equity. As a rule of thumb, flats are easier to let than houses.

Rental income is taxable, although you can deduct some expenses, including interest rates on your *mortgage* (see page 234), and genuine repairs (not home improvements). You can claim 10 per cent on depreciation of furnishings every year, and offset expenses such as buildings insurance, service charges and ground rent.

As a landlord, you may go for periods without having tenants, called 'voids'. To compensate for the risks, some mortgage lenders expect your monthly income to be at least 125 per cent of the interest payments, which are often based on the standard variable rate. They will normally require a minimum 15 per cent deposit.

If you are short of time, use a reputable letting agent to handle your rentals. The agent will find a tenant for 10 per cent of the rental income, and manage the property for a further 5 per cent. The agency fees are a tax-deductible expense.

When you resell any property except that in which you live, you are liable for *capital gains tax* (see page 132).

New *pension legislation* (see page 170) from April 2006 will enable buy-to-let property to be part of an individual's pension, with tax relief on rental income and any capital gain on sale of the property, as well as income tax relief on money invested. Financial advisers predict a boom, but some have advised caution on the basis that property is illiquid and expensive to maintain, and its value may prove volatile.

Clearing bank

A clearing bank holds deposits for the public. It uses some of the capital held to lend at a higher rate of interest. This loan is the start of a cycle known as the 'money multiplier'. The borrower buys items from a seller who deposits the money received in the bank, some of which it proceeds to lend out, so restarting the cycle.

The larger the proportion of deposits the bank lends out, the more geared is its return on them. It must assess the risk on every loan.

Every bank provides a further range of financial services to its customers.

Credit card

A credit card enables unsecured borrowing with no specific repayment period. Issued by a financial institution, it enables you to pay for anything on credit, or raise cash, and to settle later with the credit card company.

If you settle within about 25 days, you will not usually pay interest on the outstanding balance. But over a quarter of families in the UK have at least one credit card where the balance is not cleared every month, owing £2,500 on average, according to a September 2004 survey by the *Financial Services Authority* (see page 255).

If you are an active user, check in the Money section of *The Times* on Saturdays under the 'Credit Cards' column for the best rates available. Look for a credit card that has a low APR or none on outstanding balances, at least for an initial period. The APR is the annual percentage rate. It represents the interest rate and all other costs charged for a loan.

Always report a card loss or suspicion of fraud instantly. Some dubious individuals in retail organisations practise *skimming*, by which they copy details of a *bona fide* credit card onto a machine, and make a fake card. They may then use it in the owner's name until it is reported as missing and stopped.

Fraudsters also copy cards at ATMs, although new cards are being constructed with a smart chip, which is said to make the task harder than with the old magnetic chip.

Depolarisation

Depolarisation is the recent removal of the polarisation restrictions that had required financial advisers to offer either independent or tied advice. The move was initially prompted by a 1999 report by the Director of Fair Trading, which found that polarisation had not brought the consumer benefits expected.

The *Financial Services Authority* (see page 255) will have implemented depolarisation by 1 June 2005, following a six-month transitional period. Under the new regime, advisers may offer their advice from the whole of the market or a single provider as before. They may also represent a limited number of providers, and so be multi-tied. In all cases, the most suitable product must be offered.

Customers receive clearer information about the service that the adviser is offering and, for the first time, an indication upfront of the cost. The information is given through two documents: the first, the terms of business, tells the consumer about the range of products on offer, and whether the adviser is tied, multi-tied or independent; the second, a Menu document, explains the cost of the firm's services, including levels of commission, and the different payment methods, including a compulsory fee-paying option from IFAs. The sales commission for each product is compared with the market average.

The FSA expected depolarisation to result in far more choice for consumers. Under the old regime, many consumers had bought products from tied advisers representing just one company. Critics have expressed fears that, under the new regime, independent financial advisers will lose market share as the distinction between the two types of adviser becomes blurred, and that customers will not understand the difference between them, as well as being confused by the amount of paperwork given at the first meeting.

Designated territory

Designated territories are where the regulations, investor guarantees and investor compensation are as good for local funds as they are in the UK. They include the Channel Islands, Isle of Man, Ireland and Luxembourg.

Discount broker

The discount broker sells discounted financial products to the public, often by post and telephone. The discount is in the form of a rebate on some upfront commission, and is possible because the broker gives no advice to the client.

Home income plans

Home income plans are a specific type of equity release plan. Borrowers raise money by taking out a loan on their property and the cash released is used to buy an annuity. The annuity is an investment which provides borrowers with a regular guaranteed income for life. Part of the income pays the interest on the loan and the rest can be used however the borrower chooses.

This type of plan used to be popular, but tax changes, the removal of tax relief on mortgage interest in 1999, and sharp reductions in annuity rates, mean that they are now less popular and are really only suitable for homeowners aged 80 and over.

Home reversion plans

Home reversion plans enable homeowners to release equity in their homes and remain living there rent-free. They are aimed at the elderly who have property but perhaps lack cash. With these plans, an investor company buys a share of your home and pays a tax-free sum to you, based on your life expectancy. Your home is sold when you die or require long-term care, and the investor recovers its share of equity.

The plans are low risk as they have a fixed equity cost. But if you die soon after taking out a plan, it may not offer god value.

Independent financial adviser

An IFA advises consumers on suitable personal finance products across the market place. The firm, unlike the *appointed representative* (see page 231), has independent status. Under the new *depolarisation* (see page 233) regime, it must offer customers the choice of being charged on a fee basis, rather than on a commission.

By early 2005, some IFAs had been offered deals by large financial institutions to switch to being multi-tied financial advisers, and plan to take this up. How many opt to stay independent remains to be seen. How genuinely independent some IFAs ever were is open to question.

Mortgage and property purchases

A mortgage is an arrangement where an asset, typically a property, is used as security on a loan. This means that if, as borrower, you are unable to make the agreed repayments, the lender can sell the property to repay your debt. Just over two-fifths of families in the UK have secured debts (mainly mortgages), with an average balance of £67,662, according to a recent survey by the *Financial Services Authority* (see page 255).

There is now no tax relief on mortgages for the purchase of your home. On 5 April 2000, mortgage interest relief at source (MIRAS) was scrapped in the UK. It had been introduced to encourage people to buy their own homes, which the government no longer sees as so necessary as before. At one stage, MIRAS was as high as 40 per cent, but it diminished more than once before it was abolished.

A tax-efficient way of buying a property remains. Certain post codes are exempt from *stamp duty* (see page 128), a tax that the government levies on purchases of property as well as of shares. These are designated disadvantaged areas, where the property purchase price does not exceed £150,000.

Otherwise, stamp duty is payable. There is no stamp duty on properties priced up to £60,000. If the purchase price is between £60,001 and £250,000, you will pay 1 per cent stamp duty. If the price is from £250,001 to £500,000 you will pay 3 per cent and, above this level, 4 per cent. If you are considering buying a property where the asking price is just above one of these thresholds, it is a good idea to negotiate it down below this level, according to independent financial adviser Chase De Vere. One way to do this is to pay for fixtures and fittings separately, although not more than their value or this could give rise to concerns from the Inland Revenue.

Your mortgage may be repayment, interest-only, or a combination of the two. The repayment mortgage requires you to pay your lender a monthly sum that combines repayment of capital borrowed with interest on the loan. If you make all your payments, the loan will be repaid at the end of the mortgage term.

If you have an interest-only loan, you will pay interest to the lender every month. Only at the end of the term will you pay back the original debt. It will be a lump sum repayment, which you would normally prepare to meet by regularly paying amounts into an *endowment policy* (see page 166) or *pension* (see page 167), or *ISA* (see page 135). The plan is that these payments will build up a sum that, at the end of the savings term, covers your debt.

Various types of mortgage offer cheap rates for a certain period. It may be a fixed rate mortgage, which guarantees the level of monthly payments, a capped rate mortgage, which sets an upper limit, or a discount mortgage, where the rate is set at a margin lower than the lender's standard variable rate for an initial specified period. Another type is a tracker mortgage, where the interest is set at a certain margin above or below the Bank of England's *base rate* (see 'Repo rate', page 153).

An offset mortgage is where the credit that you hold with the lender is offset against what you owe on your mortgage. A variation with some appeal is the current account mortgage, where your deposits immediately reduce the mortgage amount outstanding, but it requires a disciplined approach.

Before you commit yourself to your choice of mortgage, check the lender's booking or arrangement fee, and the fee payable for the compulsory survey of the property. Note if the mortgage has early repayment penalties. This should all be clearly listed in a *key facts* illustration.

Once you own property, you can re-mortgage, or get a second mortgage, perhaps for home improvements or to consolidate other debts. If you lose your job, the state may repay your mortgage interest, but only after a time gap and for a period. Mortgage *protection insurance* is available but at a price and it has limitations. For details, see page 164.

At the time of writing, the average loan-to-value ratio in the UK has been falling, and, in the first half of 2004, only 0.03 per cent of properties were repossessed, the lowest rate since 1973.

CAT mortgage

Some mortgages have **CAT standards** (see page 132), which means that they meet government standards in Charges, Access and Terms. All fees must be disclosed before you take out the mortgage. Interest must be recalculated daily and payments credited without delay. There can be no separate higher lending charge, previously known as a 'mortgage indemnity guarantee'.

On variable rate mortgages, no arrangement fee is allowed and the interest rate must never be more than 2 percent above the Bank of England's **base rate** (see 'Repo rate', page 153). When the base rate declines, the mortgage rate must be adjusted within a month. You should be able to pay off any part of your mortgage at any time without penalty.

On a fixed or capped rate mortgage, the booking fee should be £150 or less, and any redemption charge should be a maximum 1 per cent of the amount owed for every year of the fixed period and not last longer than for the fixed period. There should be no early repayment charge if you move home but stay with the same lender, or once the fixed period is over.

If after you have taken out the mortgage, your lender is no longer able to offer you the CAT terms, it must give you six months' notice. If you get into arrears, interest should be payable at a normal rate and only on the money owed.

National Insurance

National Insurance is a UK social security system that covers various forms of sickness or incapacity, as well as unemployment benefits, widowhood benefits, and the basic pension. It is financed by regular contributions.

Class 1 National Insurance Contributions (NICs) are paid by employees and employers, and are based on the part of the employees' earnings between defined lower and upper earnings limits. Class 2 and Class 4 NICs are paid by the self-employed. Class 3 NICs are voluntary and are paid by low earners.

National Savings and Investments

National Savings and Investments started life in 1861 as the Post Office Savings Bank. As the UK's second largest savings institution, it has more than 26 million customers who have invested more than £66 billion.

The institution promotes secure, sometimes tax-free, government-backed savings products, but the returns tend to be low. Interest rates may be fixed, variable or index-linked. Variable rates are linked to the Bank of England's *base rate* (see 'Repo rate', page 153) while fixed rate products are affected by the performance of the government *bonds* market (see page 71).

You can save in an investment account, receiving a savings book and tiered rates of interest, paid gross, or in the card-based easy access savings account, which replaced the ordinary account in 2004. There are index-linked savings certificates, which are guaranteed to outstrip inflation, as well as fixed interest savings certificates. Both are tax free.

Children's bonus bonds enable you to invest tax free for your child's future. They are available in separate issues and pay a fixed rate of return for five years, and a predetermined bonus on the fifth anniversary. After the five year term, you can cash in the bond, or reinvest until your child is 21, when a final bonus is added.

Guaranteed equity bonds offer stock market growth potential with no risk to capital. Income bonds pay tiered interest at a variable rate into your bank or building society account. For the over-60s, there are pensioners' guaranteed income bonds, available on one-, two- or five-year terms, which provide a guaranteed, fixed-rate monthly gross income and full security of capital.

Fixed rate savings bonds offer guaranteed tiered interest rates with growth or income options for a fixed term, and a 90-day loss of interest for early withdrawal. Capital bonds are a five-year investment, with fixed rising interest rates, and a guaranteed lump sum at the end of the term.

Offshore bank accounts

Offshore bank accounts may not pay a higher rate of interest than onshore, but will enable account holders to delay paying tax. They will not enable tax avoidance because the interest must be disclosed to the Inland Revenue. Depositors domiciled outside the UK may avoid UK tax liability altogether provided that they do not remit the interest to the UK. Cash on deposit can roll up in a larger quantity than if net interest was paid.

Phishing

Phishing is to trick people into revealing their bank account details and passwords, or similar sensitive information by e-mail or via the internet.

The most popular variation is when the fraudsters send you an e-mail announcing that your bank account has problems but if you log onto a given website, they will be resolved. The site may display your bank's logo but it will be a fake. You will be asked for your banking details and, if you provide them, money will be stolen from your account.

Reported cases of phishing have been rising at the rate of 34 per cent a month since July 2004, according to the **Financial Services Authority** (see page 255).

Premium Bonds

Premium Bonds were launched in 1956 and are available from National Savings & Investments. They are an investment that gives savers a chance to win one or more of over 1 million tax-free prizes.

You can buy your Premium Bonds through your post office, online, over the telephone, or by post. The minimum investment is £100, which buys you 100 bonds, all with an equal chance of winning. Within a two-hour period, the computer ERNIE (Electronic Random Number Indicator Equipment) selects random numbers for prizes ranging from £50 to £1 million to be awarded to bondholders, every month. The odds of winning any prize are 24,000 to 1.

Thousands of prizes go unclaimed, mainly because people fail to inform the bond office when they move house. Bondholders can use the online prize checker at www.nsandi.com to see if they have been a winner.

Sandler Review

This was a review of the medium- and long-term financial services savings industry by Ron Sandler, a former chief executive officer of **Lloyd's of London** (see page 173), which the government commissioned in June 2001.

The Sandler Review found that consumers were not saving enough money, and that savings and investment products were insufficiently transparent, which made price comparisons difficult. Products were found not to offer value for money, partly because of the cost of regulation.

Sandler proposed a range of simple regulated products. There was a mutual fund as a simple version of a unit trust and a reformed with-profits product, both in the style of the previously established **stakeholder pension** (see page 168). He said that **ISAs** (see page 135) should be simplified.

He said that *plain English* warnings should be provided, so consumers could buy financial services products without help from an authorised financial adviser. The concept of mis-selling should be clarified, and there should be tax measures aimed at simplifying the regime for retail savings products.

The **Financial Services Authority** (see page 255) welcomed the reform proposals. Industry practitioners have given them a cautious reception. They appreciate less regulation, but feel that new cheap products combined with a focus on commissions may reduce attention to clients' savings needs.

Timeshare

Timeshare is an industry with a mixed reputation. The product has given a lot of people pleasure, but it is often bad value for money and has been associated with deceitful and high-pressure selling. The press has played the part of vigilant commentator over the years, and some of the more unsavoury elements of timeshare have become less prominent.

The product is holiday ownership that gives you the right to use self-catering accommodation on a resort for a week or longer every year. The agreement will extend over a long lease period or in perpetuity. There are 6.2 million owners of timeshares in the world, and 5,300 timeshare resorts, of which 1,400 are in Europe.

As a timeshare owner, you may have a fixed week, which is at the same time every year. There is also a floating system, including points clubs, which gives you a week within a seasonal period, and the ability to choose your week within it. As an owner you can rent, bequeath, or sell your timeshare. You must pay annual maintenance fees which cover cleaning, maintenance and local taxes. You can join an exchange company for an annual fee, which enables you to exchange your timeshare.

There are four exchange companies serving UK citizens, the largest of which is Resorts Condominiums International (RCI), followed by Interval International, and then Dial-an-Exchange and World Resort Exchange. There is also access to Timex, a small, internet-only exchange business operated from Australia. Generally, there is a pecking order of resorts, and the exchange is usually between those of similar quality, in a similar time period.

A good resort should have an owners association or club. Resorts in the summer season are in most demand, as are two-bedroom apartments. The highest rated resorts are described as *gold crown* by RCI or *five star* (also *premium*) by Interval.

If you buy a timeshare in the UK, you have a statutory right under The Timeshare Act 1992 to a minimum 14-day cooling off period in which no deposit may be taken, subject to some exceptions.

If you are a UK citizen, or buy from a UK registered company, you have the same protection buying in other EU countries. If you are not a UK citizen, you have a minimum 10-day cooling off period, with some exceptions. Some non-EU countries have their own laws.

Once you own a timeshare it is very hard to resell it. There are agencies that offer an optimistic resale service but their success rate is very low and not usually revealed.

There are other areas of sharp practice in timeshares. You may buy and find that a resort in which you bought a timeshare has not yet been built, or that, shortly after you have bought, the maintenance fees suddenly double. As an owner, you will often be invited to buy more.

Some developers have promised existing owners to resell their timeshares, not necessarily on the same resort, within a few weeks on condition that they should immediately buy another timeshare from them. But the resale almost never happens and the mark is left holding two timeshares. It was largely for such a fraud through his Tenerife timeshare resorts that John 'Gold finger' Palmer, a self-made businessman, was jailed for eight years in May 2001.

Will

A will is a formal arrangement to distribute your assets after your death. To be valid, it must be in writing, signed by the testator, and witnessed. You can draw up a will yourself, either buying a will kit from the shops, or online, but if you fail to follow the correct procedures or phrase your requirements badly, later attempts by the executors to sort out the confusion may incur substantial legal fees. Most people prefer to use a solicitor or professional will writer, which can involve a quick, not too expensive procedure.

If you do not make a will, your estate will be distributed under the laws of intestacy. The identity of the recipient will depend on such factors as whether you are married. An unmarried partner will receive nothing where there are no children. A spouse, where there are children, may receive only the first £125,000 of the estate and a life interest in the remainder or, in the absence of children, only the first £200,000 and half the rest. The balance would go to others, including parents and siblings of the deceased. If you have no relatives, your assets will go to the Crown.

If your estate is worth more than £263,000 (tax year 2004/5), it will be subject to rules on *inheritance tax* (see page 134).

Wrap account

A wrap account is an online account through which investors may view all their financial assets on one platform, with real-time pricing. These assets can range from cash deposits and bonds to unit trusts and shares. Investors may pay an annual or monthly management fee, but no transaction fees for switching investments within the wrap.

This approach has been popular in the US and Australia, and is now expanding in the UK, where Seven Investment Management launched the first wrap account in 2002.

Quotations, share issues and capital markets

Introduction

A company can issue equities or debt. It may launch a new issue in the primary market, or a subsequent issue in the secondary market. There are rights issues, scrip issues and consolidations.

In this section, we will look at the key terms and issues.

American Depositary Receipts

American Depositary Receipts (ADRs) are US domestic securities that represent ownership of a foreign stock. They are available through brokers that deal in US shares.

The ADRs work out slightly more expensive than the underlying securities, making this market unpopular, but it gives access to proper reporting information and fast news flow.

Unsponsored ADR programmes are when a depositary bank has created ADR facilities without agreement with the non-US issuer. They are declining in number compared with sponsored programmes, in which the issuer works with the bank.

Level 1 ADRs are the most basic sponsored ADR programme. In this case, the issuer is not raising capital in US markets. It will not be listing its ADRs on an exchange or on *NASDAQ* (see page 271). The level 1 ADRs are traded on the over-the-counter market.

Level 11 ADRs are listed on a US securities exchange or quoted on NASDAQ. At this level, they must comply with full registration and reporting requirements of the *Securities & Exchange Commission* (SEC; see page 260).

Level 111 ADRs are created when the issuer has made a public offering of ADRs in the US. This is the most ambitious sponsored programme. The issuer will list the shares on a US exchange or NASDAQ, and must comply with a wide range of SEC requirements.

Some companies raise capital privately in the US by issuing restricted securities under Rule 144A. No SEC review is required.

See 'Global Depositary Receipts' (page 244).

Beauty parade

The beauty parade is when banks compete for the leading role of *book runner* (see page 243) and/or global coordinator in a *new issue* (see page 245), or secondary placing, of securities.

The *pitching* process is an open secret, and the names of the winning banks are often leaked in the press before they are confirmed.

If a candidate bank has an existing relationship with the company, such as being its corporate broker, it may be a stronger candidate.

In larger deals, two banks are typically appointed, and it is important that they are able to work well together. There must be no perceived conflict of interest.

The book runners, once appointed, may be in no hurry to start the process if, for instance, market conditions are poor. When they are ready, they will appoint a syndicate of banks to help place stock with institutions and private clients, and will announce an overall fee structure. Every bank in the syndicate is given a prestigious title such as co-lead manager or co-manager.

The concept of a beauty parade also applies when brokers make competing sales presentations to clients with the aim of winning their business.

Book build

The book build is when a *book runner* (see page 243) and its syndicate build the book of demand for the issue of shares or debt.

The first step is pre-marketing, in which the book runner informs institutions of the deal. Based on their reactions, it fixes a *price range* (see page 246). It ideally needs a couple of big investors to cornerstone the issue.

A *road show* (see page 248) takes place. The book runner will price the deal according to demand, and not fair value. It takes a percentage of money raised, so the higher the issue price, the more it stands to make.

A traditional book build lasts perhaps two to three weeks, or longer in difficult market conditions. The bulk orders tend to come in the last couple of days. If interest is very low, the price may be reduced or the deal cancelled.

The longer the book build, the more time there is for something to go wrong, including share price volatility arising from short selling by hedge funds. Bad press can play havoc with institutional demand, and public relations agencies have the task of managing journalists' perceptions.

Accelerated book build

An accelerated book build arises when a single bank or broker offers a seller's equity stake in a company to institutional investors at a maximum 10 per cent discount to the existing share price.

The deal is sprung as a surprise and it tends to be completed in a day. This avoids exposure to *hedge fund* (see page 158) trading, including *short selling* (see page 159).

Book runner

This is the bank that has charge of structuring and pricing a debt or equity issue, and appointing other banks to the syndicate. It will keep the books.

In a large issue, there will probably be joint book runners, one of which is also global coordinator.

Bought deal

This is when an underwriter or syndicate buys securities from an issuer, and resells them in the market. Because it takes the risk onto its own books, the underwriter will need to have confidence in the deal.

Capitalisation issue

Another term for *scrip issue* (see page 248).

Consolidation

A share price consolidation is a *share split* (see page 249) in reverse. For example, a company may issue one new share for five old ones.

Dual listing

A dual listing is where a company is listed on more than one exchange simultaneously. This can raise extra capital. It increases liquidity of the shares, and enhances corporate visibility. At the time of writing, many consider London to be more attractive for a listing than New York, where the *Sarbanes-Oxley Act* (see page 228) applies.

The *London Stock Exchange* (see page 270) is encouraging companies listed abroad to arrange a secondary listing in London. The *Alternative Investment Market* (see page 262) is also available for this purpose.

Flipping

This is when investors subscribe to shares in a *new issue* (see page 245) and sell them quickly after flotation. It is the same as *staging*.

The practice is prevalent in bull markets, where investors aim to profit from the sharp, probably temporary, rise in the share price that is likely to follow the flotation.

The *book runner* (see page 243) may try to discourage flipping, but will want an element of it to enable liquidity in the stock after it has been issued.

Global Depositary Receipts

Global Depositary Receipts (GDRs) are domestic depositary receipts that allow ownership of a foreign stock. They allow issuers to raise capital in more than one market simultaneously.

European Depositary Receipts (EDRs) are depositary receipts offered mainly or exclusively in Europe.

(See 'American Depositary Receipts', page 241, and 'Dual listing', page 243.)

Introduction

An introduction is the cheapest way in which a company may come to the market. It offers no new shares to investors and raises no new capital.

IPO

This stands for Initial Public Offering. It is the US term for a *new issue* (see page 245) of shares. In 2004, the *London Stock Exchange* (see page 270) attracted 175 IPOs to its main market and the *Alternative Investment Market* (page 262), accounting for 80 per cent of all IPOs in Western Europe. The two markets raised £7.6 billion in new issues, up 64 per cent on 2003.

Lockup

A lockup requires venture capitalists and private equity firms to hold shares in a company for a specific period following a share offering. The lockup is typically for six months or a year, but it could be for longer.

New issue

A new issue (see 'IPO', page 244) brings securities to the market for the first time. With large *equity* (see page 117) or *bond* (see page 71) issues, the normal procedure is through a *book build* (see page 242). In small equity issues, a broker places the shares in a more low-key way.

UK government stocks, known as *gilts* (see 'Bonds' page 71), are sold by auction, which replaced the tender as a favoured sales method in the late 1980s. The auction is planned a year in advance, and includes enough stock to meet the government's financing requirements.

The auction, run by the Debt Management Office, aims to sell all the stock. Bidders will be allocated stock at the price at which they bid or, for small allocations, at an average of accepted bids.

Offer for sale

An offer for sale is a way of issuing shares to the public. A set number of shares are offered for sale to institutional and private investors. The newspapers will publish a prospectus and an application form.

The offer may be at a fixed price. If this is oversubscribed, large allocations may be scaled down, and small allocations may receive especially favourable treatment.

If there is a tender offer, investors are invited to apply for the shares they want and to name the price that they are prepared to pay. A strike price will be set, and anybody who has bid below it will receive no shares.

If an offer for sale is undersubscribed, its underwriters will buy up shares that were not acquired. These will overhang the market, perhaps adversely affecting the share price. When the price is right, the underwriters will sell out.

Pink Sheets

The Pink Sheets is an unvetted list of small US companies whose shares are tradable over-the-counter. It is provided by the National Quotation Bureau.

In the past, some companies listed on the Pink Sheets have turned out to be fraudulent.

Placing

A placing is a way to issue shares. The broker places a company's shares privately with institutions, at least some of which will be its own clients. Retail investors do not usually have a chance to buy.

Brokers often use a placing to launch small companies on the *Alternative Investment Market* (see page 262).

Placing and open offer

This is an open offer to existing shareholders that takes place simultaneously with a *placing* (see previous entry).

This dual approach is used to place shares in already quoted companies. It can be a quicker, more reliable way to raise relatively small sums than a *rights issue* (see page 247), particularly in difficult markets.

The shares are placed provisionally with institutions. It is subject to claw back by shareholders who choose to exercise their right to take up shares under the open offer. Sometimes, key shareholders will undertake to take up some shares.

Premarketing

See 'Book build' (page 242).

Price range

The price range of a securities offering is decided at the premarketing stage (see 'Book build', page 242). The perimeters are those within which the share issue will later be priced. The *book runner* (see page 243) may make the range public, and its *analysts* (see page 65) may publish supportive valuations.

Occasionally, the book runner changes the range, which shows that it had incorrectly anticipated either demand for the shares or market conditions. It usually prices the deal within the range but, in extreme market conditions, there have been some notable exceptions.

Prospectus Directive

The Prospectus Directive is part of the *Financial Services Action Plan* (see page 253), and has the objective of opening up primary markets in equities and bonds throughout Europe. Issuers need only a single approval of their prospectus before marketing the issue throughout Europe. The Directive should increase shareholder bases and reduce costs. It may also create a new market in high-risk start-ups, where investor numbers are limited in individual jurisdictions, but not so much collectively across Europe.

Following implementation of the Directive, large EU issuers will be winners, but non-EU issuers will be losers because they are required to use *International Financial Reporting Standards* (see page 215), according to Mike Duignan, Primary Markets Policy Manager, Financial Services Authority.

UK small companies fear that they will find the cost of complying with the Directive, as with others, disproportionately burdensome. For instance, a company on the *Alternative Investment Market* (see page 262) can no longer make a seamless move to the main market, but must produce a prospectus.

Pump and dump

Pump and dump is a manoeuvre aimed at manipulating investors into buying shares at spiralling prices in order to generate profit for the promoters. In the UK, it could attract a regulatory investigation of potential **market abuse** (see page 258).

The promoters buy stock cheap, typically under nominee names, and then organise a campaign to sell shares in the same company to the public. They may recommend the stock through pseudonymous postings on the bulletin boards of financial websites.

Once the share price has peaked, the promoters will sell their holdings. The share price will tumble, and small investors will rush to sell but too late. The shares will be transferable, if at all, only in small sizes, and at an unfavourable price.

Rights issues

A rights issue is when a company raises capital from shareholders by issuing new shares to them *pro rata* to their existing holdings. For example, in a one for three rights issue, shareholders will have the right to buy one new share for every three they already hold.

The new shares will be cheaper than the existing shares. In difficult markets, the discount might be as high as 40–50 per cent. This is a deeply discounted rights issue, which is more likely to succeed.

Following the issue of rights, the share price will even out slightly to a *pro rata* balance of the old shares and the cheaper new shares issued, which will make it slightly lower than before. In assessing **capital gains tax** (see page 132) the Inland Revenue considers the new shares to have been acquired at the same time as the original shares.

If a UK company wants to raise more than 5 per cent of its existing **market capitalisation** (see page 217), it has no option but to go for a rights issue.

Generally, the rights issue takes more time than a conventional share offering, which makes it risky. Shareholders will already have indicated their commitment, but if the market turns particularly bearish, they may back off. They are under no obligation to participate.

A rights issue can fail, in which case the underwriter, usually a major bank, will take up the rights. It will charge a sometimes hefty fee for the service. Some rights issues are not underwritten, which is a high-risk strategy by the issuer, mitigated perhaps if there are assurances of support from major shareholders.

A rights issue is more likely to go well if institutional investors are convinced that the company will use the cash raised properly. They will assess the plans of the issuer. If it intends to use the cash to pay off debt, they will consider whether it is enough to achieve this. If the issuer plans to use the money to make an acquisition, investors will scrutinise the target company.

If a rights issue is well conceived, it gives shareholders a welcome opportunity to acquire new shares without having to pay a stockbroking commission. Shareholders in an **ISA** or **PEP** (see pages 135 and 137) may take up rights only if they have enough money in the account for the purpose.

Shareholders not interested in a rights issue may sell the rights to which they have not subscribed, which are known as 'nil paid rights'. After they have received the proceeds, and the share price has adjusted down as a result of the rights issue, they will be in a cash neutral position.

The rights not subscribed for are known as the 'rump'. The book runner will later sell them to new investors in an accelerated **book build** (see page 242).

Road show

A road show is the series of meetings in which the **book runner** (see page 243) presents to its clients the company for which it is organising a securities issue.

If the deal is large, the road show visits London, Scotland (where many institutional investors are based), and continental Europe, as well as the US. If it misses an important country, it may use video-conferencing.

Parties likely to speak at the group meetings include corporate financiers and analysts at the book runner, and the issuer's chief executive officer, finance director, and head of corporate communications.

With the biggest clients, categorised as *first tier*, the book runner may establish one-to-one meetings on significant transactions.

Scrip dividends

These are extra shares that a company issues instead of a **dividend** (see page 210). They are worth the same in cash terms. No dealing charges or stamp duty are applicable.

The scrip dividend was popular when companies were not required to pay advance corporation tax on it, but became less so from April 1999, when this tax was abolished.

Scrip issue

A scrip issue, also known as a capitalisation issue, is when free shares are issued to existing shareholders through a transfer within the company's *reserves* (see page 222). The price of the shares is then reduced so that the total new holding is worth exactly the same as the old one. It consists of more shares but they are priced proportionately lower.

Following a three for one scrip issue, one share priced at 100p will be changed into four shares priced at 25p each. A scrip issue is similar, but not identical, to a **share split** (see next entry).

Share split

A share split is when the **nominal value** (see page 218) of a share is split. As a result, the number of shares is multiplied and the share price diluted in proportion.

The split does not involve the accounting procedure involved in a **scrip issue** (see page 248), but the practical effect is the same.

The wording used to describe each differs slightly. A five for one share split means that one share is split into five shares. But in a five for one scrip issue, a share will be split into five in addition to the original share, making six.

A company's share price will often rise on news of a planned share split or scrip issue. Investors prefer to have low-priced shares than high-priced ones. The reverse of a share split is a **consolidation** (see page 243).

Stabilisation

Stabilisation sometimes takes place after a **new issue** (see page 245) of shares. It is when the **book runner** (see page 243) buys shares in the market to counteract selling pressure and so keep the price from declining below the offer price. In the UK, there must be disclosure through a daily notice, and it can last for only 30 days.

Another version of stabilisation is when a country buys and sells its own currency to maintain its value.

Stagging

This is the same as *flipping* (see page 244).

Syndicated loan

This is where a lead bank structures and places a large loan for a single borrower. It leads a syndicate of participating banks. From the borrower's perspective, a syndicated loan is cheap.

Venture capitalist

The venture capitalist (VC) provides funding to small companies in return for part of their share capital. To reduce the risk, the VC prefers to back market-leading companies with experienced management, usually in a growth sector. It looks for a compound annual return of at least 25 per cent, and an exit route of a strategic sale or flotation. Another VC may later provide second-round financing.

Regulation and compliance

Introduction

Following recent high-profile financial failures, financial services firms are anxious to comply with regulatory requirements. In the UK, these are set and enforced by a single regulator, The Financial Services Authority, which was set up by the Financial Services and Markets Act 2000.

In this section, we will examine the key aspects of regulation and compliance. See also Section A, which includes conflicts of interest affecting analysts, and Section O, which covers corporate governance.

Approved person

An approved person is approved by the ***Financial Services Authority*** (see page 255) to perform a controlled function, which involves dealing with customers or their property, or which is likely to exercise significant influence on the firm's regulated activities.

If the FSA thinks that the person is not fit and proper, it can withdraw approval. It will publicise any such withdrawal with reasons on its website. The person may take the FSA to the Financial Services and Markets Tribunal to appeal the decision, paying any required legal fees, and the case will be heard afresh. The hearings are open to the public and have so far attracted press coverage.

Authorisation

A firm that engages in regulated activity, such as dealing or arranging deals in investments in the UK, must be authorised by the *Financial Services Authority* (see page 255) or fall within an exempt category, such as a central bank, failing which it is committing a criminal offence.

Banking regulation

UK banking regulation has been weak, as shown during the banking crisis of 1973–5, when the *Bank of England* (see page 195) was the informal regulator. The *Financial Services Authority* (see page 255) now regulates the banking sector. It is working with the Basel Committee, the European Union and the banking industry to develop its policies for implementing *Basel 2,* the new capital adequacy framework (see 'Basel Accord', page 225).

Big Bang

Big Bang describes the deregulation of the London Stock Market on 27 October 1986. It was part of a broader move to reduce the influence of the *London Stock Exchange* (see page 270) as a private club that controlled its members according to its own rules, and to stop a flight of capital from London.

Following Big Bang, overseas securities firms could for the first time become members of the London Stock Exchange. Trading on the floor of the Exchange was replaced by a screen-based system. Fixed stockbroking commissions and single capacity were abolished.

The jobber who had quoted wholesale share prices to the stockbroker became obsolete, but there was the opportunity to become a broker dealer.

Bundled brokerage and soft commission

Bundled brokerage is where a broker is paid an agreed rate for every transaction and, in return, provides a fund manager with a range of services in addition to basic trade execution.

Soft commission is where a broker pays for goods and services supplied by a third-party fund manager in return for the fund manager agreeing to route a proportion of its business to the broker. Unlike bundled brokerage, soft commission is in return for specific business and it involves third parties.

In April 2003, the Financial Services Authority proposed to limit the range of goods and services that could be bought with commission, and to require fund managers to value goods and services that could be *softed* or *bundled*, and rebate an equivalent amount to their client funds. The industry objected and the regulator gave it until Christmas 2004 to come up with an alternative disclosure regime.

The FSA published draft rules on 31 March 2005, and said it favoured the proposed industry solution. These, together, would limit investment managers' use of dealing commission to the purchase of execution and research services. Investment managers would be required to disclose to customers details of how these commission payments had been spent and what services had been acquired with them. In the relationship between investment managers and brokers should be incentives to secure value for clients in expenditure on execution and research. The playing field in the production of research should be levelled.

Broadly speaking, these measures would introduce greater disclosure into unbundling and ban soft commissions. The regulator was confident that they would improve transparency and management of conflicts of interest. It was to publish the final rules in the third quarter of 2005. The US, unlike the UK, has planned to keep soft commission in a restricted form.

Committee of European Securities Regulators (CESR)

The Committee of European Securities Regulators (CESR) is a trade body with the role of improving coordination among European securities advisers, advising the EU Commission, and working to ensure more consistent and timely legislation in member states.

Financial Action Task Force (FATF)

The Financial Action Task Force (FATF) is an agency set up by the Vienna Convention in 1988, which seeks international compliance with its standards against *money laundering* (see page 259). The agency, which is not a law enforcement body, operates a system of mutual valuation by which FATF member countries check on each other's compliance with its recommendations. In the past, it has used systems of self-assessment.

Members of FATF in May 2004 were Argentina, Australia, Austria, Belgium, Brazil, Canada, Denmark, Finland, France, Germany, Greece, Hong Kong, China, Iceland, Ireland, Italy, Japan, Luxembourg, Mexico, the Netherlands, New Zealand, Norway, Portugal, Russia, Singapore, South Africa, Spain, Sweden, Switzerland, Turkey, the UK, the US, the European Commission, and the Gulf Cooperation Council.

The FATF publicises its blacklist of non-cooperative countries and territories, and has asked financial institutions in its member countries to use verification procedures, described as 'countermeasures', against them. It has acknowledged that not all money laundering is attributable to the banking systems in the blacklisted countries.

After the 11 September 2001 terrorist attacks on New York and Washington, the US tried to coax FATF, of which it was a founding member, to stop focusing on Anglo-Saxon tax havens in its blacklist and give priority to *axis of evil* countries. It brought the ***International Monetary Fund*** and the ***World Bank*** (see pages 149 and 156) into the fight against money laundering. The FATF has claimed some collaboration with these organisations, and its blacklist has been diminishing.

Until early 2004, the future of FATF was in the balance. By May of that year, it was known that its member countries would fund it for another eight years.

Financial Services Act, 1986

The Financial Services Act, 1986 came into force in April 1988. It introduced a regime of self-regulation within a statutory framework, which was based on proposals commissioned by the Government from Professor Jim Gower.

It was an uneasy compromise that did not work properly, as subsequent regulatory scandals proved, but it was a step in the evolution of financial services regulation that has led to today's regime under the ***Financial Services Authority*** (see page 255).

Under the Act, financial services firms and their key staff required approval from the regulators in order to operate. The Securities and Investments Board (SIB), the FSA's predecessor, led the regulatory regime and was directly responsible to the Chancellor of the Exchequer.

The SIB had responsibility for overseeing the regulatory bodies that were called 'self-regulatory organisations'. They included The Securities Association (TSA), which authorised stockbrokers, and the Association of Futures Brokers and Dealers (AFBD). The two later merged and became the Securities and Futures Association (SFA).

Other self-regulatory organisations were the Life Assurance and Unit Trust Regulatory Organisation (LAUTRO), which authorised life assurance firms, and the Financial Investment Managers and Brokers Regulatory Association (FIMBRA). These later merged into the Personal Investment Authority (PIA).

The fifth self-regulatory organisation was the Investment Managers Regulatory Organisation (IMRO), which authorised fund managers. Each self-regulatory organisation had its own rulebook. It had authority only over its own members, but was statutory in all but name.

Financial Services Action Plan (FSAP)

This is a programme that aims to develop a single European market in financial services and includes legislation. It stems from the EU Single Market programme in the early 1990s and aims to create deeper, more liquid capital markets in Europe, a bigger pool of investors, and more choice for issuers and investors.

At the heart of FSAP is the Lamfalussy process. This is a four-level approach to resolve shortcomings in the regulatory and legislative system for securities in Europe. It was outlined in a report of 15 February 2001 by the Committee of Wise Men, chaired by Baron Alexandre Lamfalussy, a former Belgian central banker. The report originally covered only securities, but was later extended to include banking, insurance and pensions.

The first level of the Lamfalussy process consists of legislative acts in the form of Directives, proposed by the EU Commission following consultation, and adopted by the Council and the European Parliament. The Market Abuse Directive was adopted in December 2002, the *Prospectus Directive* (see page 246) in 2003, and the Markets in Financial Instruments in April 2004. Political agreement was reached on the Transparency Directive in May 2004.

The *Committee of European Securities Regulators* (see page 252) is active in carrying out some aspects of Lamfalussy. Regulators from various jurisdictions, including the *Financial Services Authority* (see page 255) in the UK, make proposals through CESR to the Commission.

At the European Council in Lisbon in April 2000, it was agreed that the FSAP should be completed by the end of 2005. By January of that year, 39 of 42 measures, of which about half are legislative, had been completed. Among EU states, Scandinavian countries have been among the fastest to cooperate, and France has caused the most delays.

The FSAP, in conjunction with the *euro* (see page 145) has enabled Europe to move from fragmented markets to a Single Market in just five years, but integration of the retail markets has proved much more difficult than of wholesale markets.

Financial Services Compensation Scheme

The Financial Services Compensation Scheme is a fund of last resort in the UK to which investors have access if their stockbroker defaults.

The Scheme will pay the first £30,000 of any proven claim in full, and 90 per cent of the next £20,000. It will pay a maximum £48,000 in compensation to any single claimant. Overall, the fund will not pay more than £100 million in any one year.

Financial Ombudsman

The Financial Ombudsman Service is an independent organisation that has statutory powers to address and settle individual disputes between consumers and financial services companies.

The Ombudsman can award up to £100,000 in compensation. His decision is binding on the firms, but not on the complainant, who is entitled to take the matter to court.

The service costs £28 million a year to operate and is financed by a levy on the various financial institutions.

Financial Services Authority

The Financial Services Authority is the regulator for financial services in the UK. Under the Financial Services and Markets Act, 2000, it is required to maintain confidence in the UK financial system and promote understanding of it, to secure consumer protection, and to reduce the potential for financial services firms to be used for financial crime.

As a statutory organisation, the FSA is accountable ultimately to the Treasury and Parliament. It answers to a committee of non-executive members, as well as to consumer and practitioner panels, and is funded by the financial businesses that it regulates.

In order to carry on regulated business in the UK a firm must be authorised and key employees must be approved. The FSA will authorise firms only if it is satisfied that they are competent, financially sound, and treat customers fairly. It may give permission for a firm to engage in particular regulated activities. Authorised firms are listed on the FSA's register (available on its website at www.fsa.gov.uk).

The FSA supervises activity and takes action against parties who fail to meet the required standards. It is a private company, but has statutory immunity from being sued for actions taken in its official duties, except where the act or omission was unreasonable or human rights were breached.

Regulatory standards required by the FSA are in two categories. The first is prudential standards, which cover the financial soundness and overall management of the firms. The second is conduct of business regulation, which covers how firms deal with their customers. The FSA does not seek to remove all risk from the market.

As part of its supervisory role, the FSA carries out routine checks of documentation required to be submitted by firms, and visits to firms. The regulator works closely with firms to identify issues and set timetables to resolve problems.

The FSA is the UK listing authority, and approves prospectuses for those companies that plan to start trading their shares on the main market of the London Stock Exchange. It is responsible for the authorisation and supervision of deposit taking, insurance investments and, from late 2004, it has regulated mortgage lending, mortgage advice and general insurance advice, which has put some strain on its resources.

The Authority is given power to write rules, codes and provisions as well as principles. They are all contained in the *FSA Handbook,* which consists of 19 folders. The regime is based more on principles than on rules. The onus is on senior management of authorised firms to make their own decisions, and there is a culture of cooperation with the regulator.

The FSA spends up to two-thirds of its time considering European financial services legislation, and deciding how to implement and integrate these measures into the form of domestic legislation and its own Rulebook.

In general, the FSA is a sophisticated regulator, and its principles-based regime is seen as a flexible alternative to the rules-based approach of the US **Securities & Exchange Commission** (see page 260). However, in common with many public sector employers, it cannot afford to pay its staff as much as they could earn in City firms, and has been criticised for employing people who do not all fully understand the industry that they regulate.

In the view of many commentators, the FSA has a tendency to adopt a rather premature stance against firms that it suspects of breaching its rules and principles and only then set about preparing its case. This process has been known to take up to two years or longer. In early 2005, the regulator started trying to shorten its enforcement procedures.

An appeal in late 2004 by Legal & General against a £1.1 million regulatory fine for alleged mis-selling of endowments may have been a turning point. In January 2005, the Financial Services & Markets Tribunal concluded that the FSA had not proved most of the mis-selling claims and that its process of extrapolating from a sample of alleged mis-sales into a wider customer population had been flawed, although it upheld the finding that the insurer's compliance procedures had been inadequate.

This was not the first tribunal appeal hearing in which the FSA's methods had been criticised. It demonstrated that the regulatory system was self-correcting, as it was designed to be. But there was a widespread perception that Legal & General's appeal had resulted in a pyrrhic victory for the FSA that had weakened its status as a protector of consumer interests.

Many lawyers have concluded that the FSA may take enforcement in one of two directions. It could go down the negotiated settlement route, where it achieved limited success in late 2004, with its £17 million fine imposed on Shell for **market abuse** (see page 258) and breach of the listing rules, and a subsequent £195 million settlement with split cap **investment trust companies** (see 'Investment trusts', page 284).

From the FSA's perspective, a negotiated settlement saves a lot of time and money that would be spent on enforcement action. On the other hand, it does not necessarily act as a deterrent for the industry, given that the parties may admit no liability and the fine may be limited. The FSA's role is not to extract money but to regulate.

Alternatively, the FSA could opt to take on only those relatively few cases where the chances of success were very high. It could adopt a more aggressive approach, and the regulator's current emphasis on cooperative relationships with firms could give way to US-style lawyer-driven negotiations.

Glass-Steagall Act

The Glass-Steagall Act usually now refers to the aspects of the Banking Act, 1933 that legally separated commercial and investment banking. The Act was a reaction to US banking failures. By 1933, more than 11,000 banks had failed or merged, reducing the overall number from 25,000 to 14,000.

The failure was mainly due to unit banking within US states, and a ban on nationwide banking. The Banking Act, 1933 did not address this. It introduced deposit insurance, and a wall between most commercial and investment banking, although commercial banks could continue to underwrite government bonds.

In 1999 Congress passed the Financial Services Modernization Act (also known as the Gramm-Leach-Bliley Act) which finally eliminated the Glass-Steagall separation of commercial and investment banks.

The above should not be confused with the Glass-Steagall Act, 1932, which was bookkeeping-related legislation that enabled the Treasury to balance its account.

Hawala

Hawala is the transferring of money, usually across borders, without physical or electronic funds movement. The *hawaladar* receives cash in one country, and a colleague in another country gives an identical amount, less fees and commissions, to the person specified by the payer.

The system has been used to avoid taxes and duties, and for ***money laundering*** (see page 259), including in conjunction with drug trafficking and terrorism. Hawala may have been the means of funnelling funds to Osama Bin Laden's al-Qaeda network, according to money laundering specialists.

Insider dealing

This is illegal dealing in or related to shares by, or instigated by, parties with knowledge of unpublished, price-sensitive data. It is an offence under the 1993 Criminal Justice Act. Criminal prosecutions are rare but do happen.

In December 2004, a jury at Southwark Crown Court found Asif Butt, a former vice-president of compliance, Credit Suisse First Boston (CSFB), and four co-defendants guilty of conspiracy to commit insider dealing. They had used price-sensitive information to place spread bets. CSFB was not accused of wrong-doing. In January 2005, Butt was jailed for five years and the other four were each given jail sentences ranging from nine months to two years.

Under the ***market abuse*** (see page 258) regime, civil as well as criminal actions for insider dealing are possible.

Lamfalussy process

See *Financial Services Action Plan* (page 253).

Market abuse

Under the Financial Services and Markets Act, the *Financial Services Authority* (see page 255) is able to impose financial penalties for market abuse, which may have involved misuse of information, misleading statements and impressions, or market distortion. It has brought successful actions for all three.

The regime applies to conduct in the regulated financial services industry on or after 1 December 2001. The FSA is able to pursue market abuse, including insider dealing, as a civil case, requiring proof *on the balance of the probabilities,* or as a criminal case, with the much higher standard of *beyond reasonable doubt.* It said that it would not pursue both types in a single case. This flexibility was intended to make it easier to bring an action for *insider dealing* (see page 257), which had previously required the criminal standard of proof.

The UK, like the rest of Europe, is now subject to the Market Abuse Directive, part of the *Financial Services Action Plan* (see page 253). At the time of writing, the FSA expects implementation in the UK by about May 2005, so it should be in force by the time this book is in your hands. Only one country, Lithuania, had met an earlier October 2004 deadline. Because the UK's regime already in place surpasses the Directive's requirements, the changes will not be enormous.

MAD, as it is known, is concerned not just with enforcement, but also with prevention, including issues such as the disclosure of conflicts of interest and directors' dealings. One significant change in the law which will be brought about by implementation of the Directive is the requirement to keep insider *lists* of those who have insider information. It requires enhanced enforcement, including joint investigation and enhanced information sharing. If regulators should not agree, mediation is available.

For shareholders, MAD seeks to understand the expectations of the 'reasonable investor', a concept less familiar in some EU jurisdictions than in the UK. Delays in disclosure must not be detrimental to potential or actual investors. Information must be released to the market in a way that is not just timely but synchronised across jurisdictions.

The financial services industry is concerned about how to cope with the increased record-keeping requirements of MAD. Cross-border implementation of the Directive is seen as certain to lead to inconsistent interpretations. The FSA has taken account of firms' requests for greater regulatory guidance.

Market timing

Market timing is an *arbitrage* (see page 276) technique designed to capitalise on inefficiencies in the way mutual funds value and price their shares. It works because some funds value their shares using stale prices. These may be fixed, for example, at the closing time of an exchange in another time zone, which means that they do not reflect the fair value of underlying securities when the final net asset value (NAV) is calculated.

Late trading occurs when an investor buys or sells securities after the official market has closed but at the closing price. Such an investor can profit from events arising after the market close that will not have been discounted in the closing price. It usually involves collusion between fund managers and market professionals to circumvent a firm's internal procedures on timing of trades.

In December 2003, the US *Securities & Exchange Commission* (see page 260) proposed rules that will require *mutual fund* (see page 287) companies to divulge their market-timing policies in sales material and other documents. The Commission had been investigating their market timing and late trading.

In the same year, the *Financial Services Authority* (see page 255) conducted its own investigation of market timing in the UK. In March 2004, it concluded that market timing had taken place in collective investments but did not appear to have been a major source of detriment to long-term investors. It said that most occurrences were short-lived and fund managers had quickly terminated relationships with clients who tried to time funds.

Markets in Financial Instruments Directive (MiFID)

The Directive is part of the *Financial Services Action Plan* (see page 253), and was formerly known as ISD. MiFID should be implemented in 2007, and will establish EU-wide standards in some main areas of investment business, including client classification and best execution. It extends capital requirements to a wide range of investment firms.

Money laundering

Money laundering is the process that criminals use to conceal the origin and ownership of criminal proceeds in an effort to avoid prosecution. It has been linked to global terrorism and, in geographical terms, particularly with Eastern Europe, parts of Africa and certain offshore jurisdictions.

The process starts with the placement of dirty money into the financial system, and is followed by layering, which consists of financial transactions aimed to separate the proceeds from their criminal origin. The third stage is integration, in which the launderer creates a plausible explanation for the source of the funds.

The financial services industry is an outlet for laundering money. According to the FSA, areas perceived as particularly vulnerable include spread betting, contracts for difference, foreign exchange, and mortgages and pensions.

The UK's anti-money laundering regime was strengthened by the Proceeds of Crime Act, 2002, and firms started submitting more 'Suspicious Activity Reports' to the National Criminal Intelligence Service (NCIS). The firms are required by law to make these reports, which are based on exceptions in patterns of setting up accounts identified by their computer systems.

On 1 March 2004, the scope of money laundering regulations was broadened to cover non-financial-sector firms such as estate agents and lawyers. In the 11 months to November 2004, NCIS received 144,000 reports, against 9,500 in 2003 as a whole, but the police have investigated a negligible number of cases.

If money launderers are caught, they are likely to serve a substantial prison sentence, particularly in the US, although plea bargaining there can enable a reduction in sentence. But nothing yet serves as a deterrent to the major players, who do not usually get caught. Percentage estimates from a variety of sources suggest that money laundering is between 2 and 5 per cent of global GDP, but this is little more than guesswork.

See also *Financial Action Task Force* (page 252) and *Hawala* (page 257).

Securities & Exchange Commission

The Securities & Exchange Commission (SEC) is the government-backed securities regulator in the US. It was established by Congress in 1934 to enforce new securities laws, promote market stability and protect investors.

The SEC has about 3,100 staff spread over 18 offices in four divisions, and a headquarters in Washington, DC. Five Commissioners are appointed each for five years by the President. They meet, usually publicly, to discuss the meaning, amendment, introduction and enforcement of rules and laws.

The corporation finance division checks documents that public companies must file with the SEC, including annual and quarterly filings, and filings related to mergers and acquisitions. The market regulation division seeks to maintain standards for fair, orderly and efficient markets, and the investment management division regulates and supervises investment managers and advisers. The enforcement division investigates potential violations of securities laws, recommends action, either criminal or civil, and negotiates settlements.

Unlike the *Financial Services Authority* (see page 255) in the UK, the SEC has a stringent rules-based regime. Every year, the Commission brings 400–500 civil enforcement actions against individuals and companies in breach of the securities laws. It issues substantial fines, and is open to negotiated settlements.

To promote investor protection, the SEC offers educational material to the public on its website at www.sec.gov. It works closely with Congress, other government agencies, stock exchanges, state securities regulators and private sector organisations.

Serious Fraud Office

The Serious Fraud Office (SFO) is an independent government department with up to 300 permanent staff, and is part of the UK criminal justice system. It started operating in April 1988 and has jurisdiction only over England, Wales and Northern Ireland. It is headed by the Director, Robert Wardle, who is answerable to the Attorney General, appointed by the Prime Minister.

The department investigates and prosecutes serious or complex frauds exceeding around £1 million in value. It selects cases on the basis of various criteria such as whether they have a significant international dimension, give rise to widespread public concern, or are complex and require the input of specialists such as forensic accountants or securities lawyers. Under the Criminal Justice Act, 1987, SFO staff have the power to require a person to assist for the purpose of an investigation.

The SFO has a mixed track record. It has had some high-profile successes, including BCCI, which led to six convictions, the latest in April 1997, and Barlow Clowes, where the principal defendant Peter Clowes was sentenced to 10 years in February 1992. In the Guinness case, following an SFO investigation, the four principal defendants were convicted in September 1990.

The failures have been no less publicised. One was the Blue Arrow trial, which cost tax payers an estimated £40 million. Another was the 1996 indictment of Ian and Kevin Maxwell, sons of Robert Maxwell. They were found not guilty of fraud charges after a trial that had lasted eight months and cost tax payers £25 million. This is one of the cases that led to Government proposals to scrap jury trials in complex fraud cases on the basis that juries do not understand complex fraud. The House of Lords has so far rejected them.

Over the last 10 years, the SFO has maintained a high media profile. More recent cases have included Versailles, Facia, Corporate Services Group and Wickes. The SFO has become better resourced, although critics say that it still does not attract the best investigative staff because it cannot afford to pay private-sector rates.

Cases tend to have a four to five year gestation period, and so annual results are not an accurate barometer of the SFO's output. The number of defendants has been under 80 a year, and typically under 50, so a few successes or failures have varied the annual conviction rate significantly. The cumulative conviction rate is the most reliable figure and it stands at about 70 per cent a year.

Securities exchanges and markets

Introduction

In this section, we will look at securities exchanges and markets. We will cover market makers, electronic trading and settlement. We will define the main stock market indices.

Alternative Investment Market

The Alternative Investment Market (AIM) was created by the **London Stock Exchange** (see page 270) in 1995 to meet the needs of small growing companies.

More than 1,300 companies, with a **market capitalisation** (see page 217) ranging from less than £2 million to more than £100 million, have been admitted to the AIM since it opened in 1995 and, as at December 2004, 999 companies were trading on it. More than £11 billion has been raised.

The AIM is a non-EU regulated market, although it has exchange-regulated market service as *prescribed* within the UK regulatory regime. Disclosure requirements are less rigorous for AIM companies than for their fully listed counterparts. For a full listing, a three-year trading record (with some exceptions) is required and 25 per cent of shares must be in public hands. On the AIM, these rules do not apply.

Because the AIM is a high risk/high reward market, stocks traded on it can be volatile. Every AIM candidate must have a **nominated adviser** (see page 271).

In recent years, the London Stock Exchange has been promoting the AIM to companies abroad as a means for a secondary stock market listing while they retain a main listing in their own country (see 'Dual listing', page 243). Among countries targeted are Benelux, China, Australia, India, Russia and Kazakhstan. The first Chinese company to join AIM was China Wonder on 1 October 2004.

American Stock Exchange

The American Stock Exchange is a securities trading facility in the US that operates as an auction market. Prices are decided by public bids to buy and offers to sell. Order flow is centralised on the trading floor, and investors are ensured the best possible price.

A specialist on the trading floor oversees the trading in every Amex security, bringing together buyers and sellers and helping them to trade with each other.

Back office

The back office is the part of a financial institution that deals with contracts and settlement. It is separated from the sales, research and trading functions.

Baltic Exchange

The Baltic Exchange is a membership organisation in the global maritime marketplace. It provides independent daily shipping information, maintains ship broking standards, and resolves disputes. In April 2004 the membership consisted of 520 companies and 1,600 individuals.

Black Monday

Black Monday happened on 19 October 1987. The US-based *Dow Jones Industrial Average* (see page 268) fell 22.6 per cent on the day, after an overnight decline in Far East stocks, and the UK's *FTSE All-Share index* (see page 265) fell 9.6 per cent and, the following day, a further 11 per cent.

CREST

CREST was set up in 1996 to replace the Stock Exchange's Talisman system, and is a *recognised clearing house* (see page 272). It is a computerised system for settling transactions in UK and international shares, UK government bonds, UK money market instruments, covered warrants and international securities such as Eurobonds.

CREST offers delivery versus payment settlement, with a simultaneous transfer of cash and securities, and an electronic title transfer. It is owned by 70 firms and is operated and administered by CRESTCo Ltd, an independent body.

In September 2000, CRESTCo merged with Euroclear, the world's largest provider of cross-border settlement and related services. In 2004, CREST was settling around 250,000 transactions in more than 9,000 securities each day.

Dead cat bounce

The dead cat bounce is when the *market maker* (see page 270) moves the share price down for a long period, then briefly and sharply up. It generates trading interest.

Euronext

Euronext is the first, and only genuinely multinational, exchange organisation in Europe. It is the result of a merger completed in September 2000 between the Amsterdam, Brussels and Paris stock and derivatives markets. In 2002, LIFFE, the international derivatives exchange, and BVLP, the Portuguese exchange, joined the exchange. Euronext offers a range of integrated services, including the listing of financial instruments, trading in securities and derivatives, clearing through its associates *LCH.Clearnet* (see page 269), market data dissemination and IT solutions and support.

Euronext has created a single market for cash products by making all its listed stocks available on a single trading platform, NSC, cleared through a single system, Clearing 21®, under a single set of market rules. In 2004 Euronext maintained a previously established position as the leading European exchange by value and number of shares traded on its electronic order book. Over the year, 134.5 million share transactions were completed on Euronext's cash markets, representing a 15 per cent turnover rise year on year. Euronext new listings raised €8.5 billion, which was more capital than on any other stock market in Europe over the year.

Euronext.liffe

Euronext.liffe is the international derivatives business of Euronext, comprising the Amsterdam, Brussels, LIFFE, Lisbon and Paris derivatives markets. It has created a single market for derivatives by making all its derivatives products available on a single system, LIFFE CONNECT®.

Indices

Stock market indices measure market performance. The vast majority of indices are an arithmetic mean, which is a simple average of percentage returns for the time period. The older indices may be a geometric mean, which reflects the compound rate of return. Most well known indices are calculated every minute, but many others, including most sector indices, only at the close of each trading day.

To have a market overview, it is helpful to watch more than one index. The major UK indices are produced by FTSE Group, which is jointly owned by the London Stock Exchange and the *Financial Times*. It produces 60,000 indices across global markets. Media such as *The Times* that want to publish its indices receive FTSE index data through subscribing, either through FTSE Group or through a data provider such as Reuters or Bloomberg.

Globally, FTSE has some significant competitors, including the MSCI index from Morgan Stanley for its Global Equity Index series and, in the US, S&P and Dow Jones.

The major indices are described below.

UK

FTSE All-Share index

This is the most comprehensive index of UK stocks and accounts for 98–9 per cent of UK listed companies by ***market capitalisation*** (see page 217). The All-Share is an arithmetic mean of more than 700 securities, comprising the constituents of the FTSE-100, FTSE-250 and FTSE-SmallCap indices (see below for details).

The index is weighted by the market capitalisation of individual companies, which means that the larger the company, the more impact it has on the index's performance. It is split into sub-indices according to industrial sector. Investors who track the index have historically achieved an average 8 per cent real return.

FT Ordinary Share index

The FT Ordinary Share index, known as the FT 30, is a geometric mean, consisting of 30 large companies that represent the breadth of UK industry. The opening index value was 100, from which it started on 1 July 1935, and is now real time. It is unweighted, meaning that component stocks contribute equally, regardless of size.

FTSE-100

The FTSE-100 index is the most widely used measure of the UK stock market. The index started in January 1984 from a base of 1,000. In the last decade it has reached well over the 6,000 level at its height but, in December 2004, was a more modest 4,700. It is updated every 15 seconds.

The index is an arithmetic mean of the 100 largest companies by market capitalisation listed on the London Stock Exchange, which is around 80 per cent of the eligible market. It is capitalisation weighted, meaning that each stock is included proportionately to its market value.

The index is amended quarterly. Companies are ranked by their market cap on the close of the day before an independent committee meets to review the index constituents. For inclusion in the FTSE-100, a company must rank 90th place or above. If an existing FTSE-100 company falls below 110th place, it will move to the FTSE-250 (see below). At the time of writing, the market capitalisation of stocks included in the FTSE-100 ranges from £1.1 trillion to £1.4 billion.

FTSE-250

The FTSE-250 is a real time index created in 1992. It consists of the 250 companies listed on the London Stock Exchange that are largest behind those in the FTSE-100, representing around 18 per cent of the UK stock market capitalisation. Constituent companies have a market capitalisation from £2.5 billion to £200 million.

FTSE UK Style Indices

This index measures performance of value and growth companies within the FTSE-350.

FTSE-350

This real time index is a combination of the FTSE-250 and the FTSE-100. It covers 96.8 per cent of the FTSE All-Share Index.

FTSE-350 Supersector

These give investors 18 real time sector indices for the UK market, derived from the FTSE-350 (above). They were launched by FTSE Group in September 2004, and use a new *Supersector* level of industry classification based on the Industry Classification Benchmark, a collaboration between the FTSE and Dow Jones indices.

These indices are highly tradable. Claimed features include cheaper product management costs, and low tracking errors. There is high average stock liquidity, given an inclusion of large and mid cap stocks, but not of the less liquid small cap stocks.

FTSE-SmallCap

This consists of companies that are too small for the FTSE-350 and represents 2 per cent of the UK market capitalisation.

FTSE-Fledgling index

This consists of about 700 listed companies that are too small to be included in the FTSE All-Share index, but qualify for inclusion in an index. The market capitalisation ranges from about £100 million to £250,000.

The FTSE All-Small index

This consists of the FTSE SmallCap index and the Fledgling index.

FTSE AIM index

This is made up of about 900 companies traded on the **Alternative Investment Market** (see page 262). Constituent companies have a widely varying market capitalisation. At the top end, First Calgary is capitalised at £1.6 billion, and Nelson Resources at £840 million, and at the lowest end, Azure Holdings is capitalised at only £110,000.

FTSE TMT

This index includes companies in technology, media and telecoms. It is designed to minimise exposure to individual large constituents through a tiering system.

FTSE techMARK All-share

This was created in November 1999 and consists of all companies included in the London Stock Exchange's techMARK sector. They are innovative technology companies.

FTSE techMARK 100

This consists of the top 100 companies in the FTSE techMARK All-Share index, excluding the very largest such as Vodafone. It is much more popular than the FTSE techMARK All-share.

Europe

FTSE Eurotop 100

This consists of Europe's 100 most highly capitalised companies. It is the index covered in *The Times*, but there is now a preference for the new *FTSE Eurofirst* index, which better tracks European indices and includes only liquid stocks.

FTSE EuroMid

This index is made up of medium capitalisation pan-European equities.

US

NYSE composite index

This includes all stocks listed on the **New York Stock Exchange** (see page 271) and is weighted by market capitalisation.

Amex composite index

This includes all companies listed on the **American Stock Exchange** (see page 263). It is a weighted index, which was developed with a base of 550 in December 1995.

Wilshire 5000 Total Market
This index includes all stocks of US-headquartered companies for whom price data is available.

Dow Jones Industrial Average
The Dow Jones is widely followed as a measure of the US stock market. It is based on the closing price of 30 companies adjusted by a current average divisor, and is not weighted. Companies included are from a wide range of sectors, excluding transportation and utility.

S&P Composite 500
The S&P Composite Index, known as the S&P 500, is akin to the FTSE-100 in that it is generally considered to be the US large cap index. It is based on 500 stocks listed on the New York Stock Exchange, and is weighted by market capitalisation.

NASDAQ composite index
This includes all domestic and international stocks on the **NASDAQ** (see page 271) stock market. It has a knock-on effect on technology stocks across the world. The index started in February 1971 with a base of 100.

Russell 2000
This measures the performance of 2,000 small quoted companies.

World

MSCI
These are global equity indices, which are the most widely used benchmark by institutional investors. They run across 23 developed and 27 emerging markets and are used by 2,000 organisations.

FTSE Global Equity Index series
The series represents 80–90 per cent of the world's investable stocks.

Social responsibility

FTSE4good
A Socially Responsible Investing (SRI) index series. There are UK and European versions. It covers areas such as environment, human rights, and stakeholder relationship development.

Dow Jones STOXX Sustainability Index
A main competitor to the **FTSE4good** (see previous entry).

International Order Book

The International Order Book, known as IOB, is an electronic order book for trading of liquid overseas securities on the *London Stock Exchange* (see page 270). Some will have graduated from *SEAQ International* (see page 273).

International Petroleum Exchange

This is the largest energy futures and options exchange in Europe. It is a recognised investment exchange, and more than US $2 billion daily in underlying value is traded on it. The Exchange was founded in 1980 and the first contract, for gas oil futures, was launched in 1981. In June 1988, the IPE launched Brent crude futures. In 1997, the IPE started trading its first non-oil contract with the launch of its natural gas futures.

Trades are cleared by *LCH.Clearnet* (see next entry), which acts as a central counterparty, guaranteeing financial performance of contracts.

LCH.Clearnet

LCH.Clearnet is Europe's leading central counterparty clearing house organisation. It provides clearing services for a significant share of all European equity trading, almost all European repo and global cleared interest rate derivative markets, one-third of European exchange-traded futures and options, and the great majority of European commodities markets.

The organisation was created from the merger of Clearnet and the London Clearing House, which aimed to consolidate counterparty clearing house infrastructure in Europe and, ultimately, across the world, with cost benefits to users.

In its business model, LCH.Clearnet offers ownership and governance rights to users and trading platforms, and does not discriminate across its customer base.

London International Financial Futures and Options Exchange

The London International Financial Futures and Options Exchange, also known as LIFFE, was established in 1982 as a financial futures and options exchange. In about 1992, it merged with the London Traded Options Market and, in 1996, with the London Commodity Exchange. In 2002, it became part of *Euronext* (see page 264), where it operates as Euronext.liffe.

London Stock Exchange

The London Stock Exchange is Europe's largest stock exchange and the fourth largest in the world, listing stocks with a total *market capitalisation* (see page 217) of £3.4 trillion. It started in the London coffee houses of the 17th century. In 2000, the LSE transferred its role as UK Listing Authority to the *Financial Services Authority* (see page 255) and, in 2001, it listed on its own Main Market.

The LSE has two primary stock markets, the Main Market and the *Alternative Investment Market* (see page 262). It provides trading platforms such as *SETS* (see page 274) and *SEAQ* (see page 273) used by broking firms globally to buy and sell equities, bonds and derivatives, including covered *warrants* (see page 115). EDX London is the LSE's international equities derivatives exchange.

The Exchange provides news, real time prices and other data to the global financial community. It watches markets for potential *insider dealing* (see page 257), passing on suspicious cases to the Financial Services Authority within days for investigation.

City commentators have criticised the LSE for its overcautious approach and for unwillingness to embrace technological advances. The Exchange has remained independent, but it may not stay that way.

In 2001, merger discussions with Deutsche Borse failed. In December 2004, they re-emerged. The German Exchange put in a £1.3 billion offer which the LSE rejected, sending its shares soaring, and continued negotiations despite some apparent political resistance within Germany. Euronext, the French Exchange, approached the LSE with a view ultimately to making a possible offer and, at the time of writing, the outcome is unresolved.

Market maker

The market maker is a securities firm that is a wholesaler of shares. It deals with *stockbrokers* (see page 128), and makes its money from the *spread* (see page 275). During mandatory market hours, every market maker is required to make a two-way price in at least the normal market size for stocks in which it makes a market. It is required to answer the telephone or resign its status.

The market maker has responsibility towards the companies in whose shares it makes a market, its clients, and to brokers and shareholders. Sometimes a market maker and stockbroker are part of the same firm. If so, *Chinese walls* (see page 68) should separate the two divisions and so prevent conflicts of interest. See also 'Retail service provider' (see page 273).

NASDAQ

The National Association of Securities Dealers Automated Quotation System (NASDAQ) is the second largest US electronic stock market, with about 3,300 stocks listed. It is well regulated and transparent.

The companies have potential for high growth, and cover all areas of business, but the bias is technological. More than 500 *market makers* (see entry above) offer to buy and sell NASDAQ stocks internationally.

New York Stock Exchange

The New York Stock Exchange, founded in 1792, is the world's largest Stock Exchange. It operates a system with brokers, who deal with the investing public, and specialists, who match orders or deal on their own account.

Nominated adviser

The nominated adviser, known as Nomad, advises any company seeking to list on the *Alternative Investment Market* (see page 262) and, following the listing, stays with it. The Nomads are included on a list approved by the *London Stock Exchange* (see page 270).

Nominee accounts

Nominee accounts are where investors have their shares registered in the name of a nominee company but retain beneficial ownership. The account is run by their broker.

Nominee accounts are pooled, which means they hold shares for a number of investors. This enables electronic settlement through *CREST* (see page 263), which is quicker and cheaper than when using traditional paper share certificates. Online brokers sometimes only deal with clients who will use this system.

In nominee accounts there is a risk of fraud, which is why the investor should use a broker with insurance cover. The investor loses shareholder perks and cannot vote at shareholder meetings or receive an annual report and accounts. But *dividends* (see page 210) are paid and regular account statements are provided.

Normal market size

The normal market size is the minimum number of shares in which a *market maker* (see page 270) in a share must quote a firm bid and offer price.

Ofex

Ofex is an independent, self-regulated UK growth market which enables you to buy, sell or follow the prices of its small unlisted companies. Ofex is self-regulated but overseen by the *Financial Services Authority* (see page 255).

Once a trading facility rather than a market, Ofex was always considered reputable. A continual criticism was that its shares were not especially liquid, based on the previous system of a sole *market maker* (see page 270), stock exchange member firm J P Jenkins. In July 2004, a competing market maker system was launched, and quoted prices have become more reliable. For up to a third of Ofex companies, the *spread* (see page 275) has since narrowed by an average 30 per cent.

In October 2004, Ofex Holdings, the AIM-quoted company that owned Ofex, raised £3.1 million in a slightly oversubscribed share placing. The aim was to fund its business expansion, including to overseas markets. The quoted company changed its name to PLUS Markets Group. The founding management left, and the team was strengthened with executives from the London Stock Exchange.

In early 2005, 140 companies were included on Ofex, which in number was second only to the *Alternative Investment Market* (see page 262) among growth markets in Europe, and the combined *market capitalisation* (see page 217) exceeded £1 billion.

Companies typically raise up to about £2 million through share offerings on Ofex. Some raise no new cash but their shares are traded, perhaps to obtain a valuation for acquisition purposes, or to value employee share options. Since Ofex was launched in 1995, about 95 companies have moved to either the AIM or a full listing, which Ofex sees as a vital part of its role.

For investors, Ofex remains a risky market, but at the time of writing it is simplifying its rules and increasing investor protection. You may trade Ofex shares through your stockbroker like other UK markets, thanks to the competing market maker system.

For Ofex stocks, *capital gains tax* (see page 132) taper relief and *inheritance tax* (see page 134) relief may apply. There is also *venture capital trust* (see investment trust, page 284) and *Enterprise Investment Scheme* eligibility (see page 134). More detailed guidance on tax benefits is available directly from Ofex on 020 7553 2000.

Recognised clearing house

The recognised clearing house (RCH) enables swift settlement of a share trade and guarantees it. The contract *is novated,* which means that one party has a contract with the clearing house to sell the shares and another to buy them. The buyer and the seller do not need to liaise. In London, the two RCHs are ***CREST*** (see page 263) and ***LCH.Clearnet*** (see page 269).

Retail service provider

The retail service provider (RSP) is a specialised form of ***market maker*** (see page 270) that provides an automated dealing system to retail intermediaries such as banks and stockbrokers. The RSP evolved after the creation of ***SETS*** (see page 274), with the aim of getting fair prices for retail clients, something which traditional market makers were perceived as having failed to do.

SEAQ

Stock Exchange Automated Quotations (SEAQ) is a quote-driven market for mid-cap stocks listed on the ***London Stock Exchange*** (see page 270) and for the most liquid stocks on the ***Alternative Investment Market*** (see page 262).

Competing ***market makers*** (see page 270) display continuous buying and selling prices throughout the day via more than 100,000 terminals globally. They are required to deal at the prices and in at least the minimum size that they have specified on SEAQ.

The SEAQ screen shows the ***touch*** (see page 275), and it identifies the market makers in the stock.

The ***spread*** (see page 275) is wider on SEAQ than on ***SETS*** (see page 274) because the market makers need to make a profit.

SEAQ International

SEAQ International is a market for some overseas equities traded actively in London. It provides continuous market quotes for more than 160 global securities.

Operating during London market hours, SEAQ International guarantees some liquidity for every buy or sell order. The more liquid securities will graduate to the ***International Order Book*** (see page 269).

SEATS Plus

Seats Plus is the Stock Exchange Alternative Trading Service. It is an electronic trading facility for less liquid securities listed on the ***London Stock Exchange*** (see page 270), and for stocks on the ***Alternative Investment Market*** (see page 262). It combines an order-driven service with competing quotes.

Settlement

Settlement is when investors pay for shares bought and are paid for those sold. Payment is through ***CREST*** (see page 263). Until July 1994, it was done through a 14-day account period at the end of which a net figure stated what the investor was to pay or receive. The cash flow advantage for investors was that early trades did not need to be settled until the entire account period was over.

Subsequently a rolling settlement was introduced, with every transaction a standard 10 business days after it took place, known as T+10. It was later reduced to five-day rolling settlement, or T+5. In February 2001, it became the present standard, which is three-day settlement, or T+3. For nil and fully paid rights, settlement is T+1 (see Section Q, Rights issues, page 247).

Prices quoted on the **London Stock Exchange's** (see page 270) trading services are firm when settlement is the standard T+3, but are negotiable for non-standard settlement. For an on-Exchange trade, the maximum settlement period is T+25 and brokers will sometimes offer this, particularly on trades in volatile or speculative stocks.

Several million shareholders in the UK now hold traditional paper share certificates. They are used in perhaps 15 per cent of UK transactions. The settlement period here remains T+10, which is non-standard.

SETS

The Stock Exchange Electronic Trading Service (SETS) started in early 1997. It is the **London Stock Exchange's** (see page 270) electronic order book used for trading UK FTSE Eurotop 300 securities. This includes all in the FTSE-100, and the most liquid in the FTSE-250.

It is an order-driven market with high transparency. One trader puts in a price at which it will buy, and another a price at which it will sell and, once these are matched by computer, the trade takes place.

There are about 160,000 SETS trades a day, a figure that has been rising. In October 2004, there was a record month in which there were more than 174,000 trades a day; in November the daily figure reached 182,000.

SETSmm

SETSmm was introduced by the **London Stock Exchange** (see page 270) and went live in November 2003. It is an electronic trading service in mid-cap securities with continuous liquidity provision from **market makers** (see page 270). It combines features from both **SETS** (see previous entry) and **SEAQ** (see page 273).

Shaking the tree

Shaking the tree is a tactic to encourage sellers in a rising market. The **market maker** (see page 270) will reduce the share price sharply, and some shareholders will sell out. It will then raise the price again, and some of the recent sellers will repurchase the stock.

Spread

The spread is the difference between the bid and offer price on a security, as quoted by **market makers** (see page 270) and **stockbrokers** (see page 128). *Bid* means the price at which you can sell, and *offer* that at which you can buy. A spread of 8–10 means that you can sell at 8p or buy at 10p.

Suspension

A stock exchange can suspend dealing in a company's shares. It may act on its own initiative, or at the company's request. The likely reason for a suspension is that the issuer failed to explain trading irregularities satisfactorily, or to follow disclosure regulations. Once suspended, a company may or may not return to the market.

Touch

The touch, also known as 'touch price', describes the most competitive buying and selling prices at any given time on **SETS** (see page 274), or on **SEAQ** (see page 273) or **SEAQ International** (see page 273).

Worked principal agreement

A worked principal agreement (WPA) is an *off-the-order book* order. A **London Stock Exchange** (see page 270) member firm will enter a WPA if it has a large order, rather than put it on **SETS** (see page 274) where it would be transparent and so make the market suspicious.

Trading and takeovers

Introduction

To trade shares or other financial instruments is to buy or sell in the short term. For traders, timing is more important than fundamental values, and a system is required. In this section, we will cover the key aspects.

There are a number of other sections relevant to trading. In particular, see Section L, on loss prevention and money management, and Section H, which includes coverage of short selling. See also Section D, on derivatives, Section Q, on new issues, and Sections L, K, V and W, which cover aspects of technical analysis.

Arbitrage

Arbitrage is to seek a profit from price differentials, which are often minute, between the same securities on different markets.

Agency cross trade

An agency cross trade is when a broker buys shares from one or more sellers and transfers them to one or more buyers at the same price. The broker is acting only as agent, and takes a commission.

Black box trading systems

The black box is a computerised trading system that relies on a secret, but often simplistic, method of generating the buy, sell and hold signals. It is sometimes based on *moving averages* (see page 183) crossing. Access to the system is usually expensive.

Correction

This describes a situation where the market moves strongly in one direction then makes a sharp, often short-term, move in the opposite direction. It is a technical analysis term.

Dawn raid

This is when a predator makes a sudden, unexpected purchase of a large number of shares in a target company at the market opening. It is a way to build a stake before making a formal bid.

Directors' dealings

If a director buys or sells a significant number of shares in relation to his or her stake, it can be a signal for investors to follow. If other directors are doing the same, it adds conviction.

A telling period is two months before a company releases its results. This is the last chance for directors to buy or sell shares before they enter the closed period when they are barred from dealing.

All directors' dealings in shares must be reported to the **London Stock Exchange** (see page 270) within five days, and are published by the *Stock Exchange Weekly Intelligence*.

Encryption software

Encryption software includes online brokers among its users. It ensures that information exchanged with clients via the internet is scrambled and so inaccessible by outsiders.

Fantasy share trading

Fantasy or paper share trading is when you go through the procedures required to buy and sell shares but do not commit real money. It is a useful educational experience, but it does not give that feeling in the pit of your stomach that comes when you play hardball with real money.

Front running

Front running is when a broker takes a position in equities to take advantage of a known future position with a foreseeable outcome that his or her firm will take. This illicit practice is also known as 'forward planning'.

the**share**centre:

the one place you need to go for buying and selling shares

At The Share Centre we believe buying Tesco shares should be as easy as buying Tesco's beans. That's why we've made The Share Centre the place to get the information, advice, choice and fair value you need to share in the wealth of the stock market.

We'll share our know-how and experience by giving you practical advice to help you choose the investments that are right for you - and give you that advice free of charge.

We recognise that investing in the stock market isn't right for everyone; after all, it's well understood that share prices, their value and the income from them can go down as well as up and that you might not get back what you originally invested. So if you're not sure whether it's appropriate for you we'd recommend you seek independent financial advice.

But when the time's right for you to invest in the stock market, we're here to help. And the very fact you're reading this book suggests this could be a good time to find out what we can do for you. There's a range of straightforward services available, from investing through a Child Trust Fund account to look after your child's financial future, right up to a self-invested pension account to look after yours.

So when it comes to investing in the stock market, choose The Share Centre. To find out more, or for your free introductory guide to investing, call us on 0870 400 0260.

The Share Centre is a member of the London Stock Exchange and is authorised and regulated by the Financial Services Authority under reference number 146768.
The Share Centre P O Box 2000 Aylesbury Bucks   HP21 8ZB. Registered in England No. 2461949.
Registered office: Oxford House Oxford Road Aylesbury Bucks HP21 8SZ.

thesharecentre:

where buying shares in
Tesco is as easy as buying
a tin of beans in Tesco.

Visit www.share.com or call 0870 400 0260

The Share Centre is a member of the London Stock Exchange and is authorised and regulated by the
Financial Services Authority under reference number 146768.
The Share Centre P O Box 2000 Aylesbury Bucks HP21 8ZB.   Registered in England No. 2461949.
Registered office: Oxford House, Oxford Road, Aylesbury, Bucks HP21 8SZ.

Grey market

This is the market for trading in shares that have not yet reached the official market. One inter-dealer broker, Tullett & Tokyo Liberty, has a lion's share of it.

Spread betting (see page 114) firms sometimes offer a grey market in the form of bets on how new issues of equities will perform in early secondary market trading. This applies only to some large, popular new issues. The take-up of bets is small but the bookmaker's price often achieves disproportionate publicity and has been known to influence institutional take-up of the actual shares.

Level II data

Level II data is enhanced market information which until relatively recently was only available to professional investors. Level II data is real time, and shows bid offer spreads currently available from the *market makers* (see page 270), along with a trade history. It is now offered by some online brokers, such as TD Waterhouse, and is a very useful tool for frequent traders – effectively putting them on a level footing with the professionals.

Livermore, Jesse

Jesse Livermore, born in 1887, was reputedly one of the great stock market speculators. He learnt his trade in the US bucket shop share dealers of the early 1900s, and made a fortune *short selling* (see page 159) in the 1929 stock market crash. He later went bankrupt and, in 1949, shot himself dead.

The *boy wonder*, as he was nicknamed, was a patient trader, and was willing to stay out of the market when it did not feel right. He followed the principle of going with the market flow, and he did not blame the market for losses or question why they had happened. In his view, the share price was never too high to start buying, or too low to start selling.

Livermore's techniques are detailed in a loosely disguised biography, *Reminiscences of a Stock Operator* by Edwin Lefevre, which was first published in 1923 but remains in print today.

Pairs trading

Pairs trading is to take a long position in one stock and a short position in another stock at the same time. *Contracts for difference* (see page 108) are often used for the purpose.

The position is intended to cover both downturns and upturns in the market, so reducing exposure to large-scale market movements. If a position does well, the trader lets the profits run. Conversely, if a position proves a loser, it must be sold.

Pound cost averaging

This is to spread your investment over a period through a series of regular payments. It smoothes out extreme price levels, and can reduce the risk.

Pyramid trading

Pyramid trading is to use profit made from a position in shares or commodities to acquire further positions. If a stock that you have bought rises in value, you will acquire more of it. To reduce the risk, you may take smaller positions than you did the first time. The strategy can be highly profitable in a bull market.

If your shares are declining in value, you may use pyramid trading to average down. You will buy additional shares in the same stock, but more cheaply than before, so reducing the overall average cost.

Scalping

Scalping is to trade securities with the aim of snatching small trading profits frequently, rather than fewer but larger profits. The trader may move in and out of the same stock several times a day. The strategy can be very profitable but it requires watching the market constantly.

Stale bull

This is a trader who has a position in a commodity or similar with a paper profit but which cannot be sold because there are no buyers at the level it is priced.

Stop loss

See page 193.

Takeover

Trading

Actual, rumoured or expected takeover activity can give a boost to the target company's share price. The predator could be making a friendly (see *white knight*, page 283) or hostile move. The most likely target is an underperformer, or a cash-rich company, and the benefit of the move could be synergies that would offer advantages to the combined group.

In many cases, takeover talk comes to nothing, but you can buy shares of apparent targeted companies and, provided you sell before the talk deflates, you can often make a quick profit. You may profitably buy shares in a predatory company, but check that it has a broad acquisition strategy and management experienced in takeovers.

Mechanics

If a takeover is to go ahead, the predator must obtain more than 50 per cent of the target company's voting shares. Once its stake has reached 30 per cent, it must make a formal offer to all shareholders.

If shareholders decline to take up an offer, a buyer can acquire their shares compulsorily if holders of 90 per cent of the voting shares have accepted. The acquirer pays for a target company's shares either with cash or with its own shares.

Under the Companies Act, 1989, anybody acquiring more than 3 per cent of a public company's share capital has to notify the company within five days. If it does not, the *Takeover Panel* (see next entry) will intervene.

A takeover may need approval from the Department of Trade and Industry. In its turn, the DTI can refer a bid to the government-appointed UK Competition Commission or, in multinational takeovers, to the European Competition Commission, either of which can block a bid on competition grounds.

See also *Dawn raid* (page 277). For details of the abolition of *merger accounting*, see 'International Financial Reporting Standards' (page 215).

Takeover Panel

The Takeover Panel is an independent regulatory body with no statutory powers but which is supported by bodies backed by statute. It is widely respected in the City.

The Panel enforces The City Code on Takeovers and Mergers, which has been endorsed by the *Financial Services Authority* (see page 255). It aims to make sure that shareholders in takeover bids are treated equally.

Turtles

The Turtles was a group of futures traders established after commodities trader Richard Dennis and his trading partner Bill Eckhardt had a dispute over whether great traders are born or made. Dennis believed that great traders could be taught from scratch and Eckhardt that ability and genetics mattered most. To test the point, they advertised for novice traders in Chicago with a view to training them and putting them to work.

In early January 1984, 13 trainees, selected from over 1,000 applicants, started trading small accounts. They were called 'The Turtles', based on Dennis's plan to *grow* traders as turtles were grown in Singapore, which he had visited. The Turtles traded liquid futures on US exchanges in Chicago and New York and, over four years, earned an annual compound rate of return of 80 per cent. It went a long way to proving that trainee traders could be taught from scratch.

Trading in the Turtles style is as follows. If the latest securities price is the highest for a given period, you will take a long position, and close any short trades, or if the price is the lowest for the period, you will go short, and close any long trades. The full rules are much more detailed. They are considered not to work as well as they once did.

Vendor placing

This is when the seller of a business has received shares in the acquiring company and sells them to investors for cash.

War chest

This is cash that a company keeps to help make an acquisition, or to protect itself against a hostile takeover.

Whipsaw

A whipsaw is when the price moves in one direction and then quickly in the other, and then back in the first direction. It is a feature of volatile markets.

The trader who has been whipsawed will have taken a position on the first signal, sold out when it reversed, and then resumed his or her first position.

White knight

A white knight is a company that makes a friendly *takeover* (see page 281) offer for a company that a predator has targeted with a hostile takeover.

Unit trusts and similar

Introduction

In this section we will look at unit trusts and comparable funds. Hedge funds are covered in Section H.

Exchange-traded fund

The exchange-traded fund was launched in the UK in April 2000 and is continuously quoted on the London Stock Exchange's extraMARK market. Structurally, it combines elements of a *unit trust* (see page 288) and an *investment trust* (see below).

You can buy your ETF on *margin* (see page 110), and settle using the underlying shares instead of cash. Unlike with a unit trust , there are no set-up charges, and anybody completing a trade will immediately know at what price.

The EFT trades like an ordinary share and it tracks an entire index or sector. It usually pays a *dividend* (see page 210) and its price tends to be at a small discount to net assets. The price can change at any time during stock market opening hours.

Like a unit trust, the EFT can issue an unlimited number of units to meet demand. Because it is based offshore, there is no *stamp duty* (see page 128) on units purchased. You can also sell it *short* (see 'Short selling', page 159).

Investment trust

An investment trust is categorised as an investment company in *The Times*. It is a quoted company that invests in other companies' shares. It pools money from investors but, unlike a *unit trust* (see page 288), it is not categorised as a collective investment scheme as defined by the *Financial Services Authority* (see page 255).

Investors do not necessarily have access to the *Financial Ombudsman* (see page 254) although, if the fund is purchased through a manager-sponsored wrapper product such as a savings scheme or *ISA* (see page 135), or through a financial adviser, there is access to the *Financial Services Compensation Scheme* (see page 254). The trust employs a fund manager, who is answerable to the trust's board of directors.

Investment trusts vary in the type of stocks in which they invest. Some aim to generate high income and others go for capital gain, or a combination of both. Some invest in large blue chip companies and others in small companies, which is riskier. Also contributing to the risk profile is the geographical location: trusts that invest in emerging markets are more speculative than those that stick to Western Europe.

Unlike a unit trust, the investment trust is a *close-ended fund,* which means it cannot issue more shares to meet demand. It can issue new shares on occasion, subject to shareholder approval, but because most investment trusts tend to trade at a discount, this is not common. Unit trusts expand and contract in size according to demand, but investment trusts have a fixed number of shares in issue at any one time, so for every buyer of an investment trust share, there must be a seller. The trust can keep its assets in cash, and has the flexibility of being able to raise cash by borrowing, and so can be highly geared. It can invest in unquoted shares.

Any gains made by an investment trust on shares are not subject to *capital gains tax* (see page 132). But investors may be liable to any CGT if they should sell the trust, subject to their annual exemption allowance (£8,200 in the tax year 2004/5), unless it is sheltered within an *ISA* (see page 135). The trust distributes *dividends* (see page 210) after a 10 per cent income tax deduction.

The share price of an investment trust fluctuates with supply and demand, and according to the value of the net assets. Unless the fund management is considered exceptional, the share price will tend to trade at a discount to *net asset value* (see 'Net Assets', page 218).

Investment trusts, unlike unit trusts, don't have trustees. Instead, they have an independent board of directors to oversee the management of the investment trust. In extreme cases, the board might choose to take the management contract elsewhere. Investment trusts have the flexibility to do this because they are companies in their own right.

Some investment trusts have monthly savings schemes, for which the managers may reduce or waive dealing costs. They are sometimes promoted as a flexible way to repay the capital on a *mortgage* (see page 234), enabling investors to stop and restart contributions without penalty. On balance, investment trusts are slightly riskier than unit trusts because their discount or premium to net assets may vary and they are geared, perhaps to a high level.

Many investment trusts have no initial charge, unlike on a unit trust, and the annual management fee tends to be lower. The *spread* (see page 275) is usually narrower than on unit trusts, although it can be wider. Advertising of investment trusts is allowed only in the case of wrapper products, and investors gain from the cost savings. However, there will be a stockbroker's commission on trades, and buyers must pay *stamp duty* (see page 128). Inclusive of all fees to the investor, investment trusts, in common with unit trusts, often fail to beat the market average.

In November 2004, the Treasury started consultation on whether there should be further regulation of investment trusts. The catalyst was a mis-selling scandal surrounding split capital investment trusts.

Split level investment trust

The split level investment trust is a type of investment trust that has more than one class of share capital. Usually, one type of share is for income and the other for capital gain. The income shares on a split capital investment trust will receive all the income generated by the trust, even when much of it is from other shares.

The trust will have a fixed life span, perhaps seven years, as compared with the open-ended life of other investment trusts. At the end of its life, its remaining assets are distributed among shareholders.

In the bear market from March 2000, split capital investment trusts were highly geared and they saw their share prices plunge. When one fund collapsed in value, others followed suit – a number were linked by cross share holdings in each other. By December 2003, 26 out of around 95 split capital investment trusts were either in liquidation or had suspended dealing. The *Financial Services Authority* (see page 255) found substantial evidence of wrong-doing.

On 24 December 2004, the FSA agreed a final £194 million negotiated settlement with 18 out of 22 of the firms under investigation, with no admission on their part. It was perceived as a climb-down from the £350 million that the FSA had originally demanded, although the four firms that declined to partic-ipate in the settlement together had 30 per cent of the turnover.

Multi-manager funds

Multi-manager funds take the concept of diversification one step further. There are two main types. The first is a *fund of funds,* where a manager invests in a variety of managed funds. The second is a *manager of managers* scheme, where a number of fund managers are each given part of the fund to invest in the stock market.

Fund managers give multi-managers privileged treatment because they invest so much money. Multi-manager funds have recently shown superior investment returns as well as diversifying the portfolio widely. But fund of funds can work out expensive. The fund selectors can negotiate discounts on the annual fees and a waiver of the initial fee for funds in which they invest, but pass on the remaining extra costs to investors. Manager of manager schemes cost less because they instruct managers rather than invest in an existing fund. Either way, performance depends on the skill of the stock selector or selectors.

Mutual fund

This is the most usual kind of collective investment in the US. It is an actively managed fund that pools money from its investors to buy a wide variety of securities.

The *loaded* mutual fund has sales charges, which compensate the commission-paid salespeople who promote and advise on it. The *no-load* fund charges only a management fee.

OEICs

The open end investment trust (OEIC) was launched in the UK in 1997. It is still better known in continental Europe, but many UK institutions have now converted their funds into OEICs with the consent of their investors. They prefer the more modern fund structure.

Like an **investment trust** (see page 284), the OEIC issues shares on the London Stock Exchange, and uses the money so raised to buy shares in other companies. Like a **unit trust** (see page 288), the OEIC is open ended, meaning that the manager may create shares to meet investor demand.

All shares in the OEIC are bought and sold at a single price. Any initial charge is shown separately on your transaction statement. It is more transparent than for unit trusts, which have different buying and selling prices, in which charges are included.

The OEIC is often set up under an umbrella structure that allows easy and cheap switching between funds. Unlike an investment trust, the OEIC always trades at **net asset value per share** (see page 218). It can be held in an **ISA** (see page 135).

Property investment fund

Property investment funds (PIFs) are the planned UK equivalent to real estate investment trusts (REITs) in the US. Over the last 30 years, REITs have outperformed most benchmarks. They came to the US in 1960 and are now popular in Australia, Japan, Hong Kong, France and the Netherlands.

REITS buy and manage properties. They must distribute most of their earnings as dividends to shareholders, but are exempt from income and capital gains tax. In the UK, property stocks do not have this tax exemption and trade at only up to 40 per cent of their net asset value (NAV). But PIFs, like REITs, could trade at about their NAV, according to analysts.

In March 2004, the Labour Government introduced a consultation paper on PIFs. The move caused a big jump in the share prices of UK property companies and the Government has been expected to introduce legislation. It sees PIFs as a way to boost property investment. Previous governments have feared that such products would reduce tax income.

The new funds are expected to have restrictions on gearing, and to be required to invest a proportion of their assets in residential property. This should assist the Government's aim of increasing the supply of affordable rental accommodation. However, some representatives of the property industry have found the government proposals too prescriptive.

Tracker fund

A tracker fund aims not to beat the market but simply to track a popular market index. The fund charges no initial fee to investors because it has no active management, and its annual charge is usually low. The better known the index, the lower the charge tends to be.

Tracker funds attract UK investors who have lost faith in the ability of active fund managers to beat the market average. In bull markets, it can pay off and UK trackers have often outperformed the majority of managed funds, once dealing costs are taken into account. Continental European trackers have done less well. In bear markets, tracker funds have been less successful than many actively managed funds, partly because they have not had the facility to protect their value by holding cash.

Tracker funds may vary in their investment return, even when they are based on the same index. This is due to differences in the tracking method as well as in the fee structure. The closest way in which a fund can replicate the index is to buy every stock in it in proportion to its weighting. A simpler way is to buy representative shares or relevant derivatives.

Unit trust

A unit trust is a collective investment scheme, first launched by M&G in 1931. Like others, it is designed for those who lack the time and, perhaps, the expertise to look after their own investment portfolio. As with *investment trusts* (see page 284), investors will buy into a professionally managed fund with a variety of assets, so diversifying risk and reducing dealing costs. They may invest a lump sum, or regular monthly payments.

The trustees, usually banks or insurance companies, appoint the fund managers, and choose the types and classes of assets in which the fund invests, according to its investment objectives. There are many variations. Some unit trusts invest in large blue chips, others in small companies, some in the UK and others abroad. Investment may be split between shares, bonds and property, usually with a small amount kept in cash to cover any redemption.

The unit trust charges an initial fee of about 5 per cent of the amount invested, most of which goes to the adviser who sells the investment, and an annual fee of about 1 to 2 per cent, covering the costs of running the fund, such as management, administration and brokerage. If there is no initial charge, there may be an exit charge for investors who want to sell within five years. If the fund invests overseas, the fees are higher to cover related costs.

Unlike an investment trust, the unit trust trades at net asset value and is open ended, which means it can issue unlimited units to meet demand. The price is reset usually once a day, based on a reassessment of the trust's value, divided by the number of units in issue. In a few cases it may be reset weekly or less often. Anybody who buys or sells will not know the price until the fund is next revalued.

The maximum offer and minimum bid prices are set as required by the **_Financial Services Authority_** (see page 255). To calculate the maximum offer price, also called the 'creation price', the assets are valued in the trust at their mid-price, at the daily fixed time known as 'valuation point'. The value of any other trust property such as uninvested cash, less expenses, is added to reach the net asset value. Notional dealing costs of buying the portfolio are added, and the total is divided by the number of units in issue. The initial charge is added, and the total is rounded to four figures.

The minimum bid price, also called the 'cancellation price', is reached by a similar process. The portfolio's net asset value is calculated as above, and notional dealing costs of selling the portfolio are deducted, with the total divided by the number of units in issue.

The bid/offer **_spread_** (see page 275) is, at its widest, the difference between the maximum offer and minimum bid prices explained above. It is usually narrower because managers do not pass on all notional dealing costs to investors. The managers may widen the spread when either buyers or sellers predominate.

The trustees will supervise the trust's management and pricing, and will keep a register of investors. They will collect the income on the unit trust on the investor's behalf. For income units, they will pay the income out as a dividend share. For accumulation units, they will reinvest it.

Income paid out from a unit trust is net of 10 per cent income tax. Lower and basic rate tax payers will pay no further tax, and higher rate tax players will pay more tax. ***Capital gains tax*** (see page 132) is payable on profits, subject to the annual exemption.

Unfortunately, the vast majority of unit trusts underperform the market average, after all costs are taken into account. This is where ***tracker funds*** (see page 288) seek to rest their case, but their limitations have paved the way for the current proliferation of ***multi-manager funds*** (see page 286).

Volume and open interest

Introduction

Technicians in particular consider trading volume and open interest significant. In this short section, we will examine the concepts.

Granville, Joseph

Joseph Granville is a US-based technician known for his theory that trading volume drives share price movement. He invented *On balance volume* (see page 185), a widely used technical indicator.

In the 1970s and early 1980s, Granville became famous as a stock market guru. His showman's approach achieved great popularity but, like others in his line of business, he eventually fell from favour.

Open interest

Open interest is the number of options or futures contracts that have not been exercised or delivered, or have not expired, on a given day.

The higher the open interest, the more liquid is the market. Increasing open interest confirms price direction. Open interest only increases when a new buyer and a new seller meet. If one side of a trade is closing an open position, while one is opening a new position, open interest remains unchanged.

Trading patterns can distort the level of open interest. When an options or futures contract starts trading, open interest rises, and when the contract gets close to expiry, it falls.

Volume

Trading volume is useful to confirm price movement, according to technicians. The principle accords with **Dow Theory** (see page 294). The most favoured way to measure volume is by the number of securities traded, with buyers balanced against sellers. Alternative measures are by value of the securities, or by the number of trades.

Volume is shown in a histogram below the price chart, facilitating comparison. The *scale* on the histogram is normally arithmetic (see page 88).

In thin markets, volume may fluctuate too much to give any signal that technicians consider meaningful. The higher the volume, the more weight they see as behind the trend. They prefer to assess volume in busy markets, and often in conjunction with *open interest* (see page 291). In a bull market, rising volume is said to indicate strong commitment from buyers, and in a bear market, strong seller commitment.

If a rally is accompanied by declining volume, or if a price decline is accompanied by rising volume, a trend reversal is likely, according to technicians.

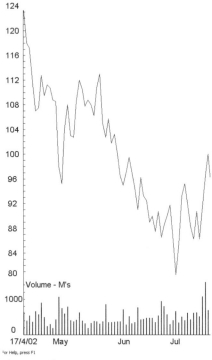

Figure V1 Share price vs volume

Waves, cycles, trends and Dow

Introduction

Waves, cycles, trends and Dow are aspects of technical analysis. Cycle theory emphasises time. Wave theory focuses on patterns and ratios, and has been influenced by Dow Theory.

In this section, we will take a look at how they all work. In particular, I would draw your attention to the trend, which is the most important concept in technical analysis.

Berry cycle

This is a 25–35 year cycle discovered by Brian Berry in 1991. It is based on infrastructure development.

Cycle

A cycle is a regularly recurring price pattern within a specified time period. Technicians use cycles to measure time, often in an attempt to optimise other technical tools. The classic cycle starts low, rises to a high, and then returns to the low, in a smooth movement. Analysts will mark a cycle from one low point to another.

Cycles in financial markets may reflect observable cycles in nature, including seasonal changes, according to technicians. Many cycles of unrelated events are considered synchronised.

However, cycles that may be used for trading financial markets are not always present. Only 23 per cent of price motion is oscillatory, and open to prediction, according to pioneering cycle technician J M Hurst.

Dow Theory

Dow Theory is the basis for modern *trend* (see page 300) theory, which is fundamental to modern technical analysis. Financial journalist Charles Dow started developing it in the late 19th century after he noticed that stocks tended to rise or fall together. He introduced two stock market indices: the Industrial Average, which consisted of 12 blue chip companies, and the Rail Average, which had 20 railroad companies.

William Hamilton, a subsequent editor of the *Wall Street Journal*, developed Dow's findings into an early version of Dow Theory that he published in 1932. Robert Rhea later added structure and refinements.

Dow Theory says that the share price reflects *everything* that is known about a stock. There are three trends in the stock market – primary, secondary and tertiary – and they may all be operating simultaneously.

The *primary trend* represents the broad direction of the market. To assess this is considered the most important aspect of successful speculation. The trend lasts for between one and several years and is in three phases.

The *secondary trend* lasts from about three weeks to three months. It interrupts the primary trend, retracing between one- and two-thirds of the gain or loss.

A *tertiary or minor trend* represents daily fluctuation. It lasts for between one day and three weeks. It is significant only for very short-term traders.

One way in which a trend will end is when the share price fluctuates for two to three weeks within a 5 per cent range, which creates a line. The longer and narrower the line, the more powerful will be the *breakout* (see page 90), which, by definition, will lead to a new trend.

To validate Dow Theory, the line should arise on either or both of the Industrial and the Rail Averages, depending on which version you follow. Together, they convey a stronger message, complementing each other, and which gave the first signal is unimportant.

Volume counts but is a secondary consideration, according to Dow Theory. An overbought market has lower volume on rallies and higher volume on declines. An oversold market has the reverse.

Dow historians claim that the Theory has an impressive track record. Taken over the first half of the 20th century, shares bought on Dow indications beat the market massively, even after trading expenses. More recently, Dow has attracted criticisms that it is out of date. Defensive technicians claim that the Averages have modern equivalents, and note that indices can be traded through *contracts for difference* (see page 108) or *spread betting* (see page 114).

Dow Theory is not infallible, and was never intended to be. Its signals come late, which means that early potential profit is reduced, but so are most false signals.

Elliott Wave Theory

Elliott Wave Theory proposes a structure to financial markets. Ralph Nelson Elliott, a technical analyst, published his original version in 1939. He was influenced by **Dow Theory** (see previous entry).

Elliott died in 1948, but his theory lived on. Today, Elliott Wave Theory is applied to stock market indices as well as, beyond Elliott's original conception, to commodities, currencies and bonds.

The basis of Elliott Wave Theory is that market cycles have an impulse wave of five parts, which reaches new highs, followed by a corrective wave of three parts. Five-wave patterns always develop in the direction of the current degree trend, whether that trend is up or down. The result is an eight-wave cycle. There are nine of these eight-wave cycle degrees, each with its own time span. The largest is the *grand super cycle,* which lasts between 150 and 200 years and consists of five super cycles.

Every super cycle has five cycles, each of which has five primary waves. Every primary wave has five intermediates, each of which lasts about one or two years and has five minors. Every minor lasts between three and five months and breaks up into five minutes. Every minute consists of five minuettes, each of which has five sub-minuettes. The sub-minuette may last only a few hours. These subdivisions represent the fractal nature of price patterns in liquid, traded markets.

The underlying assumption is that every individual wave is both split into smaller ones and belongs to the next larger wave. If a wave precedes a larger advancing wave of which it is part, it subdivides into five waves. If it moves against the direction of this wave, it subdivides into three parts.

The proportional relationship of the waves is linked to **Fibonacci** (see next entry) numbers. Elliott Wave theorists use these numbers to set price objectives, to forecast percentage retracements, and to set time targets following a trend change.

A common complaint about Elliott is that it is difficult to count the waves and some question its validity. This is more due to a lack of understanding of the principle. Elliott Wave Theory is sometimes misunderstood but, used in conjunction with Fibonacci ratios and an understanding of crowd behaviour, can be made into a very powerful tool, according to Steven W Poser, former chief US technical analyst at Deutsche Bank, and author of *Applying Elliott Wave Theory Profitably.*

Figure W1   Elliott wave movement

Fibonacci

Leonardo Fibonacci was a mathematician born in about 1170, who is best remembered for his sequence of numbers, also used before his time in the Ancient World. In his book *Liber Abaci*, Fibonacci explained that his numbers were based on how a population of rabbits could develop numerically if one pair gave birth to another.

The numbers start with 1, 1, 2, 3, 5, 8 and 13. Any two numbers added together are equal to the next highest number (for example, $5 + 8 = 13$). The sequence continues in this vein to infinity.

After the first four numbers, any number's ratio to its next highest is about 0.618, which mathematicians call 'phi'. The ratio of any number to its next lowest is about 1.618. Alternative numbers have a ratio of 2.168, or its inverse, 0.382. The higher the number, the more precisely the ratios are attained.

Followers of Fibonacci claim that a logarithmic spiral based on the Fibonacci ratio of 0.618 or 1.618 is constant in all areas of nature. It is created from arcs drawn between the corners of squares within a *golden rectangle* constructed from a *golden mean*. The squares have infinite capacity for expansion and contraction. The sunflower demonstrates the spiral in action. It has 89 curves, which is a Fibonacci number. Of the curves, 34 turn in one direction and 55 in another, and both are Fibonacci numbers.

In financial markets, Fibonacci retracements are the most popular application of the Fibonacci numbers. These are constructed initially from a ***trend line*** (see page 301) drawn between two extreme points, with horizontal lines intersecting it at Fibonacci retracement levels, 0 per cent, 23.6 per cent, 38.2 per cent, 50 per cent, 61.8 per cent and 100 per cent, and further. After the price has risen or fallen substantially, it will often retrace a large part of the move, finding ***support and resistance*** (see page 299) at Fibonacci levels.

Fibonacci fan lines are similarly based on a trend line between two extreme points. A vertical line through the second point is visualised, and trend lines drawn from the first point will pass through it at Fibonacci levels of 38.2 per cent, 50 per cent and 61.8 per cent. These are support and resistance levels. The fan lines may be combined with the retracements to emphasise the levels.

Fibonacci arcs are three in number, centred on a second extreme point to which a trend line extends from a first one. The arcs intersect the trend line at Fibonacci levels of 38.2 per cent, 50 per cent and 61.8 per cent. Fibonacci Time Zones, another variation, are vertical lines spaced in line with Fibonacci numbers.

Gann, William D

William D Gann was a US-based stock trader and mathematician (1878–1955). He pioneered Gann Theory, a form of technical analysis based on mathematical principles and their relationship with the market.

A basis of Gann Theory is that price and time are proportionally related. For example, two units of price might match one unit of time. To find tops and bottoms, Gann squared price and time, representing the relationship as fan lines. Like Elliott, he considered trading volume significant. He paid special attention to highs and lows.

To determine prospective ***support and resistance*** (see page 299), Gann invented the Cardinal Square. It has numbers in rows and columns, which intersect within the square. The numbers included in the vertical and horizontal lines passing through the centre of the square are known as the Cardinal Cross and are the most likely support and resistance levels, followed by the diagonal lines through the centre.

Certain numbers recur in the movement as well as price of shares, and in dates, according to Gann Theory. The number 7 is a milestone because it represented the days in the week, and Gann noted multiples of it such as 49. A year, 18 months and 2 years are seen as significant, as are the anniversaries of highs and lows.

Percentage numbers play no less of a part. If a share price rises 100 per cent, the move is probably complete, and any fall will be thwarted at the 0 per cent level, according to Gann Theory. Other significant percentages include 50 per cent, followed by multiples of 8 such as 12.5 per cent, 25 per cent, 37.5 per cent, 62.5 per cent and 75 per cent, and multiples of 3 such as 33 per cent and 67 per cent.

Gann split the 360 degrees in a circle. Turns of 30, 90 or 120 degrees indicate a potential change in market conditions. The degrees may be applied to the share price in pence, making 90p or 360p *natural* levels of support and resistance. Gann's most significant trend line is at 45 degrees, which represents an absolute balance between price and time. If prices are above the line, there is a bull market, and if below it, a bear market. To breach the line means to reverse the trend.

Gann has his modern-day disciples, including promoters of expensive courses based on his trading methods. Many critics say that Gann was more successful at selling books and courses than trading. It did not help his reputation that he had studied Indian sidereal astrology in India and included astrological symbols on his charts.

Harmonicity principle

This principle holds that two cycles in sequence are related by a consistent number. It is usually two, indicating that one cycle will be followed by another of half, or double, the length.

January barometer

This is the theory that if share prices rise in January, they will end the year higher and, if they fall in January, will end lower.

Juglar cycle

This is a 7–11 year cycle of economic activity reflecting investment in machinery and equipment. It was discovered by Clement Juglar in 1862.

Kitchen wave

This is a 3-5 year cycle of economic activity, based on investment in inventories, especially for consumer goods. It was discovered by Joseph Kitchen in 1923.

Kondratieff wave

This is an approximately 54-year super-cycle that technicians may apply to most stock and commodity markets. It was discovered by Nikolai D Kondratieff, a Russian economist in the 1920s, based on research into capitalism back to the Industrial Revolution of 1789.

Kondratieff found that capitalism worked well as a model: speculation expanded resources and caused inflation, which self-corrected to enable new growth. His conclusions did not please the Stalinist regime and he was sent to a Siberian labour camp where he died at the age of 40.

Earlier this century, Austrian economist Joseph Schumpeter described the Kondratieff wave as the single most important tool in economic prognostication, but some have found little evidence that it works, particularly in the post-World War II economy.

Kuznets cycle

This is a 15–20 year cycle of economic activity, based on investment in building construction and housing. It was discovered by Simon Kuznets, a 20th century economist born in Russia.

Left or right translation

Left or right translation describes the inclination bias of a cycle peak.

If the cycle peak moves more to the left of the ideal level, it is a left translation, which is a bearish signal. The price is below the ideal, indicating a decline in the long-term trend.

If the peak moves to the right of the ideal level, it is a right translation, which is a bullish signal. The price is above the ideal, which indicates a rising long-term trend.

Presidential cycle

This is a cycle based around the four-yearly US presidential election. As Election Day approaches, stock prices are claimed to rise in anticipation of a strong economy, but subsequently the first three years will be weak.

Proportionality principle

This means that, the longer a cycle is, the wider is its amplitude (which measures height).

Return line

See 'Trend channel' (page 300).

Strauss and How cycle

This cycle arises every 80 to 90 years, and includes four generations, each with a distinct personality. It was formulated by US futurists William Strauss and Neil How.

Summation principle

This is the principle that all price movement consists of cycles added together.

Support and resistance

Support and resistance lines are the boundaries of a trading range on a chart. The support level is the *lowest* point to which a share or index may fall within a trend. Here the buyers move in. The resistance level is the *highest* point to which a share or index may rise within a trend. Here, sellers become prominent.

Once the share price has risen above the resistance level or fallen below the support level, it has *penetrated* the trend. The longer that a support or resistance line has proved impenetrable, the stronger it is considered. It is also held to be a sign of strength if the line is recent, or if it is a memorable round number, a high or low, or is accompanied by heavy volume.

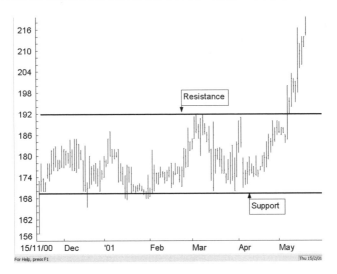

Figure W2   Support and resistance

Synchronicity principle

This is that cycles and waves have a tendency to turn together.

Trend

Technical analysts believe that a share price moves in trends, on the same principle as business trends. A trend is believed to be in force until it is unequivo-
cally broken. If the trend is steadily up, investors should buy, and if it is down,
they should sell.

A trend may be in many time frames simultaneously, including but not
confined to, short, medium and long, and these can overlap. If the short-term
trend is moving in the direction of a longer-term one, it is seen as more likely to
endure.

Trend channel

This shows share price fluctuation between a ***trend line*** (see next entry) and a
parallel line known as the 'return line'. Some technical analysts buy and sell
stocks only within the channel. They divide it in the centre by a horizontal line.
When the share price moves above this line, they buy, and when it slips below
it, they sell.

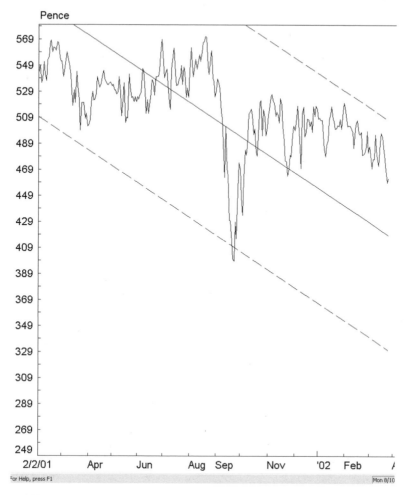

Figure W3 Trend lines and trend channels

Trend line

The trend line shows the rate at which a price changes during a trend. It can be a useful signal of a slowing trend.

To form the trend line, a valid trend must exist, and you must be able to draw a straight line on it. The price needs to *respect* the line, ie to almost or completely touch it at three points in order to validate it. If it respects only two points, the trend line will be tentative.

If you are measuring an uptrend, you must draw your trend line through the lows. If you are measuring a downtrend, you must draw it through the highs.

Exclusions

Introduction

'Ex-' denotes exclusion from the share price. There is a cut-off point at which the price is adjusted to reflect the exclusion, and it is then called 'ex'. In this section, we shall look briefly at the main variations.

XA

This is ex-all. It describes the share price after a *capitalisation issue* (see 'Scrip issue' page 248), dividend distribution, and *rights issue* (see page 247).

XC

This means ex-capitalisation issue. The XC share price has been revised down after a capitalisation issue, also known as a *scrip issue* (see page 248).

XD

This stands for ex-dividend. When the shares become XD, the latest dividend is excluded. Because shareholders before the cut-off date are entitled to the dividend, the share price will be reduced accordingly.

XR

This denotes ex-rights. The XR share price is adjusted down after the cut-off date to reflect the fact that the shares no longer include rights issue participation.

Your portfolio and the cost of capital

Introduction

Your portfolio represents the spread of your investments. In this section we will look at how it can be made up and valued, particularly in relation to Modern Portfolio theory.

Arithmetic mean

This is the average return for investors over a fixed period. It is the sum of the returns in a period, divided by the number of years included. Expressed as a percentage, this is the arithmetic mean. (See 'Geometric mean', page 309.)

Benchmark

A benchmark is a standard against which to measure performance. For investments, it is usually a *market index* (see 'Indices', page 264).

Beta

An equity beta measures the sensitivity of a firm's share price to movements in the general stock market. In more technical language, this is *systematic risk* (see page 313) exposure. Beta does not measure share price volatility that is not market-linked. It is used in the *Capital Asset Pricing Model* (see page 304).

If a stock has a beta of 1.00, it indicates that the share price has historically changed in line with changes in the value of the stock market. With a beta of 0.50, the change in share price has been half as much as the change in the overall stock market and, at 2.00, twice as much.

The higher the systematic risk, the higher the beta. *Cyclical companies* (see page 121) such as house builders have higher betas because earnings are linked to the economic cycle. The higher the level of a company's operational *gearing* (see page 309), the higher the systematic risk, and the higher the beta, given that the fixed costs will not decline if turnover falls due to market conditions.

The beta estimate is not always as reliable as we would like because it is based on historical data, and the characteristics of the business may change. Beta is often measured over five years, which is a balance between having enough observations for reliability but not so many that you are relying on out-of-date data.

Beta is measured by a regression of share prices against stock market indices. Errors based on imperfect measurement are addressed by a Bayesian adjustment, in which beta estimates are weighted towards 1. For details of beta data providers, see Appendix 1, Equities.

Capital Asset Pricing Model (CAPM)

The Capital Asset Pricing Model is the most accepted model for evaluating *systematic risk* (see page 313) and calculating the *cost of equity* (see 'Weighted average cost of capital', page 313). It was invented by Nobel Prize laureate Bill Sharpe.

The CAPM (pronounced *Capem*), as it is called, finds the required rate of return on a stock by comparing its performance with the market. It expresses this return as equal to the *risk-free rate* of return (see page 312) plus the product of the *equity risk premium* (see page 308) and the stock's *beta* (see previous entry).

CAPM Formula

Cost of equity = risk free rate + (equity market risk premium × equity beta).

On the CAPM model, the well diversified portfolio will see its required rate of return rise as systematic risk increases. This is shown on the *Security market line* (see page 312). The CAPM stipulates that the market does not reward investors for taking unsystematic (ie, company-specific) risk because it can be eliminated through diversification. This is in keeping with *Modern portfolio theory* (see page 310), from which the CAPM originates.

The CAPM is a theoretical model. It assumes no taxes or transaction costs, and that investors see the same investment opportunities, and have a shared time horizon and expectation of return. It assumes that investors may borrow and lend at the risk-free rate of return and that investments are properly and instantly priced according to risk levels, and that market information is made available instantly and free of charge to all investors.

In the real world, the theory is used extensively, and its limitations are acknowledged.

Alternatives to CAPM

Alternatives to CAPM are not widely used but can serve as a useful check. They are based, like CAPM, mainly on historic data.

Arbitrage Pricing Theory (APT), like CAPM, measures the required rate of return as a function of the risk-free interest rate plus a premium for risk. The difference is that CAPM has the broad stock market as its only risk premium and APT has multiple factors, not always identified, which will include the stock market but possibly general factors such as interest rates and **Gross National Product** (see page 149). Critics find the APT opaque as well as complex.

The Fama French Three Factor model has a measure similar to beta, but also considers how the company size impacts on cost of equity, and the ratio of book value to market value.

Deductive models such as the **Dividend discount model** (see page 306) are used as an alternative route to finding the cost of equity. Another is the stochastic options-pricing model, which can only be used if the shares also have traded options. It calculates the cost of capital based on **Black-Scholes** (see page 107), and uses implied volatility instead of beta. Unlike CAPM and APT, it uses both systematic and unsystematic risk in the rate of return.

Capital market equilibrium

This says that the required return on an asset must be equal to its expected return.

Cash extraction

This is when you sell your equity portfolio and put most of the proceeds in a high-interest cash account, and the rest perhaps in a highly geared investment such as covered **warrants** (see page 115).

Discounted cash flow analysis

Discounted cash flow (DCF) analysis translates future cash flow into a present value. It starts with the net operating cash flow (NOCF). You will find this by taking the company's earnings before interest and tax. Deduct **corporation tax** (see page 132) paid and capital expenditure. Add depreciation and amortisation, which do not represent movements in cash. Add or subtract the change in working capital, including movements in stock, in debtors and creditors, and in cash or cash equivalents. (See Section N, page 201 for accounting terms.)

This is the year's NOCF. It can be calculated for future years, and reduced in value to present day terms by a discount rate. **Weighted average cost of capital** (see page 313) is often used as the discount rate. If the task is to value only equity, analysts may use the flow-to-equity method, which discounts cash flows to equity, after interest and taxes, at the cost of equity (most often derived using the **CAPM** see page 304). Alternatively, the adjusted present value approach discounts operating cash flow separately from that of the benefits from the tax shields provided by corporate debt, and then combines the two.

Cash flows are likely to continue beyond the period over which it is possible to accurately assess cash generation. This can be modelled through the use of terminal value. Present and future modelled cash flows, together with the terminal value, make up the net present value (NPV) once they have been discounted at an appropriate cost of capital. The number of years over which these cash flows are discounted, and the actual future NOCF forecasts, will influence the NPV. Besides this, the larger the discount rate used, the smaller is the NPV of future cash flows.

To make an accurate forecasting scenario more likely, **analysts** (see page 65) may plot DCF models using different discount rates and different cash generation scenarios to present alternative valuations. DCF analysis tries to predict the future and this is not always possible. It is not the fault of DCF analysis that analysts have abused it in an effort to promote favoured companies, a practice that regulatory trends have now made more difficult. DCF analysis is considered the most useful valuation tool.

Dividend discount model

This is a method of valuing a share largely based on the present value of future **dividends** (see page 210) that a company is expected to pay its shareholders.

If the dividend is expected to remain constant, the share is valued at the dividend divided by the required rate of return. If the dividend is expected to grow constantly every year (a big assumption), the share is valued at the next expected dividend divided by the required rate of return, less the dividend's growth rate. This is known as the Gordon growth model.

If dividend growth is variable, the model is applied in a more complex way that involves multi-stages using phases of differing dividend growth (based on even more assumptions), and discounting dividends to their present value.

In all cases, there is difficulty in finding the most suitable rate of return. The dividend discount model works better for stocks that pay high dividends, such as in the utilities sector, than for high growth stocks, particularly where they don't pay dividends.

EBITDA

EBITDA is earnings before interest, tax, depreciation and amortisation (see Section N, page 201 for the accounting terms).

In capital-intensive companies with huge borrowings, such as in the telecoms sector, EBITDA arguably presents a more realistic valuation than conventional earnings, which are calculated after interest and tax. But EBITDA is not recognised by accountants. Because it excludes tax, you cannot compare stocks on this valuation across international borders when the respective countries' tax regimes differ.

Analysts had used EBITDA to value WorldCom, a US telecoms group which, in June 2002, was to reveal a US $11 billion accounting fraud. A month later, the company made a Chapter 11 bankruptcy protection filing. Analysts then stopped using EBITDA as a standalone stock valuation tool. See also 'Enterprise multiple' (page 308).

Economic profit

Economic profit is net operating profit after tax, less weighted average capital multiplied by capital invested in the business. It has been promoted under the name 'Economic Value Added', or EVA, a brand name developed by Stern Stewart & Co, a global management consulting firm.

Economic profit arises only in projects where all cash flow, discounted back to the present value, is positive (see 'Discounted cash flow analysis', page 305). Companies use it as a measure of management performance, and it may be linked to management incentives. Critics say that it discourages investment and best fits long-established and capital-intensive businesses.

Efficient Frontier

The Efficient Frontier consists of the portfolios with the highest return at all possible levels.

It appears as an upward sloping curve on a graph that shows average rates of return for a number of securities against their standard deviation. A portfolio along the Efficient Frontier, and not below it, will give the best return for any level of standard deviation.

The less correlated the risks of the securities in a portfolio, the lower the combined standard deviation for a given rate of return. This is a practical implementation of **Modern portfolio theory** (see page 310), and demonstrates the value of diversification.

Efficient market theory

The efficient market theory finds that securities prices at any given time entirely reflect all information available that could influence their movement. There are three levels of strength:

1. The weakest form holds that securities prices reflect past price movements and data. This would make technical analysis unable to add insight into future movements.
2. The semi-strong form goes further and says that prices also reflect published information. This would make fundamental analysis unable to add insight into future movements.
3. In its strongest form, the theory says that price reflects private as well as public information. On this basis, it would be impossible to beat the market except by chance (see 'Random walk theory', page 312). But you could still make money from an upward movement in the stock market over time.

The efficient market theory remains subject to dispute. Some successful investors, including Omaha-based billionaire *Warren Buffett* (see page 120), have rejected the theory. Many academics have upheld it, particularly in its weakest form. They cite empirical studies showing that technical analysis has generally failed to predict share prices, and that some fund managers have performed well one year and badly the next.

Enterprise multiple

This is *enterprise value* (see next entry) divided by *EBITDA* (see page 307).

Enterprise value

Enterprise value is a company's market capitalisation plus debt. It is the total value for all equity and debt investors.

Equity risk premium

The equity risk premium is the difference between the risk-free rate of return and the average stock market return. Investors require it on equities to compensate for the risk associated with investing in equities in general, and it is used in the *Capital Asset Pricing Model* (see page 304).

Ethical investment

This is when principles guide where the investor puts money, or how shareholder rights are exercised.

Ethical funds vary in their approach. Some passively exclude perceived unethical sectors of the stock market such as pharmaceuticals. Others actively select companies with ethically positive activities such as a strong environmental policy.

How far an ethical fund's performance is handicapped by the restrictions, if at all, is a subject of debate.

Fisher equation

The Fisher equation is sometimes used as a shorthand way to convert nominal into real rates of return, or the reverse. The formula is:

$$(1+r) = (1+i) \times (1+p)$$

where:
r = nominal risk-free rate of interest
i = real risk-free rate of interest
p = projected rate of inflation.

Free cash flow

Definitions of free cash flow vary slightly. It is basically operating profit, with depreciation added back, and adjusted for various cash flows, including changes in working capital, taxation and buying and selling of fixed assets (see Section N, page 201 for the accounting terms).

Gearing

Gearing represents a company's level of borrowing, or the relationship between debt and equity in its capital structure. It is most commonly expressed as debt capital as a percentage of total capital funding (ie, of debt capital plus equity capital).

The higher the gearing, the greater the risk but, as a rule of thumb, more than 50 per cent is a potential cause for concern.

Operational gearing

Operational gearing is the level of fixed assets as a proportion of total costs in a company.

Geometric mean

This is the average annual return for investors over a period. It is the square root of the ratio of the final to the initial value in the data set, expressed as a percentage. The result is either smaller than the **_arithmetic mean_** (see page 303) or, if all members of the data set are equal, equal to it.

Internal rate of return

This is the discount rate required to make the **_net present value_** (see page 311) of cash flows zero. It is more rigid than net present value in that it cannot incorporate variable discount rates.

Investment club

An investment club enables investors to share the risks and the returns of investing. It can serve beginners well. If club members share a variety of professional backgrounds, it may add extra skills and experience to the stock selection procedure, although this can also end in conflicts. Some investment clubs have made serious money but many peter out.

The club is most easily run as a partnership. It requires a treasurer, who issues monthly financial statements, and a chairman and secretary. It should hold regular meetings, which may have a strong social element, maybe in a pub. The club's investments will be financed by regular contributions from each member, perhaps £30 a month, into an investment fund. Members should be entitled to give notice and to sell their stake.

In the UK, Proshare (www.proshare.org), a non-profit-making organisation that encourages wider share ownership, has offered advice and encouragement in setting up investment clubs, and these proliferated across the country during the roaring bull market until March 2000.

Modern portfolio theory

Modern portfolio theory is about how to find a portfolio with a maximum long-term rate of return for a given level of risk. It was developed by Harry Markowitz and has been put into practice by the **_Capital Asset Pricing Model_** (see page 304) developed by William Sharpe.

The theory links risk with systematic volatility; that is to say, volatility that cannot be diversified, even within a portfolio of investments, because the systematic risks are all correlated.

Stocks with individually high **_standard deviations_** (see page 313), and that may be very risky in themselves, may actually turn out to have low systematic volatility when included in a portfolio of stocks because much of the volatility may be diversifiable.

Modigliani-Miller

This theorem, published in 1958 by Nobel prize-winning Franco Modigliani and Merton Miller, has become the basis for modern thinking on capital structure. It says that a company's market value depends on anticipated cash flows and cost of capital and is independent of how the company is financed. The conclusion is that it makes no difference whether the company raises capital by issuing shares or debt, or in any combination.

Debt costs less than equity, and so the more of it there is the cheaper the funding. But as a company increases its gearing by raising its debt, its debt and equity become riskier and so more expensive, according to the theorem. The *beta* (see page 303) increases as a result of the gearing, and when included in the *Capital Asset Pricing Model* (see page 304), leads to a higher required rate of return. Increased debt will impact adversely on gearing and some other ratios, which results in a lower credit rating, and so a higher cost of debt.

The reduction in the cost of financing accompanying a rise in debt is exactly offset by the increased cost of debt and equity, according to the theorem. On this basis, the *weighted average cost of capital* (see page 313) would be unchanged by variations in the ratio of debt to equity held by the company.

In the real world, this model does not work unadjusted. It holds only in a perfect market with no asymmetric information. There must be no corporate tax because when a company borrows money, there is tax relief, and no expenses related to bankruptcy, which becomes more of a risk as the company increases its debt.

Monte Carlo simulation

The computerised calculation of various randomly generated possible outcomes on an investment strategy.

Net present value

The net present value (NPV) is the discounted value of future cash flows minus the internal investment's value. Compare with *internal rate of return* (see page 310). If the NPV is positive, as is desirable for a business, the discounted return is more than the cost of investment.

Program trading

This is the computerised buying and selling of shares by institutional investors. It is often triggered by the difference between stock *indices* (see page 264) and *futures* (see page 108) prices.

Q ratio

The Q ratio compares the stock market's value with the replacement cost of the corporate sector's tangible assets. It was invented by James Tobin, a Yale academic, and is also known as 'Tobin's Q'. If Q is higher than 1, it is cheaper to buy the assets directly than to invest in the companies that hold them. If the ratio is less than 1, the reverse is true.

In early 2000, a high Q ratio led to forecasts that the US stock market was overvalued and would fall. They turned out to have been well founded.

Random walk theory

This holds that share prices follow a random path, unlinked with trends or past price movements. On this basis, a stock's direction is unpredictable in the short term although, in the long term, it is acknowledged that stock markets rise. The theory calls into question the validity of both fundamental and technical analysis. See also *efficient market theory* (page 308).

Risk free rate

The risk free rate of return is derived from the asset in the market with the lowest risk. This is usually taken to be government bonds, whether they are index-linked or not. The relevant return is the yield to redemption. The risk free return is used as the fundamental building block in the *Capital Asset Pricing Model* (see page 304).

Security market line

This is the linear relationship between an asset's required rate of return and its *systematic risk* (see page 313). Stocks above the security market line give an excess return against systematic risk and, if below the line, they give an insufficient return. It is demonstrated by the *Capital Asset Pricing Model* (see page 304).

Sharpe ratio

The Sharpe ratio, developed by William F Sharpe, shows the ratio of return to volatility in a fund. It is the fund's excessive return over the risk free rate, divided by the fund's *standard deviation* (see page 313).

There is no directional bias in the volatility measured by standard deviation, which means that a fund is penalised for short-term out-performance. To avoid this, the *Sortino ratio* (see next entry) was devised.

Sortino ratio

The Sortino ratio quantifies a fund's risk by measuring its return in relation to harmful volatility. It is calculated as the fund's excessive return over the risk free state, divided by the fund's downward deviation.

The ratio is less widely accepted than the ***Sharpe ratio*** (see previous entry), which differs only in that it uses standard instead of downward deviation.

Standard deviation

Standard deviation measures how far the return on a stock deviates from the average over a given period. It is a statistical measure of variance in a distribution and is without directional bias. The lower the standard deviation is, the less the return on a stock will vary from the average over a given period, and the higher it is, the greater the variation.

To calculate the standard deviation, you will need to find the square root of variance in the relevant distribution. This means the square root of the arithmetic mean of the squares of the deviations from the mean value.

Systematic risk

This is market risk and it cannot be eliminated by diversification. It includes any risk linked to the stock market or economic conditions. If the market should rise or fall, it affects all stocks systematically, although some more than others.

Systematic risk is measured by ***beta*** (see page 303) and is the opposite of ***unsystematic risk*** (see the next entry). The cost of equity in a well diversified portfolio will change only because of an increase in systematic risk, according to the ***Capital Asset Pricing Model*** (see page 304).

Unsystematic risk

This is the risk specific to a company. As the reverse of systematic risk, it is not linked to the stock market or economic conditions, and it can be eliminated by diversification. An example is a pharmaceutical company facing sudden new competition for one of its drug products.

Weighted average cost of capital

This is often abbreviated to WACC, and represents the cost of capital to the company. It is the average of the cost of equity and debt, weighted in proportion to the amounts of equity and debt capital deemed to be financing the business. ***Analysts*** (see page 65) often use WACC as the rate for discounting in ***discounted cash flow analysis*** (see page 305).

The cost of equity is the expected return on equity, which is most often measured by the *Capital Asset Pricing Model* (see page 304). It is variable because the share prices fluctuate and dividend payments may be changed. Share buyers require a higher return than debt providers to compensate for this risk, and for the fact that the company must give priority to debt repayment over dividends.

The cost of debt is more transparent. It is commonly estimated as the redemption yield on the company's bonds, and interest rates on loans and overdrafts. The yield may be broken down into the risk-free state (as on government bonds) and a margin beyond this. The higher the margin, the higher the default risk, and this is often assessed by *credit rating agencies* (see page 74).

In the real world, with corporate taxes and bankruptcy and financial distress costs, the optimum debt/equity ratio for companies is a delicate balance. Because debt is cheaper than equity, increased gearing is beneficial up to a point, but after the optimum point has been exceeded, debt and equity costs start to rise faster than the benefits from introducing more debt funding per se, and the cost of capital will increase. For details of the theoretical case that the equity/debt distribution does not make any difference to cost of capital (in a world without taxes and bankruptcy and financial distress costs), see 'Modigliani-Miller' (page 311).

Z terminology

Introduction

In this section, we will take a quick look at some key z terms that arise in the financial pages.

Zero coupon bond

This is a bond that pays no interest but is issued at a deep discount to its redemption price.

Zero coupon preference shares

See 'Preference shares' (page 127).

Zero-sum game

This is where a winner's profits are matched by a loser's losses, as in *options* (see page 111).

Z-score

The z-score is a measure of a company's solvency. It combines several standard business ratios, each weighted to give a score indicating the business's health. If a company has a z-score below 1.5, it is not far from bankruptcy.

Appendices

Appendix 1
Internet resources

Bonds

Debt Management Office (gilts), www.dmo.gov.uk

Kaunders Portfolio Management (on gilts), www.gilt.co.uk

Company financial statements and similar

Carol, www.carol.co.uk

Companies House, www.companieshouse.gov.uk

Corporate reports (subscription site), www.corpreports.co.uk

FT reports service, www.annualreports.ft.com

Complaints

Financial Ombudsman Service, www.financial-ombudsman.co.uk

Financial Services Authority, www.fsa.gov.uk

Corporate governance

Age of Transparency (US site), www.ageoftransparency.com

Corporate governance, www.corpgov.net

European corporate governance institute, www.ecgi.org

Directors' dealings

Digitallook (good general investing site as well), www.digitallook.com

Economics, statistics and money markets

Bank of England, www.bankofengland.co.uk

Bank for International Settlements, www.bis.org

British Retail Consortium, www.brc.org.uk

Bank of Montreal (economics), www.bmo.com/economic/

Chartered Institute of Purchasing and Supply, www.cips.org

Deutsche Bank research – a limited amount of free research on site, including daily commentary, www.dbresearch.com

Euro – the Official Treasury Euro Service, www.euro.gov.uk

European Bank for Reconstruction and Development, www.ebrd.com

European Business Register, www.ebr.org

European Central Bank (English site), www.ecb.int

European Commission, www.europa.eu.int

Federal Reserve, www.federalreserve.gov

Financial Reporting Council, www.frc.org.uk

Institute of Economic Affairs, www.iea.org.uk

International Energy Agency, www.iea.org

International Monetary Fund, www.imf.org

National Association for Business Economics (US-based), www.nabe.com

National Bureau of Economic Research (US-based), www.nber.org

National Statistics, www.statistics.gov.uk

Organisation for Economic Co-operation and Development, www.oecd.org

Samuel Brittan – economic commentator for the Financial Times, www.samuelbrittan.co.uk

Society of Business Economists (UK-based), www.sbe.co.uk

The Treasury, www.hm-treasury.gov.uk

WestLB Panmure – free economic research (under Markets and analysis section), www.westlb.com

Worldbank, www.worldbank.org

World Trade Organisation, www.wto.org

Equities

General

There are many sites. Here are three of the best:

ADVFN, http://www.advfn.com

Interactive Investor, www.iii.co.uk

The Motley Fool UK, www.fool.co.uk

Beta estimate providers

Barra, www.barra.com

Bloomberg, www.bloomberg.com

Datastream, www.datastream.com

Value Line, www.valueline.com

London Business School, Risk Measurement Services, www.london.edu

Research

Charles Schwab – US-based centre with access to research tools,
    www.schwab.com

Equity Development – analysts' reports commissioned by companies,
    www.equity-development.co.uk

Hoover's Online – in depth coverage of 40,000 businesses, www.hoovers.com

IDEAglobal – global financial markets, www.ideaglobal.com

Salomon Smith Barney – a limited amount of free research,
    www.salomonsmithbarney.com

Zacks.com – US site. Company reports, monthly economic outlook, and more,
    www.zacks.com

Price quotes

There are many sites that give share price quotes. Here are three:

Interactive Investor, www.iii.co.uk

Freequotes, www.freequotes.co.uk

Moneyextra, www.moneyextra.com

Exchanges

American Stock Exchange, www.amex.com

Australia Stock Exchange, www.asx.com.au

Baltic Exchange, www.balticexchange.com

BME (Spanish Stock Exchange), www.bolsaymercados.es

Borsa Italiana (Italian Stock Exchange), www.borsaitalia.it

Bourse du Luxembourg, www.bourse.lu

Bucharest Stock Exchange, www.bvb.ro

Chicago Board Options Exchange, www.cboe.com

Chicago Mercantile Exchange – largest US futures exchange, www.cme.com

Copenhagen Stock Exchange, www.cse.dk

Deutsche Borse, www.exchange.de

Dubai International Financial Centre, www.dubaiifc.com

EUREX, www.eurexchange.com

Euronext, www.euronext.com

FTSE International (details of indices), www.ftse.com

Helsinki Stock Exchange, www.hex.com

International Petroleum Exchange, www.theipe.uk.com

JSE Securities Exchange (South Africa), www.jse.co.za

Latvian Stock Exchange (Riga), www.rfb.lv

London Metal Exchange, www.lme.co.uk

London Stock Exchange, www.londonstockexchange.com

Moscow Stock Exchange, www.mse.ru

NASDAQ – the US high-tech market, www.Nasdaq.com

National Stock Exchange of India, www.nse-india.com

Moscow Stock Exchange, www.mse.ru

New York Mercantile Exchange, www.nymex.com

New York Stock Exchange, www.nyse.com

NZX (New Zealand Stock Exchange), www.nzx.com

OFEX web – market for small unlisted companies, www.OFEX.co.uk

OMX (Stockholm Stock Exchange), www.stockholmborsen.se

Oslo Stock Exchange, www.ose.no

Sao Paulo Stock Exchange, www.bovespa.com

Singapore Exchange, www.ses.com.sg

Toronto Stock Exchange, www.tsx.com

Tokyo Stock Exchange, www.tse.or.jp

Warsaw Stock Exchange, www.gpw.com.pl

Insurance

Association of British Insurers, www.abi.org.uk

Chartered Insurance Institute, www.cii.co.uk

The International Underwriting Association of London, www.iua.co.uk

Lloyd's of London, www.lloydsoflondon.co.uk

International investing

J P Morgan's ADR web site – useful on ADRs, www.adr.com

Renaissance Capital – good research on Russian markets, www.rencap.com

Investment clubs

Proshare, www.proshare.org

New issues and capital markets

Financial News, http://www.efinancialnews.com www.efinancialnews.com

News and analysis

AFX News, www.afxpress.com

Ananova, www.ananova.com

BBC News Online (Business), www.bbc.co.uk/business

Bloomberg News, www.bloomberg.co.uk

Breakingviews, www.breakingviews.com

Citywire, www.citywire.co.uk

Dow Jones Newswires, www.dowjones.com

Estates Gazette, www.egi.co.uk

FT.com, www.ft.com

MergerMarket.com, www.mergermarket.com

PA News, www.pressassociation.press.net

PrivateEquityOnline.com, www.privateequityonline.com

Red Herring magazine – US high tech company developments,
    www.redherring.com

Reuters, www.reuters.co.uk

ShareCast.com, www.sharecast.com

Personal finance

Alternative Investment Management Association, www.aima.org

Association of Investment Trust Companies, www.aitc.co.uk

Lipper (Reuters on funds), www.lipperweb.com

Micropal (Standard & Poor's on funds), www.funds-sp.com

Moneynet, www.moneynet.co.uk

Moneyweb, www.moneyweb.co.uk

Moneyextra, www.moneyextra.com

Pension Advisory Service, www.opas.org.uk

William Burrow Annuities – tables showing annuity rates on open market, www.williamburrows.com

Regulators, standard setters and related trade bodies

Accounting Standards Board, www.asb.org.uk

Autorite des Marches Financiers – French financial regulator, www.amf-franc.org

British Bankers Association, www.bvca.co.uk

British Building Societies Association, www.bsa.org.uk

British Venture Capital Association, www.bvca.co.uk

Committee of European Securities Regulators (CESR), www.cesr.eu.org

Competition Commission, www.mmc.gov.uk

Consob – Italian financial regulator, www.consob.it

Corporation of London, www.cityoflondon.gov.uk

Department of Trade and Industry, www.dti.gov.uk

Ethical Investment Association, www.ethicalinvestment.org.uk

Federation of European Securities Exchanges, www.fese.be

Financial Services Authority, www.fsa.gov.uk

International Organization of Securities Commissions (IOSCO), www.iosco.org

International Securities Market Association, www.isma.co.uk

National Association of Pension Funds, www.napf.co.uk

Office of Fair Trading, www.oft.gov.uk

Securities & Investment Institute, www.securities-institute.org

Serious Fraud Office, www.sfo.gov.uk

US Securities & Exchange Commission, www.sec.gov

UKSIP (UK member society of the CFA Institute), www.uksip.org

Settlement

CREST (part of Euroclear), www.crestco.co.uk

Euroclear, www.euroclear.com

LCH.Clearnet Limited, www.lch.com

Spread betting

Onewaybet.com – our favourite web site about spread betting,
www.onewaybet.com

spreadbets.net, www.spreadbets.net.

Spread betting explained, www.spreadbettingexplained.com

Tax

Inland Revenue, www.inlandrevenue.gov.uk/home.htm

Technical analysis

General

DecisionPoint.com – material on charting, some free, the rest for subscribers
only, www.decisionpoint.com

Dorsey Wright Associates – point-and-figure charting,
www.dorseywright.com

murphymorris.com – technician John Murphy addresses subscribers,
www.murphymorris.com

Prudential – US site with free daily technical report from Ralph Campora,
www.prudential.com

Society of Technical Analysts, www.sta-uk.org

StockCharts.com – general site on charting, www.stockcharts.com

Technical software

Indexia, www.indexia.co.uk

Omnitrader, www.omnitrader.com

ShareScope, www.ShareScope.co.uk

Synergy, www.synergy.com

Updata, www.updata.co.uk

Trading

DayTraders.com, www.daytraders.com

Hollywood Stock Exchange – fantasy trading in film stars and musicians as
practice for stock market trading, www.hsx.com

Trade2Win, www.trade2win.com

Unit trusts and other aggregated investment schemes

Association of Investment Trust Companies, www.aitc.co.uk

Investment Management Association, www.investmentuk.org

Morning Star, www.morningstar.co.uk

S&P Micropal, www.funds-sp.com

TrustNet, www.trustnet.com

Unlisted stocks

AngelBourse – investor access to early growth company investments, www.angelbourse.com

J P Jenkins Limited – a market maker in unquoted and unlisted securities, www.jpjl.co.uk

ShareMark – an electronic auction market for small company shares, www.share.com

unquoted.co.uk – news, information, interviews and message boards on OFEX companies, www.unquoted.co.uk

535x – a share price and financial information service for UK unquoted companies, www.535x.com

Appendix 2
Further reading

To follow up on this guide, choose from the recommended books below. You can buy online from global-investor (www.global-investor.com) or Amazon (www.amazon.co.uk).

Accounting

Interpreting Company Reports and Accounts, Holmes, Sugden and Gee, FT Prentice Hall, 2002

The Motley Fool UK Investment Workshop, David Berger and Bruce Jackson, Boxtree, 1999

The City and its markets

The City: Inside the great expectation machine, Tony Golding, Pearson Education Ltd, 2001

The Economist Guide to Financial Markets, Mark Levison, Profile Books, 2000

How to Read the Financial Pages, Michael Brett, Random Books, 2000

The Money Machine: How the City works, Philip Coggan, Penguin Books, 2002

Corporate finance

The Penguin Guide to Finance, Hugo Dixon, Penguin Books, 2000

Streetsmart Guide to Valuing a Stock, Gary Gray, Patrick J Cusatis, and
   J Randall Woolridge, McGraw Hill, 1999

Derivatives

*How to Use Spread Betting, CFDs, Options, Warrants and Trackers to Boost
   Returns and Reduce Risk,* Peter Temple, Harriman House, 2003
Options Plain and Simple, Lenny Jordan, FT Prentice Hall, 1999
Rogue Trader, Nick Leeson, Warner Books, 1999

Economics and foreign exchange

A Question of Economics, Peter Donaldson, Penguin, 1990
The Economist Guide to Financial Markets, Marc Levison, Economist Books,
   2002
First Steps in Economic Indicators, Peter Temple, FT Prentice Hall, 2003
Free Lunch, Easily Digestible Economics, David Smith, Profile Books, 2003
The Investor's Guide to Economic Fundamentals, John Calverley, John Wiley,
   2003
The Penguin Dictionary of Economics, Graham Bannock, RE Baxter and Evan
   Davis, Penguin, 1998

Equities and bonds

The Big Tech Score, Michael Kwatinetz, John Wiley, 2001
First Steps in Bonds, Peter Temple, FT Prentice Hall, 2001
The Intelligent Investor, Benjamin Graham, HarperBusiness, 2003
How to Make Money in Stocks, William O'Neil, McGraw-Hill Professional,
   2002
The New Buffettology, Mary Buffett and David Clark, Simon & Schuster, 2002
One Up on Wall Street, Peter Lynch and John Rothschild, Simon & Schuster,
   1990
The Zulu Principle, Jim Slater, Orion, 1997

Hedge funds and short selling

Bear Essentials. The Secrets of Forensic Accounting and Profitable Trading,
   Simon Cawkwell, T1ps.com, 2003
Hedge Funds. An investment professionals' guide, Matthew Ridley, Kogan
   Page, 2004

Investment clubs

The Company of Successful Investors, Terry Bond, FT Prentice Hall, 2002
Proshare Investment Clubs, Looseleaf Manual, Proshare

Personal finance and tax

Fear and Loathing in my Bank Account, Sean Coughlan, Kogan Page, 2002
The Ultimate Guide to Shredding Pounds off Your Bills and Saving Money off Everything, Martin Lewis, Random House, 2004
Your Money or Your Life, Alvin Hall, Coronet, 2003

Trading and takeovers

Come into My Trading Room, Alexander Elder, John Wiley, 2002
The Disciplined Trader, Mark Douglas, NYIF, 1990
Practical Speculation, Victor Niederhoffer and Laurel Kenner, John Wiley, 2003
Takeover, Peter Waine and Mike Walker, John Wiley, 2001

Technical analysis

Applying Elliott Wave Theory Profitably, Steven Poser, John Wiley, 2003
The Candlesticks Course, Steve Nison, Marketplace Books (Wiley), 2003
The Complete Guide to Point-and-figure Charting, Kermit Zieg and Heinrich Weber, Harriman House, 2003
Forecasting Financial Markets, Tony Plummer, Kogan Page, 2003
Getting Started in Technical Analysis, Jack Schwager, John Wiley, 1999
The Investor's Guide to Charting, Alistair Blair, FT Prentice Hall, 2002
Martin Pring's Introduction to Technical Analysis, Martin Pring, McGraw-Hill Education, 1997
Technical Analysis of the Financial Markets, John Murphy, NYIF, 1998

Regulation and corporate governance

Essential Director. An Economist guide, Bob Tricker, Economist Books, 2003

Index

Index of advertisers